The Mesa Verde World

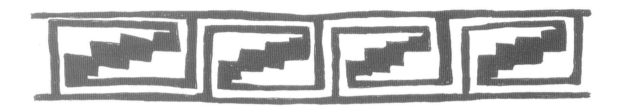

The publication of this volume was made possible by generous gifts
from Maggie and Christian Andersson for the Loretto Chapel of Santa Fe,
William S. Cowles, and Melinda Burdette for Crow Canyon Archaeological Center.

CROW CANYON
ARCHAEOLOGICAL CENTER

The Mesa

Edited by David Grant Noble

A School of American Research
Popular Southwestern Archaeology Book

Verde World

Explorations in Ancestral Pueblo Archaeology

School of American Research Press
Santa Fe, New Mexico

School of American Research Press
Post Office Box 2188
Santa Fe, New Mexico 87504-2188
www.press.sarweb.org

Acting Director: Catherine Cocks
Copy Editor: Jane Kepp
Design and Production: Cynthia Dyer
Maps: Molly O'Halloran
Proofreader: Kate Talbot
Indexer: Ina Gravitz
Printed in China by C&C Offset Printing

Library of Congress Cataloging-in-Publication Data
The Mesa Verde world : explorations in ancestral Pueblo archaeology / edited by David Grant Noble.
p. cm.
"A School of American Research popular southwestern archaeology book."
Includes bibliographical references and index.
ISBN 1-930618-74-3 (cl : alk. paper) — ISBN 1-930618-75-1 (pa : alk. paper)
1. Pueblo Indians—Colorado—Mesa Verde National Park—Antiquities.
2. Pueblo Indians—Colorado—Mesa Verde National Park—History.
3. Pueblo pottery—Colorado—Mesa Verde National Park .
4. Excavations (Archaeology)—Colorado—Mesa Verde National Park.
5. Mesa Verde National Park (Colo.)—Antiquities. I. Noble, David Grant.

E99.P9M46 2006   978.8'27—dc22
2006002577

Cover photograph (front): Ruins in Hovenweep National Monument, courtesy David Grant Noble, photographer.
Cover photograph (back): Kiva Plaza in Balcony House, courtesy George H. H. Huey, photographer.
Frontispiece: Spruce Tree House, Mesa Verde National Park, courtesy George H. H. Huey, photographer.

Contents

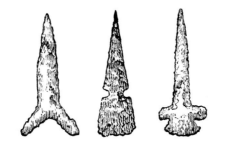

Acknowledgments

The contributors to this book deserve enormous credit for devoting time and effort to writing these chapters amid their busy schedules. I especially thank Mark Varien, Rich Wilshusen, Bill Lipe, and Larry Nordby for their guidance along the way.

Liz Bauer, Jerice Barrios, Deborah Confer, Mary Etzkorn, Jonathan Haas, Larry Harwood, Rebecca Lintz, Linda Martin, Ruth Meria, Elaine Hughes, Cary McStay, and Stephen Nash helped me find photographic illustrations in collections at the Colorado Historical Society, Crow Canyon Archaeological Center, the Field Museum of Natural History, the Museum of New Mexico, the Museum of Northern Arizona, and the University of Colorado Museum of Natural History. James Brooks, Catherine Cocks, Jonathan Lewis, and Jason Ordaz of SAR Press provided critical editorial, technical, organizational, and moral support.

Three institutions especially deserve credit for their support of this project as it evolved from

Pictographs, Grand Gulch, Utah

rough concept to finished book: Crow Canyon Archaeological Center, Mesa Verde National Park, and the School of American Research.

Other people who helped me on the book include Victoria Atkins, Kevin Black, Fred Blackburn, Lauren Blauert, Sheri Bowman, Cory Breternitz, Joel M. Brisbin, Laura Casjens, Ian Crosser, Jim Duffield, Jerry Fetterman, Paul Folwell, Larry Harwood, Adriel Heisey, Laura Holt, Bruce Hucko, George H. H. Huey, Elaine Hughes, Louann Jacobson, Jim Judge, Jane Kepp, J. R. Lancaster, Laurie Logsdon, Minnie Murray, Eric Polingyouma, Jim Potter, Bob Powers, Alvin Reiner, William Stone, Linda Towle, Ruth Van Dyke, Ruth Wright, Mara Yarborough, and Mike Zeilik.

Finally, for their financial contributions, which enabled this book to be so finely produced, I thank Bill Cowles, Maggie and Christian Andersson, and Melinda Burdette.

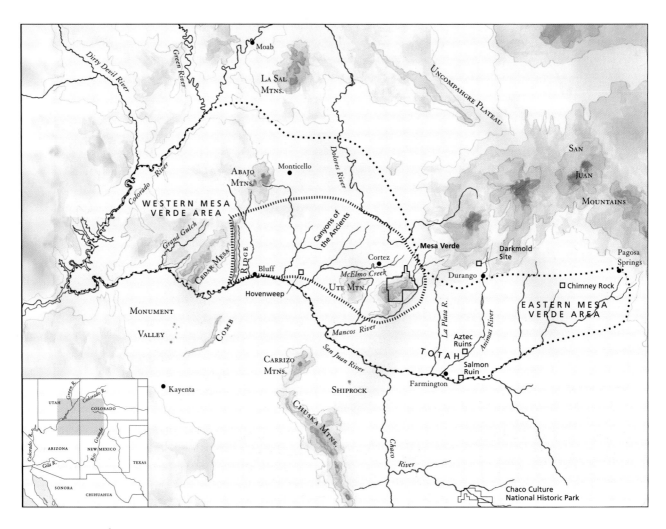

Map 1. Mesa Verde region.

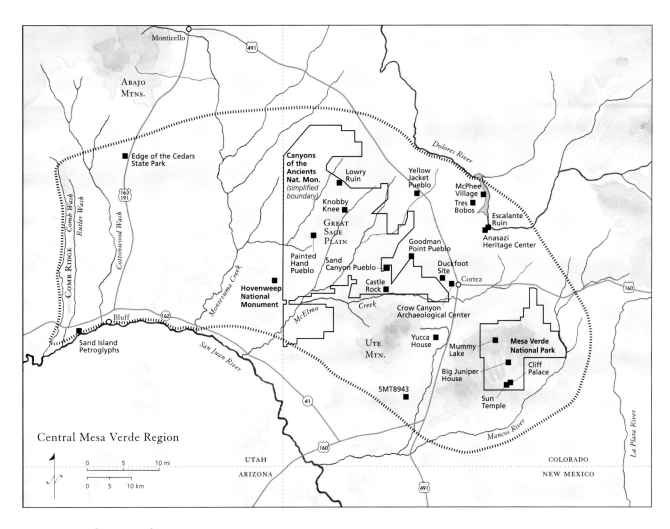

Map 2. Central Mesa Verde region.

A Short Archaeological Chronology for the Mesa Verde Region

Before 6000 BCE	Paleoindians present in or near the Mesa Verde region.
6000–1000 BCE	Shift to Archaic lifeway.
1000 BCE–500 CE	Basketmaker II people occupy areas near present-day Durango and in southeastern Utah. First corn cultivation.

Common-era dates

500–750	Basketmaker III period. Farming settlements become more widespread; pottery appears.
750–900	Pueblo I period, marked by first large pueblos.
900–1150	Pueblo II period. Ancestral Pueblo population swells. Chaco-style great houses appear between 1075 and 1135.
1150–1300	Last major prehistoric Pueblo occupation. Appearance of large villages, many cliff dwellings, and towers.
After 1100–1300	Numic and Athapascan speakers present in the region.
1776	Escalante-Domínguez expedition travels through the area, recording archaeological sites and Indian tribes.
1874–1878	First scientific archaeological documentation, by W. H. Holmes and W. H. Jackson.
1888	Wetherills find Cliff Palace and other Mesa Verde cliff dwellings.
1891	Gustav Nordenskiöld and Richard Wetherill excavate some Mesa Verde sites.
1891–1903	Collecting and reconnaissance expeditions in the region.
1906	Mesa Verde National Park (MVNP) established.
1907	A. V. Kidder and S. G. Morley survey in McElmo area.
1908–1922	J. W. Fewkes active in MVNP.

1913–1940	E. H. Morris excavates many sites in region.
1921–1929	Research in Chimney Rock area by Jeançon and Roberts.
1923	Hovenweep National Monument established.
1929–1939	Paul Martin conducts research in region and excavates Lowry Pueblo.
1940s–1950s	Excavations in MVNP by D. O'Bryan and J. A. Lancaster.
Late 1950s–early 1960s	Wetherill Mesa, Navajo Reservoir, and Glen Canyon archaeological projects.
1965–1971	University of Colorado records more than 1,600 sites during survey of sites on public land.
1966 to present	National Historic Preservation Act and other legislation protect sites on public land and lead to many "cultural resource management" projects.
1972	Ute Mountain Ute Tribal Park set aside to protect ancient Pueblo and Ute sites.
1972–1975	Cedar Mesa Project: survey and testing in western part of region.
1977	University of Colorado completes survey of MVNP; almost 4,000 sites now recorded there.
1978–1985	Dolores Archaeological Program (DAP) researches area to be covered by Lake McPhee.
1982–2005	Archaeological Conservancy acquires 11 sites on private land to ensure their preservation.
1983–1997	Four Corners Archaeological Program follows up on DAP.
1983–present	Crow Canyon Archaeological Center (CCAC) conducts survey, mapping, and excavations at many sites in central Mesa Verde region.
1996–2003	More than half of Mesa Verde National Park is burned by wildfires, with archaeological consequences.
2002	Beginning of Animas–La Plata Project just outside Durango.
2005	CCAC and National Park Service begin research collaboration at Goodman Point Pueblo.

Note: BCE stands for "before the common era," and CE, for "common era."
Many field schools, academic research projects, and cultural resource management projects in addition to those listed here have made valuable contributions to our understanding of Mesa Verde archaeology. Some of them are credited in the chapters of this book.

The Mesa Verde World

Spruce Tree House in snowstorm.

Introduction

David Grant Noble

One November day some years ago, my wife, Ruth, and I drove up onto Mesa Verde, where I hoped to catch the late afternoon light in a photograph. As we climbed the escarpment into the park, the weather began to deteriorate, large snowflakes plastering the windshield. By the time we arrived at Chapin Mesa, it was no longer snowing, but the temperature had dropped and the light had faded. Still, with photography, you never know, so lugging my camera and tripod, I set off down the trail to Spruce Tree House. It was then that the storm renewed itself, accompanied by a gusty wind. At the edge of Spruce Canyon, with the cliff dwelling faintly visible through a screen of swirling snowflakes, I made the picture.

The experience brought to mind accounts of Richard Wetherill and Charlie Mason's first view of Cliff Palace in 1888. They, too, saw it through a curtain of snow, an event later fictionalized by Willa Cather in her book *The Professor's House*. Beauty, romance, and mystery have become part of the aura of Mesa Verde, drawing visitors—including archaeologists—from around the world.

Centuries ago, the Mesa Verdeans themselves must have deeply felt and appreciated the beauty of their world. It is reflected in their craft arts and architecture and apparent still in the culture of their descendants. But they were not visitors to their green mesa, with its rugged canyons and sheltering caves and alcoves. They lived there. They grew crops, hunted and foraged, built homes, raised families. They dealt with the variable weather, changing seasons, marginally productive land, fires, and floods, not to mention accidents and illnesses. For many generations they made it work, both on Mesa Verde and throughout the surrounding region. Then, in the thirteenth century of the common era

(CE), the difficulties of survival intensified. Many families simply packed up and left. How many perished from malnutrition, disease, or strife may never be known.

Today, when we visit the Mesa Verde region, the ruins we see date mostly to the twelfth and thirteenth centuries, for it was then that the region's inhabitants built large villages and enduring stone architecture. But by the time of the cliff dwellers, Basketmaker and earlier Puebloan people, residing in scattered farmsteads and hamlets, had already grown corn in this part of the world for many centuries. They moved about with relative frequency as they adapted to the vagaries of the climate and searched for water, fertile ground, wild game, and edible plants. And humans' experience of the region goes even further back than this, to a time long before the cultivation of maize. In that distant era, people were nomadic and survived entirely by hunting and foraging, leaving little behind for archaeologists to find. Theirs is a little-known chapter in the Mesa Verde story.

Another low-visibility chapter involves the Numic and Athapaskan speakers who came after the Puebloans. Archaeological research has not yet revealed precisely when the ancestors of the Ute and Navajo people began settling in Mesa Verde country. Like the Paleoindian and Archaic peoples of early times, they were hunter-gatherers who left little trace of their presence on the landscape. The Utes and Navajos have their own stories, and beginning in the late 1700s, Americans of European descent wrote accounts of their encounters with these indigenous tribes. But archaeologically speaking, their record is meager and ambiguous.

Archaeologists first focused their research on the Mesa Verde proper, where the sites they found were especially striking and well preserved. In the past 30 years, they have paid increasingly more attention to the larger region, especially to sites in the Montezuma Valley and in what members of the Hayden survey called the "Great Sage Plain" (see map, p. ix). One factor behind the refocused research was legal. As David Breternitz explains in chapter 20, federal laws since 1963 have mandated that archaeological resources on public land be inventoried and, when threatened by activities such as road construction and mineral extraction, researched. As a result, "cultural resource management" projects now produce vast amounts of new data and information. Another reason lies in archaeologists' recognition that most of the ancestral Pueblo population resided not in cliff dwellings but in ordinary farmsteads, hamlets, and villages in the fertile land to the west and north of Mesa Verde. Still another factor was the founding in 1982, near Cortez, Colorado, of Crow Canyon Archaeological Center, whose professional staff and students have been energetically surveying, mapping, excavating, teaching, and publishing for more than two decades.

As might be expected, since the mid-1970s the archaeological database for the Mesa Verde region has grown by leaps and bounds. Unlike proof in the "hard" sciences, archaeological proof is often elusive, and evidence, seldom conclusive. So the practitioners of the discipline draw inferences and arrive at tentative conclusions and interpretations about how ancient people behaved. Because these often require amendment as new data are obtained, archaeology is a dynamic field. By now, much of the information has been digitized, and with a few mouse clicks, interested people around the world can read online reports ranging from major publications such as those about the excavations at Sand Canyon Pueblo to minor ones about lithic scatters along a planned pipeline or haul road to a mine. What is more, as Tim Kohler explains in chapter 8, computers have made possible new types of archaeological studies and expanded the ways in which we can think about the past.

All of these exciting developments stimulated me—in collaboration with the School of American Research Press and Crow Canyon Archaeological Center and with the cooperation of the National Park Service—to produce this book on Mesa Verde archaeology, in order to introduce readers to some of the new research and findings. I wanted the chapters, like those of other books in the School's Popular Southwestern Archaeology Series, to be written by the people who had, themselves, done the work in the field and laboratory and invested so much personal time in studying the subject. I feel fortunate to have been able to bring on board some of the leading researchers and thinkers in this exciting field.

The first five chapters describe the natural environment of the Mesa Verde segment of the Colorado Plateau and offer insights into how human culture evolved there from Paleoindian times until the late thirteenth century CE. On the basis of their research into material culture, archaeologists divide prehistory into a series of temporal-cultural categories. These categories for the Mesa Verde region, often referred to in the text, appear in the chronology on pp. x–xi.

Eleven authors have focused their chapters on specific topics: pottery, mural painting, craft arts, cliff-dwelling architecture, reservoirs, the sacred landscape, archaeoastronomy, violence, migration, wildfires and archaeology, and computer simulation. These chapters reflect new and ongoing research and fresh interpretations.

Some living Indian groups have strong cultural ties to the Mesa Verde region. After the Pueblo ancestors left this part of the world centuries ago, they passed on stories and traditions to subsequent generations. Inevitably, much of this oral traditional knowledge has not survived, while some has changed—as stories do in the telling—and still more is kept private by clans and tribes. This book includes two perspectives from Native Americans: the principal one is from Tessie Naranjo, a scholar from Santa Clara Pueblo in New Mexico, and the other is a story that a Hopi elder recounted in the 1860s.

Finally, Mesa Verde archaeologists have developed a history of their own, one that began when William Henry Jackson and William Henry Holmes first recorded archaeological sites in southwestern Colorado in 1874 and 1875, respectively. The last two chapters, whose authors have spent many decades digging sites themselves, are dedicated to the archaeologists' story.

The people involved in the business of archaeology are an interesting lot. Not unlike our nomadic ancestors, they are at ease tramping across rough and remote landscapes in weather fair or foul. As they hunt and gather their evidence (albeit with the aid of maps and compasses), they spot bits and pieces of old things on the ground that most of us would miss. Anyone who took walks with Alden Hayes will remember how he would casually lean down and pick up a stone flake or potsherd and tell you about the person who made or used it. His words always conveyed deep respect. I think that many would agree with Winston Hurst and Jonathan Till that landscape "remains as sacred to those of us who value historical knowledge and cultural understanding as it was to the ancient peoples whose record it contains."

This is not to romanticize archaeologists, who have erred in their practices for years, having done their work with little regard for the feelings and knowledge of the descendants of the people whose history they were researching. Today, that situation has significantly improved. Archaeologists now routinely consult Native Americans about how to do their research with cultural sensitivity, as well as within legal guidelines.

The stereotype of the Southwestern archaeologist has changed over time too. We see photographs from the 1920s of him supervising his laborers in the field, dressed in a suit and tie. Fifty years later, there he is laboring down in the hole himself—trowel or shovel in hand, bearded, shirt off. Today, more than likely, she will be in the hole, or standing by it showing her students what to do, or sitting at a computer building simulations of settlement patterns and agricultural productivity.

Today, when you walk the trails of Mesa Verde National Park or Canyons of the Ancients National Monument, you hear many languages being spoken. Most people (regrettably not all) regard the archaeological sites of the region as national treasures. It is my hope that this book will move readers to a deepened appreciation of these places, of the need to preserve them, and of the value of studying them. If that is the effect, then I encourage you to join

organizations such as Crow Canyon Archaeological Center, the Archaeological Conservancy, and the School of American Research.

The study of how people in the past behaved is relevant to our present lives. To give an example, while I was working on the chapters of this book that discuss drought, population, violence, and migration, a news story caught my attention. It was headlined "Tribal Clashes over Water and Land in Central Kenya Leave at Least Four Dead." Is this what happened at Castle Rock Pueblo (see ch. 17)? Recently, my own community in New Mexico has been experiencing rapid population growth and development, along with drought, and I have participated in contentious public meetings about what to do. Although the people and places archaeologists research are from the distant past, the issues they study can be current. What we learn about past human behavior and adaptation can help us deal with our own social and environmental problems.

One June evening several years ago, I made my way with my camera to a canyon edge in southwestern Colorado. Hovenweep Castle was perched precariously on the cliff across from me, and Square Tower was visible below on the canyon floor (see figs. 5.6, 16.3). The air was dead still, only a nearby canyon wren breaking the silence. Like a thousand photographers before me, I was waiting for the last light of the day. But a summer storm's dark clouds were spreading from the north, already blocking the sun. I set up my tripod and camera and sat down on a rock to wait. Being familiar with the area's archaeology, I began envisioning a scene as it might have been 700 years before—cries of children, dogs barking, adults discussing the day as they prepared supper, smoke from hearths curling into the air.

Archaeology, whatever its limitations, has made accessible to me a dimension of landscape—its history—that otherwise remains elusive. In the American Southwest, with the marks of past human presence still so poignantly visible on the land, one has the privilege of being able to sit on a rock and step back in time. The specific ancestral experience, of course, belongs to Native Americans, but to the extent that we all share a common human past, the Mesa Verde story belongs to us all.

Figure 1.1. North rim of Mesa Verde, looking toward Sleeping Ute Mountain.

Through the Looking Glass

The Environment of the Ancient Mesa Verdeans

Karen R. Adams

For Alice in Wonderland, the task was easy. All she had to do was step through a magic looking glass into a wonderful new world that was not only clear but also in full color. Our archaeological looking glass, on the other hand, is fogged, and the images we peer at seem blurry at first. Plant remains and animal bones in archaeological sites usually are broken up, and plant fragments are often black from charring. Yet as we archaeologists continue to assemble evidence from many sources, the haze in our looking glass clears, and we see in increasing detail the environment of the ancient Puebloans of the Mesa Verde region. Little by little, we understand better how they went about growing crops, foraging for wild plants, and hunting animals.

We now know that for centuries farmers have considered the Mesa Verde country of southwestern Colorado and southeastern Utah to be a great place to settle down and raise a family. Well suited to agriculture, the region receives sediment carried by winds blowing regularly from the southwest, sediment that has formed thick layers of loose, nutrient-rich farmland. In addition, nature has obliged many a Mesa Verdean farmer's need for enough moisture and frost-free days to enable crops to mature. For much of the time between 500 and 1300 CE (the Basketmaker III through Pueblo III periods), farmers raised corn (maize), beans, and squash, and they grew or traded for gourds. More recently, farmers in southwestern Colorado have experienced a century of successful dryland farming (farming by natural precipitation alone), particularly of splotchy red-and-white common beans similar to those grown by ancient farmers.

Despite the region's suitability for farming, we know that ancestral Pueblo people also experienced times of hardship caused by agricultural failures. More than once they watched their crops wither from lack of rain or succumb to killing frosts. Sometimes hunger and malnutrition pitted groups against each other, resulting in warfare and emigration. The more we know about the environment of the past, the better we can understand population spikes and declines, the movements of people, and the ways they coped with food shortages.

The diverse biotic communities of the Mesa Verde region have long included many plants and animals that humans have found useful. Studies of preserved pack rat middens (nests) tell us that the present plant and animal communities of the American Southwest have been in place for the past 4,000 years. The archaeological record verifies that ancestral Pueblo landscapes hosted many of the same wild plants and animals we see today.

Still, our ability to envision earlier landscapes has been inhibited by the appearance over the last century of invasive species originating on other continents. Tumbleweeds, summer cypress, and clovers, for example, now crowd out native plants. In addition, commercial farming, logging, and livestock grazing have cleared vast areas that once supported piñon and juniper woodlands and parklands of sagebrush and native grasses. Along with deep plowing and fire suppression, these historic activities have altered the proportions and, in some instances, the natural groupings of plants and animals. The role that ancient people played in altering their environment must also be acknowledged.

Figure 1.2. Ancestral Pueblo farmers built agricultural terraces such as these in Mesa Verde National Park to contain runoff and stabilize soil.

The Modern Environment

Seven major biotic communities grace the Mesa Verde regional landscape. Each consists of a certain group of plants and animals that is affected by and adapted to local temperature, precipitation, and soil. From the valleys, at some 4,000 feet in elevation, to mountain peaks above 12,000 feet, these plant communities are characterized by, respectively, sagebrush and saltbush shrubs; grasses; piñon and juniper woodlands; Gamble oak scrubland; ponderosa pine and Douglas fir woodlands; spruce and true fir woodlands; and low-growing alpine tundra.

Piñon-juniper woodlands, expanses of sagebrush and saltbush, and grasslands abound in the southwestern corner of Colorado, where ancient human populations were once large. Although the region includes both major rivers (the San Juan, Animas, La Plata, and Dolores) and smaller rivers and creeks (the Mancos, McElmo, Piedra, and Yellow Jacket), the springs and ephemeral drainages

have long been critical water sources for both animals and people. Over the centuries, Puebloans also constructed check dams, water diversion systems, and reservoirs to make water more accessible (fig 1.2).

All farmers know how critical moisture is to their crops. In the Mesa Verde region, mean annual precipitation ranges from 7.8 inches near Kayenta, Arizona, to more than 18.3 inches in and around Durango, Colorado. Moisture from snowmelt allows corn kernels to germinate and sustains tiny seedlings through the normally dry weeks of late spring and early summer. Later, sporadic summer rains spur rapid plant growth and ear development. On the Colorado Plateau, corn agriculture requires at least 12 to 14 inches of annual precipitation to be successful, and some developmental stages of corn growth, such as pollination and grain development, especially need water.

Pueblo farmers learned long ago that they could

direct runoff from intense summer showers to their fields by aligning stones, dirt, and brush debris. They also placed their fields in locations best suited to receiving storm runoff, such as at the bases of gentle slopes. Sometimes they also hand-carried water from reservoirs ("pot irrigation"), especially to drought-intolerant crops such as squash.

Temperatures, too, play an important role in growing crops successfully. Most varieties of corn need at least 120 frost-free days and a minimum amount of summertime heat in order to mature. The latter is measured in "corn-growing degree day" (CGDD) units; at least 2,500 units are required during a growing season.

CGDD units are calculated by summing the difference between each day's average temperature and a set base temperature (50 degrees Fahrenheit). One CGDD unit is accumulated for each degree by which the average exceeds the base temperature. A minimum of 50 degrees and a maximum of 86 degrees have been set as thresholds below and above which corn crops will not thrive.

My colleagues and I have examined modern temperature and precipitation records for the Mesa Verde region to assess the locations best (and worst) suited for farming. Our research shows that despite being above 7,000 feet in elevation, Mesa Verde proper currently has enough CGDD units, frost-free days, and precipitation to farm successfully in most years, enhanced by the fact that the broad, sediment-covered mesas tilt gently south, toward the warming sun. The Yellow Jacket, Cortez, and Blanding areas, too, receive enough moisture and summer heat to grow corn, so it is no surprise that they were all densely populated in prehistoric times.

Tree-ring samples obtained from ancient roof beams, stands of very old living trees, and even older wood lying on rocky landscapes provide data on precipitation in the past. Dendrochronologist Matthew Salzer, working in the San Francisco Peaks area, near Flagstaff, Arizona, used bristlecone pine records to reconstruct periods of relatively higher and lower temperatures for the ancestral Pueblo

centuries. He then combined the annual temperature and precipitation data to construct a 2,000-year time line of conditions critical to agriculture. To add to this, Timothy A. Kohler (see chapter 8) and his associates from Washington State University recently assembled a broad range of environmental data, information about corn yields, and estimates of human population to form the basis of a sophisticated, multicentury model of periods of farming success and failure for the Mesa Verde region.

Agricultural Success and Failure, Population Spikes and Declines

Farmers in the Mesa Verde region began growing corn, a Mexican import, sometime in the first few centuries of the first millennium CE. Before long it became both a dietary staple and an integral component in ceremonies. Why did this happen? Corn is unique among grain crops in having both large kernels and high yields. By planting a single kernel, a farmer could grow a plant that produced 300 to 600 kernels. Studies have shown that Puebloans in the last century routinely set aside approximately 350 pounds of corn kernels for one person's annual consumption (fig. 1.3). Under favorable circumstances, three to four acres of land could yield enough corn to feed a family of three to four people for a year, assuming that wild plants and animals provided additional calories, critical vitamins and minerals, and protein missing from corn. Also, around 600 CE, Pueblo people began growing common beans. When added to corn in their diet, beans gave them all the amino acids of a complete protein.

After corn became a staple, the successes and failures of corn harvests paralleled the rises and declines of the native population. By the 600s, population was on the increase, but a drought in the late 800s made dryland farming too risky. Throughout the 900s, Pueblo farmers seem to have hung on by tending small fields along drainages or by clearing fields at the bases of slopes to benefit from storm runoff. By the middle and late 1000s, while living in dispersed farmsteads and walking daily to their nearby cornfields, they were again reaping successful harvests. Between 1130 and 1180, however, drought again placed its curse on agriculture. We see its reflection in tree rings, in a

Figure 1.3. Pueblo people stored large quantities of corn, their most important food staple. The kernels safeguarded in this jar, excavated in Mesa Verde National Park, may have been specially selected seed corn.

reduction in house construction and remodeling, and in a rise in intergroup violence and strife. When that long dry spell ended, prosperity returned. By the late 1100s, population was growing and construction booming.

As the thirteenth century drew to a close, ending the Pueblo III period, the inhabitants of the Mesa Verde region once more experienced scant and unpredictable summer rains. This severe drought, which lasted from 1276 to 1299, spelled the end of eight centuries of Pueblo presence in the Mesa Verde and Four Corners region. Some communities suffered violent ends, and some people must have perished from the effects of malnutrition. Others emigrated to more promising places to the south and east to join relatives or friends and acquaintances. Chapters 5 and 6 tell more about this warfare, abandonment, and migration.

Gathering and Hunting

Over years of working in the Mesa Verde region, I have accumulated a list of important native plant foods that are found in the archaeological record or have been recorded in historic ethnographic literature. Ancestral Pueblo people collected tasty,

calorie-rich piñon nuts, harvests of which can be abundant but often are sporadic and undependable. They occasionally gathered the reliable juniper berries, whose tartness (one species is used to flavor gin) requires some getting used to. Other nourishing wild foods harvested in large quantities included the seeds or fruits of weedy goosefoot, pigweed, purslane, tomatillo, tansy mustard, yucca, globe mallow, grasses, and cacti (figs. 1.4, 1.5).

Ancient people knew when plant foods ripened and were ready to be collected. For example, starting in late spring or early summer, they gathered lemonade berries, rice grass grains, and tansy mustard seeds for immediate consumption and storage. Later in the summer, they likely gathered the tender and nutritious leafy greens of goosefoot, pigweed, and purslane. Although little evidence of the leaves and stems of these weedy plants has survived in the archaeological record, evidence for the use of their seeds is plentiful, and we assume that plants growing in farmers' fields and on midden piles produced copious seeds for harvesting.

As the growing season progressed, people ate a variety of grass grains, as well as serviceberries and sunflower seeds. By fall, everyone must have looked

Figure 1.4. The yucca plant provided large, sweet pods for food and fibrous leaves for making baskets, sandals, and mats.

Figure 1.5. Rice grass produces abundant grains that ripen in late spring. Historically, Pueblo people cut the stems and held them over a fire, allowing the toasted grains to fall into a waiting container.

stored corn and wild plants inside their dwellings, but during the warmer months they preferred cooking outdoors. They parched wild seeds over a fire or ground them up to be cooked in pottery vessels as porridge or gruel.

Ancestral Pueblo people found many other uses for plants besides food. On occasion they smoked wild tobacco, leaving burned tobacco seeds for archaeologists to find centuries later. Needing timbers for house construction, they chopped down juniper trees at lower elevations and Douglas firs and ponderosa pines on the higher mesas. They used piñon trees for building, too, but were aware that weaknesses in the wood reduced its value. Still, piñon and juniper, along with woody shrubs such as sagebrush, saltbush, bitterbrush, and mountain mahogany, provided fuel for cooking, heating, and light. And craftsmen no doubt tossed wood scraps left over from making household and agricultural tools into the fire.

In addition to knowing which wild plants to harvest, Mesa Verdean men and women also knew when and where to find each one. We infer from the investment they made in architecture, as well as from farmers' need to be near their crops during the growing season, that many lived in their dwellings and villages year-round. Because many of the wild plants they gathered thrive in disturbed habitats (we call such plants "weeds"),

forward to gathering piñon nuts, if the harvest was good, and eating prickly pear fruit, one of the few sources of natural sugar. Because juniper berries remain attached to their tree branches for a long time, they could be gathered when needed. During the winter, women regularly prepared meals of

Figure 1.6. Mule deer, which thrive in piñon-juniper woodlands, were an important source of animal protein for Pueblo people.

Cottontails, however, continued to be hunted, for they apparently thrived in the brushy vegetation that grew on recovering fallow fields. The hunting pattern differed on Mesa Verde itself, where larger populations of big game continued to be available.

Like plants, animals provided useful products other than food. People wove blankets from tur-key feathers and rabbit fur and made awls, needles, spatulas, ornaments, and flutes from turkey and deer bones. "Man's best friend," the dog, shared their accommodations, and favorite dogs were buried with due regard. Although today fishermen flock to the region's rivers and man-made lakes, we have little evidence that ancestral Pueblo people caught or ate fish. This is puzzling. Part of the reason may be poor preservation of fish parts or the fact that fish caught and eaten on the spot leave no evidence back in villages or homes. But ancestral Pueblo people might simply not have eaten much fish.

we assume that many harvests came from local agricultural fields and other places where daily living had disturbed the natural vegetation. Probably some members of each community occasionally traveled considerable distances from their pueblos to collect special plant resources.

Jonathan Driver, who has studied regional faunal records, believes that Mesa Verdeans hunted primarily local animals but occasionally sent small hunting parties farther afield. They obtained animal protein mainly from mule deer, jackrabbits, and cottontail rabbits, along with domesticated turkeys. Less often, hunters brought home bighorn sheep, pronghorn antelope, and elk. Although we find rodent bones in archaeological sites, they probably reflect natural deaths, as well as hunting and trapping.

As Driver has noted, the quantities of rabbit, deer, and turkey meat that Puebloan people consumed fluctuated over time. Basketmaker III and Pueblo I people, for example, relied on rabbits and large game and rarely ate turkeys, whereas later Pueblo II people regularly raised turkeys for their meat. After 1150, Puebloans of the Great Sage Plain (see map, p. 45) ate less big game and even more turkey meat. By then, they had overhunted deer near their settlements and diminished deer habitat through generations of tree cutting.

Anthropogenic Ecology: Humans' Effects on Their Landscape

For eight centuries, inhabitants of the Mesa Verde region farmed, foraged, hunted, chopped down trees, and did much else that affected their landscape. From time to time, intentionally or not, they also set fire to portions of forests. We refer to such human influence on plant and animal communities as "anthropogenic (human-caused) ecology."

Archaeologists Tim Kohler and Meredith Mathews were among the first to report evidence of this process, from Pueblo I village sites around Dolores, Colorado. In the ancient plant remains, they observed a shift over time in fuelwood use, from piñon and juniper trees to shrubby plants and cottonwoods. That is, as preferred trees were used up, people sought alternative fuels still locally available.

Figure 1.7. Bean farming thrives today, as it did centuries ago, in the Montezuma Valley, north of Cortez, Colorado.

for example. Did eight centuries of intermittent farming diminish nutrients in corn fields? Can we even document such trends after modern farmers have cultivated the same land? To complicate matters, it is difficult to assess the effects of historically introduced weeds that have invaded modern landscapes.

Despite such difficulties, we archaeologists continue to fine-tune our knowledge of the Mesa Verde region's past environment. Our multiple lines of evidence include plant and animal data preserved in archaeological sites; reconstructions of ancient weather; knowledge of modern plants and animals and of the best places to farm; and the responses of living indigenous groups to their environmental problems. As our archaeological looking glass continues to clear, the ancient Mesa Verde landscape comes into sharper focus—not quite like Alice's experience, perhaps, but satisfying nevertheless.

With Vandy Bowyer, I took a similar look at the Pueblo III plant record of the Sand Canyon locality near Cortez, Colorado, and concluded that although Puebloans had cut many trees and opened up land for agriculture, portions of piñon-juniper forests still remained within walking distance of their pueblos. That people consumed less corn in the late 1200s might reflect more than the onset of drought: the fertility of the land might have diminished, too, reducing its ability to produce enough food. It is clear that by this time, preferred foods, including wild game, had become scarce and people turned to foraging for wild plants. At Salmon Ruin, to the south, we know that hungry residents resorted to eating leftover corncobs, normally used only as tinder or fuel, as well as juniper bark, broad yucca leaves, animal bones, and insects.

Karen R. Adams is an archaeobotanical consultant who has been researching plant remains from archaeological sites in the American Southwest since the early 1970s. She is director of environmental archaeology at Crow Canyon Archaeological Center and coordinator of the Borderlands Ecology Project for Mexico North Research Network, based in San Antonio, Texas.

Closing Thoughts
Reconstructing past environments can be a challenge. Many facets of life affected by the environment simply are invisible to the researcher's eye—a maverick late spring frost or an early fall frost,

Figure 2.1. Basketmaker II petroglyphs of anthropomorphic figures along the San Juan River, Utah.

The Earliest Mesa Verdeans

Hunters, Foragers, and First Farmers

Mona Charles

Mesa Verde National Park is best known for its stunning architectural sites, vestiges of the ancestral Pueblo people. It is difficult to imagine that earlier people lived in the region for many millennia before the architects who built Cliff Palace, Long House, Balcony House, Sun Temple, and the rest of the alcove and cliff-top ruins. But the Mesa Verde culture as we define it today grew out of a local population that inhabited the area for many thousands of years before the cliff dwellers. My research into the hunter-gatherers and early agriculturalists of the Mesa Verde region is driven largely by my desire to learn more about "those who came before" the Mesa Verde architects. I have looked at one archaeological site in particular—the Darkmold Site in the Animas River valley near Durango, Colorado. It is contributing substantial new information about the people and the environment of this region from its earliest occupation through the introduction of agriculture.

Paleoindians

We know little about the very earliest people of the Mesa Verde region, who probably moved into the area sometime between 11,500 and 11,000 years ago. Archaeologists call them "Paleoindians." They were mostly nomadic and followed herds of now-extinct large game animals—wooly pachyderms, giant bison, and horses.

Archaeologists divide the Paleoindian period throughout the American Southwest into subperiods, largely on the basis of differences in hunting practices and associated artifacts, especially spear points. The so-called Clovis and Folsom peoples,

the earliest of the Paleoindians, lived in small groups and camped along streams and near lakes. Many of these no longer contain water, owing to a general drying trend that began with the melting of the glaciers that once covered much of North America, including parts of the San Juan Mountains north and east of Mesa Verde. It is widely accepted that Folsom and Clovis people depended on big game for most of their daily needs, such as meat and fat. They boiled and cracked bones for the succulent, nutritious marrow. They used hides for clothing and to cover temporary shelters, keeping winter winds and freezing temperatures at bay.

Other than a few isolated spear points and an occasional sparse scatter of tools and flakes, archaeologists have found little evidence of Clovis or Folsom people in the central Mesa Verde region. There is more evidence that they roamed southeastern Utah and northeastern Arizona, and still better evidence of early Paleoindians in the Gunnison Basin and the San Luis Valley, only a few days' walking distance from Mesa Verde. What attracted Paleoindians to these places and not to the central Mesa Verde region is not fully understood. Perhaps big game animals were absent around Mesa Verde. Paleontological remains of extinct fauna are extremely scarce there, even though the climate might not have differed significantly from that of the Gunnison Basin and the San Luis Valley.

In an attempt to learn more about the climate and landscape during Paleoindian times, students and staff from Fort Lewis College have carefully studied the layers of silt and sand at the Darkmold

Figure 2.2. Mona Charles (center) and Fort Lewis College students excavating a storage cist, Darkmold Site, 2005.

Site (fig. 2.2). Deeply buried, just above the Permian Sandstone, is a layer of fire-reddened soil, the result of a forest fire that swept through the area. This natural disaster was a boon for archaeologists and geologists because it left bits of charcoal that could be radiocarbon dated. From them we know that the fire blazed about 11,600 years ago—just before the time the first Paleoindians likely arrived. By studying fossil pollen from the oxidized and charcoal-enriched layers, we also know that the climate then was wetter and colder than it is today.

Later, as the climate became warmer and drier, a pine forest expanded farther into the Mesa Verde region, and grasses and sagebrush replaced colder- and wetter-adapted plant species. Smaller browsers and grazers such as elk, deer, and bighorn sheep took advantage of the rich new environment created by the receding glaciers and replaced the larger animals that were so important to the Paleoindians.

By about 7500 BCE, much better evidence exists for Paleoindians in the Mesa Verde region. Archaeologists find late Paleoindian stone tools in larger numbers and throughout the environmental zones, although actual sites are still rare. The large mammals had died out by this time, and people had adapted by hunting the smaller herd animals and incorporating even smaller mammals such as rabbits and rodents into their diet, along with wild plants. A technological advance, the atlatl, or spear thrower, made it easier to hunt the smaller animals (fig. 2.3). The question of whether these later Paleoindians settled in the Mesa Verde region year-round or occasionally visited remains open. Clear evidence exists elsewhere for habitation structures and long-term camps during the late Paleoindian period.

Archaic People

In the Mesa Verde region, a shift to what archaeologists call the Archaic period began about 6000 BCE. Archaic hunters—part of a pan-North American way of life—embraced the atlatl almost exclusively. Along with hunting the smaller herd animals, these people made use of a greater variety of locally available plants and animals than the Paleoindians had done. Vegetation patterns at the time approximated those of today. The Archaic was a period of population growth and migration. It is well represented by sites as diverse as rockshelters, campsites, rock art sites, lithic procurement sites, places where plants and animals were processed, sites where game drives took place, and perhaps even shrines.

Archaeologists often divide the Archaic into three subperiods—early, middle, and late. For the most part, the climate changes of the Paleoindian period had ameliorated by the Early Archaic, and an era of environmental stabilization began that continues today. Early Archaic sites from the Mesa Verde region are few, but unlike Paleoindian artifacts, they appear in the mountains, as well as on the mesa tops and at the heads of canyons. People of the Early Archaic continued to follow the mobile lifestyle of the Paleoindians, but they may have moved around as much for plant gathering as for hunting. Food plants in this region often grow in scattered patches, and their seeds, nuts, or fruits ripen at different times of the year. Archaic gatherers

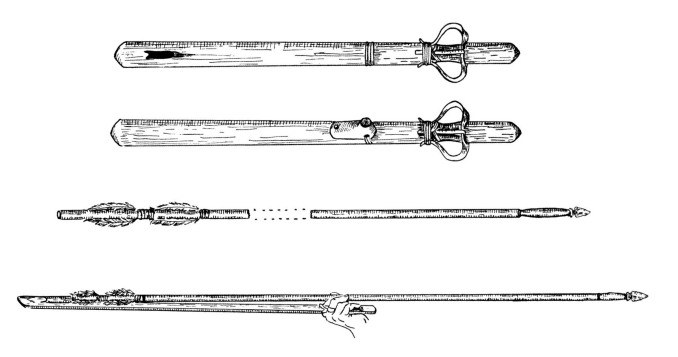

Figure 2.3. Throwing sticks, or atlatls. Used with a dart and a spear shaft, the atlatl was the standard weapon used by Archaic and Basketmaker II people.

needed to understand local plant communities thoroughly and be prepared to travel long distances to reach them at just the right time. Most likely, women directed when to move and where to camp for harvesting plant foods most efficiently.

A warming and drying trend during the later part of the Early Archaic period and into the Middle Archaic (5000 to 2500 BCE) may have pushed people into the higher elevations of the Mesa Verde region, where temperatures were slightly cooler and water from winter snow and spring rain was more available. Sites of the Middle Archaic often reveal a variety of atlatl point styles—useful indicators that ideas from beyond the Mesa Verde region, if not actual people from elsewhere, influenced local residents (fig. 2.4). Some archaeologists view the Mesa Verde Archaic population as having developed from a local, mountain-adapted Paleoindian group, the so-called Foothills Mountain Complex. Others see influences coming from the Great Basin, to the west, the San Juan Basin, to the south, and the Rio Grande Valley, to the east. I think it likely that both in-place development and migration account for the variability in Archaic artifact assemblages. As

people moved into new areas, they must have come into contact with other Archaic groups. Certainly they traded goods and exchanged ideas with one another, and they may have intermarried, all of which led to regional variations in artifacts and ideas.

Archaeologists know much more about Late Archaic people in the Mesa Verde region than about their predecessors, having found and excavated many more Late Archaic sites than those of the earlier subperiods. In addition, Late Archaic people more commonly lived in rockshelters, where the dry atmosphere preserved an array of perishable items—baskets, mats, and plain-weave sandals, for example. Split-twig figurines that resemble deer or mountain sheep have been discovered at some Late Archaic sites (fig. 2.5). Despite their overall similarities, each of these willow-twig figurines is unique. They often appear in groups in rockshelters along the Colorado River and its tributaries. Although no one knows exactly how people used them, most archaeologists think that their makers believed them to possess ritualistic or supernatural powers.

The Late Archaic was also a time of trade in exotic or hard-to-find items such as obsidian,

Figure 2.4. Archaic and Basketmaker II atlatl points. *Top row:* Basketmaker II spear points from the Darkmold Site. The point at extreme right was probably used with a bow and arrow. *Bottom row:* Early, Middle, and Late Archaic points from the San Juan Mountains, southwestern Colorado.

turquoise, and marine shells. Large and small shells were traded into the Mesa Verde region from the Pacific coast, probably via southern Arizona. By cutting off the tops of the spirals of small gastropods (species of *Olivella*) and grinding their edges smooth, people made shell bead necklaces and bracelets strung on sinew or human hair. They cut, polished, and sometimes etched decorative patterns on large abalone (*Haliotis*) shells and wore them as pendants. Artisans and perhaps even shamans drew and painted abstract images and representational life forms on the walls of cliffs, alcoves, and boulders.

Simple, easy-to-build living structures at some Late Archaic sites imply that people had begun to settle in certain areas. Nuclear families living in

these wood-and-mud houses might have survived the winters on wild plants they gathered and stored in underground cists. Experiments in plant domestication at some Late Archaic sites set the stage for what happened next—the introduction of corn agriculture and the beginning of ancestral Pueblo culture.

Basket-Making Cultivators

The Archaic way of life across the Mesa Verde region ended, for the most part, around 1000 BCE, when corn made its way into the region. Though not all groups adopted corn simultaneously, by 300 BCE it was a primary subsistence item in the region, if not the paramount one. People no doubt contin-

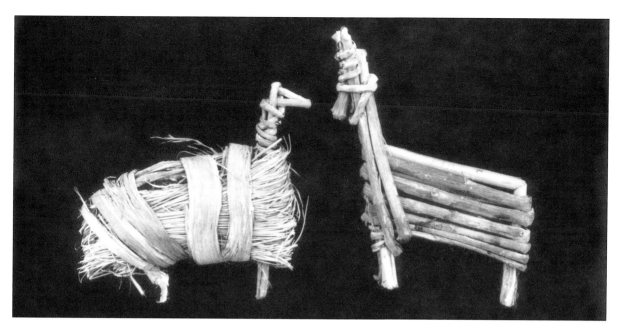

Figure 2.5. Split-twig figurines have been found in caves and rock shelters in the greater Mesa Verde region. Researchers believe that Archaic people used them for hunting magic.

ued to hunt and gather wild plants, but in time, wild food sources diminished in importance relative to corn, squash, and later beans.

Settlement in small villages or hamlets replaced the nomadism of the Archaic period. People became invested in the land in an entirely new way. For one thing, they could not leave their crops unattended for long. Somebody had to stay in the village year-round, even if only the very old or the very young were left behind to watch over the crops. Tying themselves to the land as farmers while continuing to hunt and gather confronted these people with challenges—challenges they met successfully. They became the forager-farmers of what archaeologists call the "Basketmaker II" period. (When archaeologists first codified the names of these cultural periods, evidence for the Archaic period was in its infancy, so they began the classification system with the Basketmakers. Since then, Basketmaker I has been subsumed under the umbrella of the Archaic period.)

In 1893, Richard Wetherill, a rancher-turned-explorer from Mancos, Colorado, excavated the first Basketmaker II site that we know of. In a cave in Whisker's Draw in southeastern Utah (see fig. 16.1), Wetherill came upon an occupation level below the cliff-dweller level. He called the

antecedent Puebloans who had lived there "Basket People," because of the many remnants of beautifully crafted baskets he uncovered. For a long time after this initial discovery, explorers paid little attention to sites of the Basket People, except for making relic-hunting forays into the canyon country. Not until the early twentieth century did A. V. Kidder, Jesse Nusbaum, and Samuel Guernsey undertake professional expeditions specifically to unravel the mystery of the Basket People. They excavated in sheltered sites in Marsh Pass, Arizona, and Kanab, Utah. In 1927, at a meeting in Pecos, New Mexico, archaeologists formally defined the Basketmaker II period of the Puebloan era as the "agricultural, atlatl-using, non-pottery-making stage."

It took a few decades after Kidder and Guernsey's work for new information about the Basketmaker II period to come to light. This time the information pertained to the eastern Basketmakers. While digging in the talus and rubble of a trio of sites near Durango, Colorado, archaeologists Earl Morris and Robert Burgh, along with local amateurs Helen Sloan Daniels and Zeke Flora, uncovered the remains of superimposed floors stacked against steep-sided slopes and built on man-made terraces. Log foundations for crib-roofed shelters

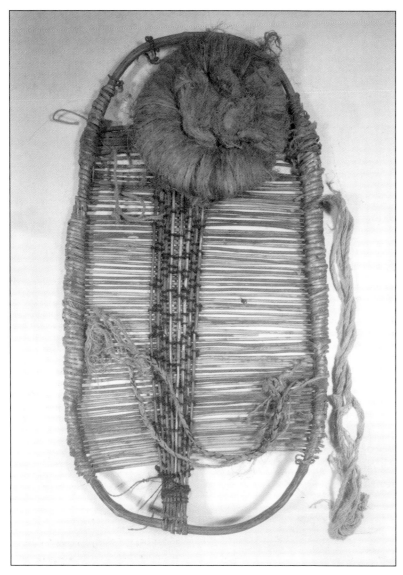

Figure 2.6. A cradleboard from the Basketmaker II period.

early explorations in Southwestern archaeology. Nevertheless, archaeologists knew little about the physical nature of the Basketmakers. Because Basketmaker skulls differed from the elongated skulls of the later cliff dwellers, people popularly believed that the Basketmakers came from a different "genetic stock." Sometime later, researchers showed that the Basketmakers had strapped their infants to soft cradleboards whereas the cliff dwellers had strapped their infants to rigid cradleboards that deformed the babies' malleable skulls. Cradleboards, not genetics, were responsible for the differenct skull shapes (fig. 2.6).

Osteological study of skeletons from recent investigations near Durango has greatly improved our knowledge of the daily lives of the Basketmakers. We now know that the Durango Basketmakers were short— the men, 5 feet 5 inches or less—compact, and muscular. The hands, feet, and knees of adult Basketmakers showed signs of healed fractures and degenerative joint diseases. They were no strangers to hard labor—lifting, stooping, kneeling, and squatting. They traveled long distances over steep terrain. Many of their crania showed signs of moderate anemia, a result of iron deficiency but not necessarily of malnutrition. Some bones showed signs of infections that could have resulted from common transmissible diseases. The teeth were heavily worn and sometimes looked polished. I attribute this tooth wear to their having chewed fibers and hides in preparation for weaving and sewing. This premise is supported by the unusually large numbers of fiber-processing tools made from animal ribs and scapulae in the Durango sites.

Besides baskets, Basketmaker II people made sandals, gopher-skin pouches, menstrual aprons, feather blankets, rabbit-skin robes, and sleeping

circumscribed the circular clay floors. Inside the mud-and-wood structures were pits for storing food, hearths for heating and cooking, pits used for burials, and areas for working and sleeping. The discovery of such substantial architecture reinforced a growing belief among Southwestern archaeologists that a significant change had taken place from the hunting-and-gathering lifestyle of the Archaic period. Not only were people now settling down in one place for long periods of time, but they were also claiming rights to the land by burying their dead among the living.

Finding Basketmaker burials and their associated funerary objects was the main goal of many

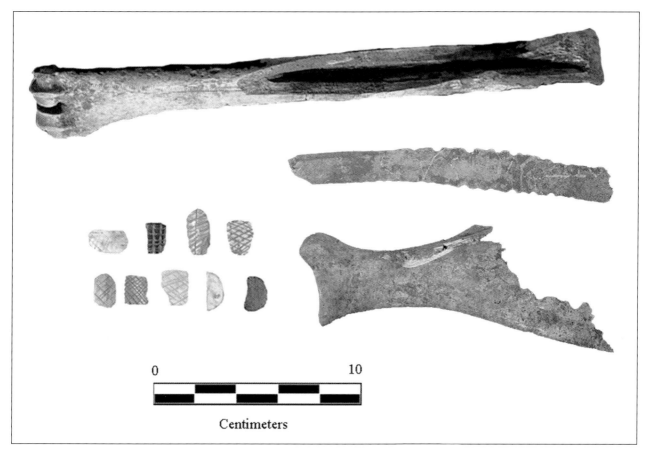

Figure 2.7. Bone tools and dice from the Darkmold Site. Basketmaker people used ribs and scapulae from deer, mountain sheep, and elk to process fibers for textiles. They fashioned long bones into scrapers to remove fat and flesh from bones. Oval, circular, and rectangular pieces of bone and antler, used in gaming, were finely polished and etched.

mats woven from reeds and juniper bark. Bone whistles, stone and clay pipes, and bone and antler gaming pieces have been found at Basketmaker II sites as distant from one another as Kanab, Utah, and Durango, Colorado (fig. 2.7). Basketmaker II people often buried their dead with elaborate gifts and ornaments, which archaeologists interpret as evidence of differences in social or economic status. Status was communicated not only by kinds and quantities of burial goods but also in rock art by the display of jewelry, flutes or whistles, clothing, masks, and body embellishments. By these measures, at least some Basketmaker II people were well off.

Basketmaker II settlement patterns often reveal regional clustering. One such cluster is near Durango, where several large sites, including the Falls Creek Shelters, the Darkmold Site, and Talus Village, were inhabited over many generations. Is it coincidental that they lie close to present-day natural hot springs? Perhaps the local Basketmakers planted near the hot springs, where the ground was warmer, in order to get an early start on the summer growing season. More significant perhaps, hot springs are therapeutic. Their importance to historic Native Americans is well-known (the Ute name for Pagosa Springs means "sulfur-spring water"), and no doubt they were important prehistorically as well.

A discussion of the Basketmaker II period is incomplete without mentioning its distinctive rock art. Basketmaker rock art appears all across the Mesa Verde region—on boulders, in alcoves, on canyon walls, and along drainages and river valleys. Images of animals, abstract forms, and human figures with realistic details were pecked, painted, or both. Elements occur as single images and as large, complex panels. This rock art was sometimes

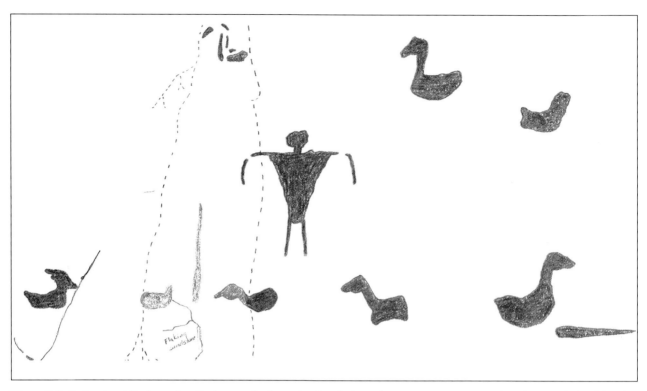

Figure 2.8. Red-painted Basketmaker II pictographs from the Watch Crystal Site, near Durango, Colorado. Broad-shouldered anthropomorphic figures and ducklike images are common in the rock art of this period.

private, made in hard-to-reach spots where few eyes ever saw it, and sometimes public. The human forms are small or life-size, and sex is sometimes indicated by genitals and by breasts and menstrual aprons. Human forms may be standing or reclining; the latter are sometimes depicted playing flutes and are called "kokopelli," from the Hopi word *kokopilau*, the humpbacked flute player. Body shape is most often triangular, but rectangular and trapezoidal forms appear as well. Heads are both rounded and rectangular, sometimes with large eyes and wearing headdresses. Masks and masklike features were popular and suggest supernatural personages. Overall, Basketmaker II rock art is remarkably consistent, despite some regional variations. Rock art specialist Sally Cole attributes this consistency to the long duration of the Basketmaker lifeway and the broad sharing of material culture, ideas, and ceremonial practices—all of which are visible in Basketmaker rock art.

Similarities and differences in Basketmaker artifacts, architecture, rock art, and burial goods and practices across the Mesa Verde region have been fodder for ideas about migration and ethnicity. Earl Morris proposed a northward migration into, or perhaps colonization of, the Durango area by Mogollon people from east-central Arizona and west-central New Mexico. Culturally sensitive artifacts such as textiles and projectile points, however, challenge Morris's migration design. Current ideas about Basketmaker origins include both migration and in-place development. R. G. Matson sees two distinct Basketmaker II populations in the Mesa Verde region: an eastern population, such as the Durango group that developed from a local population, and a western population, such as the groups in southeastern Utah and northeastern Arizona who migrated in from the Basin and Range geographic province to the south. What might be more likely is that Basketmakers across the region participated in a broad cultural tradition in which variations represented individual or group (perhaps clan) choices influenced by interregional contacts and associations. More important, the differences likely had roots among the indigenous Archaic populations.

This long-lived and highly successful period in Southwest prehistory drew to a close around 500 CE, when people began consistently to use bows and arrows instead of atlatls and to rely on pottery making more than basketry (although archaeologists continue to call them "Basketmakers" until about 750). I believe the social and economic system we see among the present-day Pueblos had its origins in the Basketmaker II tradition, in large part because of the introduction of agriculture. When prehistoric Southwesterners embraced agriculture—which they seem to have done rapidly—their lives were changed forever. Metaphorically speaking, the seeds were sown for ancestral Pueblo culture.

Acknowledgments

I thank Sally Cole for generously sharing her photographs and for her many helpful suggestions. I thank Betty Christian and Mark and Ann Dold and their children for their part in advancing the state of Basketmaker II research.

Mona Charles teaches at Fort Lewis College and directs the college's archaeological field school. Her special area of interest is the Basketmaker II period.

Figure 3.1. Household tools from the Pueblo I period.

The Genesis of Pueblos
Innovations between 500 and 900 CE

Richard H. Wilshusen

As an archaeologist who has worked in the Mesa Verde region for more than two decades, I am particularly interested in understanding the transformation of early Southwestern communities. The years between 650 and 850 CE are especially intriguing, for it is then that we see evidence of the genesis of villages, or large pueblos. These 200 years encompass most of what archaeologists identify as the Basketmaker III (500–750 CE) and Pueblo I (750–900) periods. Early Southwestern archaeologists such as Earl Morris (1889–1956) thought the cultural changes that took place in these two centuries were revolutionary enough to suggest that one culture had literally moved into the region and replaced another. We now recognize that the rapid shift to living in villages was a local innovation and not a replacement of people.

The Basketmaker III inhabitants of the Mesa Verde region were almost certainly the ancestors of the present-day Pueblo peoples of Arizona and New Mexico, and their population increased dramatically in this region after 575 CE. For almost two centuries after that time, their lives were centered on small hamlets of one to three residences (fig. 3.2). Only after about 775 did the first villages—settlements of 100 or more people—begin to appear. Yet by 850, more than half the region's population lived in such pueblos. Population increased at the same time, and it became more difficult to make a living from a mixed economy based on foraging, hunting, and gardening. People had to depend on corn agriculture and stored surplus food to get through lean times. This experiment with a more sedentary and communal way of life changed ancestral Pueblo society forever.

Some innovations, such as the increase in settlement size that we associate with villages, took hold rapidly. In areas where villages formed, an average site size of 1 to 3 households leaped to 15 to 20 households in less than a generation's time. Other changes, such as sedentism—the commitment to living in the same place year after year—evolved more slowly. When my colleagues and I compare the architecture, trash deposits, and settlement patterns of sites from around 650 CE with those from around 850, we recognize a gradual shift to a more sedentary way of life. It is evident, for example, that by the 800s villagers were building their homes more sturdily, and possibly they were accumulating more nonperishable possessions than had been usual several centuries before. It is also clear that population was growing across the region and people were making more intensive use of natural resources such as agricultural land, wild game, and woodland timber.

Yet even though regional population had grown markedly by 850, people were leaving the area just 50 years later. This pattern of rise and fall of population in the Mesa Verde region foreshadows what happened in the twelfth and thirteenth centuries (see chapters 4 and 5).

The Life and Times of Basketmaker III People
Archaeologists have found only a handful of sites to show that Basketmaker III people were living in the Mesa Verde region before about 575 CE. By the early

Figure 3.2. Reconstruction of Tres Bobos Hamlet, a characteristic Basketmaker III settlement. Note the brush-covered shelters, outdoor work areas, and pit structure with antechamber.

600s, in contrast, we see plenty of evidence: people were chopping down trees, building residences, making pottery, and forming communities. Analysis of artifacts such as the pottery and projectile points they left behind suggests that these early inhabitants immigrated there from south of the San Juan River. My own best estimate is that by 675 the region's population totaled some 1,000 to 1,500 people, living in widely dispersed communities. As on any frontier, each small community must have been highly self-sufficient, for it was a long walk to the nearest neighbors.

Ancestral Pueblo residences of this period typically consisted of one to three pithouses with small pit rooms nearby for storing food and tools (fig. 3.2). Ramadas, or brush-covered shelters, in the plaza protected some of the outdoor work areas from the sun. Looking across a plaza at a small Basketmaker III hamlet, one might have seen hearths for cooking food, racks for drying hides, and work areas for grinding corn and drying food for long-term storage. Just outside the main site area, one might have expected to find the household's garden and a nearby source of water. Resources such as firewood, water, native edible plants, and game had to be locally available, or else basic daily tasks such as cooking food and supplementing a family's diet with

desirable wild foods would quickly have become too burdensome.

A single pithouse dwelling would have housed a family or an extended family of four to eight people. The pithouse design provided a quick architectural solution to the need for shelter, because much of the earth required for the roof came from the original excavation of the building. The builder dug a large but relatively shallow pit, constructed a wooden framework roof with a brush covering over it, and then covered this construction with the surplus dirt. The wooden framework had to be substantial, for it would carry a load of 5 to 15 tons of earth. Pithouses, which were standard housing throughout the Southwest for centuries, were snug and protected their residents from cold in winter but remained cool in summer.

Although pithouses were relatively efficient to build and inexpensive in terms of labor, anyone who has ever spent time in a root cellar knows that they were also dark and musty. Yet during the coldest days of winter and the hottest days of summer, work in the pithouse—lit by a fire in the central hearth—was no doubt pleasant. Residents stored their household tools on low benches around the edges of the dwelling or in small corner bins or sometimes hung them from the rafters and beams of the roof. In winter it is possible that much of the grinding of corn and preparing of meals took place in the pithouse, and people likely crowded in to sleep on the floor in the evening. When weather permitted, however, household members probably carried out many of their daily tasks in the outside plaza or under nearby ramadas.

By looking at the features of a site and the artifacts in its trash, archaeologists can tell a lot about what the former inhabitants did there. Basketmaker III sites almost always have one or more large sandstone metates (grinding slabs) and associated manos (hand stones) for grinding corn and wild foods and possibly even for smashing up clay and temper for pottery making. The stone tools are surprisingly basic and expedient. Although some of the projectile points for arrows and darts are well made, the majority of the stone tools in Basketmaker III trash consist simply of flakes with sharp edges for the cutting and scraping tasks related to food preparation, woodworking, and processing animal hides or plant fibers. Large, heavy stone mauls or ax heads would have been hafted onto wooden handles to make small hatchets for "gnawing" down the many trees and saplings needed for house construction, firewood, and the manufacture of wooden tools such as digging sticks and hunting bows. Although pottery is found at these sites, it is relatively plain and not particularly well made. Many containers and tools probably were fashioned out of plant fiber, wood, gourds, or other perishable materials, and these are only rarely preserved in archaeological sites.

Often archaeologists can tell a great deal about how "sedentary" a society was by looking at the permanence of its facilities and the weight of its tools. The fact that many Basketmaker tool kits appear to have included many lightweight items such as yucca-fiber baskets and gourd vessels suggests that household moves were still feasible, though not easy.

Basketmakers, like the Puebloans who followed them, understandably found it difficult to carry weighty objects such as grinding stones and large quantities of stored food (corn is heavy) over long distances. Basketmaker people appear often to have kept at least a year's worth of foodstuffs in storage as insurance against poor crop yields caused by bad weather or other perils. But the relatively short use-lives of their structures and the portability of many of their tools suggest that relocating to avoid a crisis was still a very real option for them.

The Knobby Knee Site

In 1988 archaeologists excavated a stockaded Basketmaker III hamlet before it was destroyed by the construction of an irrigation canal about 21 miles northwest of Cortez, Colorado. The site, Knobby Knee Stockade, got its name from a knobby-kneed human portrayed on a prehistoric pot found at the site. It was a hamlet of one to three families that thrived from 610 to 650 CE. Over time, as children grew up and adults aged, families needed to repair and remodel their pithouses or vacate them

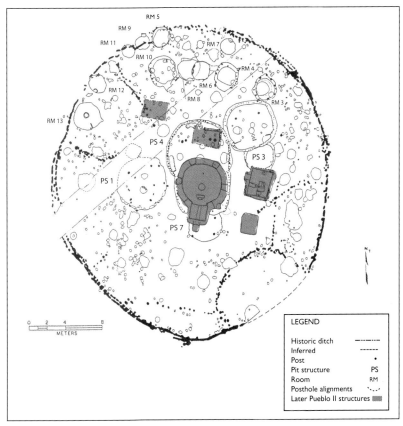

Figure 3.3. Plan of Knobby Knee Stockade, a Basketmaker III pithouse hamlet.

The Genesis of Pueblos 21

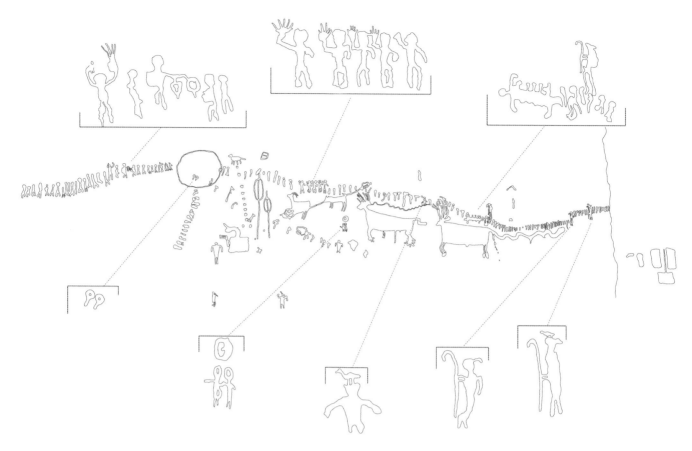

Figure 3.4. Basketmaker III petroglyph panel in the western Mesa Verde region that seems to depict many people traveling to a central gathering place, perhaps a great kiva.

and build new ones. As the archaeologists dug, they were able to recognize and record many of these changes. They also noted the remains of one unusually large pithouse and the existence of an encircling, defensive wooden stockade, which reminds me of those surrounding historic American frontier forts.

Comparing Knobby Knee with other Basketmaker III sites in areas that have been intensively surveyed, I surmise that it was part of a larger community that included other, similar hamlets in the vicinity. Factors such as intermarriage, communal ownership of farmland, sharing of daily tasks, and mutual defense must have bound the members of this community together.

When the inhabitants of Knobby Knee eventually abandoned their hamlet, they took with them most of their usable household items. They left only the heaviest things, such as a trough metate and its associated manos, and a few special items, including a miniature jar, two sandal-impressed clay tablets, and several small pendants and azurite nodules. This suggests that they were able to move almost all the remainder of their household goods and therefore stayed in the general area.

Before leaving, they set fire to their homes. They also appear to have buried a dog in the floor of one of the other structures that was burned at the site. Some archaeologists argue that intentional burning of houses and villages points to warfare, and this certainly is true in some cases (see chapter 16). But although Basketmaker people certainly knew conflict, the Knobby Knee site showed no evidence of violence at the time its inhabitants left. I believe the destruction was part of an abandonment ritual, perhaps to signal that these people still held claim to the site and the area and to preclude the possibility that their dwellings might be taken over by others. Other examples of burned Basketmaker III hamlets reinforce this interpretation.

Figure 3.5. Artist's reconstruction of Duckfoot Pueblo.

Judging from its numerous structures, relatively long history of use, and substantial stockade, Knobby Knee must have been one of the more important sites within its dispersed community. Yet it did not offer enough space or facilities for a gathering of the 100 to 300 people who likely made up its local community. Although we have not surveyed the area close to Knobby Knee sufficiently to know about this community, we know that community gatherings did take place during Basketmaker III times. There are great kivas, or immense pit structures, just to the south of the San Juan River that could have held several hundred people. And scenes that seem to depict a great kiva as a gathering place for hundreds of people are found in rock art panels in the Mesa Verde region, suggesting that the concept was well established among Basketmaker III people (fig. 3.4).

Life in Early Pueblos

Archaeologists mark the shift from the Basketmaker III way of life in the Mesa Verde region to what they call the "Pueblo I" period—beginning around 750 CE— by changes in both architecture and the way the Mesa Verdeans laid out their settlements. Duckfoot Pueblo, located in the Montezuma Valley west of Cortez, Colorado, and excavated in the 1980s by the Crow Canyon Archaeological Center, offers a good example of the increased investment people began to make in their housing (fig. 3.5). The site consists of three attached suites of aboveground rooms, each apparently housing a single extended family. Its occupants lived in the larger front rooms and used the smaller back rooms primarily for long-term food storage. The site also includes three deeply excavated pithouses, each just to the south of the suite of rooms with which it was associated. To build their hamlet, Duckfoot's inhabitants used stone and earth for the walls, timbers for the support posts and ceilings, and excavated earth from the pithouse construction to cover the roofs and finish the walls. Duckfoot's pithouses, like those of nearby hamlets, were primarily residential. Pithouses in a few larger

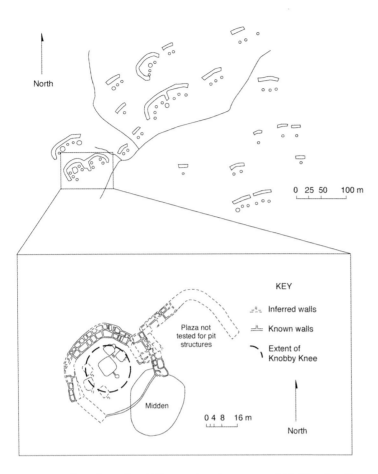

North

0 25 50 100 m

KEY

Inferred walls

Known walls

Extent of
Knobby Knee

Plaza not
tested for pit
structures

Midden

0 4 8 16 m

North

Figure 3.6. Plan of McPhee Village with enlargement of McPhee Pueblo.
An outline of the Knobby Knee site is inserted for size comparison.

When I compare the household tool kit from a Basketmaker III residence with one from a Pueblo I household, many things are not very different. In both Basketmaker III and Pueblo I sites, there is evidence of digging sticks, choppers, and hoes for work in the agricultural fields; metates and manos for grinding corn and gathered fruits, nuts, and seeds; bows and arrows and stone tools for hunting and cutting up rabbits, deer, and small game; jars and ollas for storing food and water, as well as pots blackened from cooking; woven net bags for transporting items and sandals to protect people's feet while on journeys; and numerous personal items. Yet subtle differences show how the organization of daily life gradually changed over 200 years The sheer weight of a household's possessions was greater in Pueblo I than in Basketmaker III, and this limited a family's ability to pick up and move. People had more grinding implements, more ceramic pots, and, most important, much more stored food —and they made a greater investment in the storerooms that kept it secure.

By the ninth century, the organization of communities in the Mesa Verde region had changed too. Most people lived in compact villages encompassing 15 to 50 households and populations averaging around 200. Villagers could control their local landscapes because they probably had historic claims to particular parcels of land and certainly must have had the capacity to field warriors. Still, although the villages represent a striking social phenomenon for their time, the individual dwellings remain architecturally unimpressive. When I walk through the ruins of a Pueblo I village and imagine it restored to pristine condition, it reminds me of a big trailer court.

McPhee Village, which archaeologists excavated in the 1980s in connection with the Dolores Archaeological Project (see fig. 3.6 and chapter 20), is an example of one of the largest settlements. Even a small part of this site reveals a household and community layout entirely different from that

villages, however, clearly served as venues for community meetings and religious rituals.

A Pueblo I hamlet such as Duckfoot was more substantial than even a stockaded Basketmaker III site such as Knobby Knee. Pueblo I rooms for food storage were more secure than the smaller Basketmaker III pit rooms, and a family's storerooms could now hold at least two years' worth of stored corn. By joining their houses into small pueblos, the inhabitants of a site such as Duckfoot made their aboveground structures habitable nearly year-round, and they were able to move many of their daily household activities out of the pithouses. Increasingly, pithouses served as places where the several households in a hamlet might share in work or neighborhood ceremonies. They also were sufficiently spacious and well insulated to shelter a large extended family in the coldest days of winter.

of earlier Basketmaker III villages. In 850 CE, 12 to 15 households were packed into just the western wing of one of the horseshoe-shaped pueblos in the village. Two hundred years earlier, that much space would have held only two households. With a likely population of 500 people, McPhee Village was one of the largest community centers in the Mesa Verde region. The horseshoe-shaped (or sometimes double U-shaped) roomblocks in these villages are often more substantially constructed than smaller roomblocks in the same village. The large roomblocks sometimes comprise more than 100 rooms.

The McPhee villagers appear to have cultivated fields within one to three miles of their homes and built small field houses—often no more than rama-da-type shelters—for protection from the weather while they tended to their crops. During the summer, these field houses must have offered pleasant respites from village life and allowed people some shelter and a place to make meals while they protected their crops of corn, beans, squash, and greens from the appetites of deer, rabbits, and rodents. Besides, meat was increasingly rare in the ever more populated Pueblo I landscape, so the possibility of hunting game while protecting crops was a second reason to maintain a field house. The overall arrangement of these field houses, dispersed across good patches of well-watered agricultural soils, reminds me of the settlement pattern of the Basketmaker III hamlets of 200 years before.

Although I am fascinated with villages, I still have to ask myself why, in the ninth century, people preferred living in large villages instead of small hamlets. Why live cheek by jowl with so many neighbors? Why risk the increased chance of disease? Why cope with the social problems that arise in crowded settings? Such questions are best addressed by examining some details of McPhee Village and its place within the region as a whole.

Households, Communities, and Regional Organization

Among the 19 roomblocks of McPhee Village, one in particular—McPhee Pueblo—stood out for its size and substantial construction. At its maximum, I estimate that it must have housed at least 25

households in its eastern and western wings. These households must have been closely related and economically tied to one another, but they must also have interacted daily with the larger village community. At least some of the people in these households appear to have occupied key leadership roles and helped to bring order and structure to village life.

Highly structured Pueblo I villages such as McPhee may have been better able to integrate groups from diverse kin and cultural backgrounds into a single community. No doubt people living in hamlets enjoyed freedoms not possible in densely populated settings, but the villages offered different advantages. One was greater security against raiders; another was to serve notice to smaller settlements to cooperate. The diverse settings of a village's cropland would have provided something akin to an insurance policy from crop failures caused by localized disasters such as insect infestations and early summer freezes in low-lying areas. In addition, village life probably expanded inhabitants' ability to trade, find marriage partners, and establish other advantageous relationships, which, in a hamlet, might have been restrictively controlled by one's local kin group.

Other customs may have characterized life in large villages. For example, many ethnographic accounts from other parts of the world tell of big village feasts in which food and other goods are redistributed to those in need and wealthy persons accrue prestige through giving. Archaeologists such as Eric Blinman, Jim Potter, and I have demonstrated that villagewide feasts and ritual performances during Pueblo I times appear to have been controlled by certain roomblocks or social groups within a village such as McPhee.

The new Mesa Verdean villages were dynamic centers that drew people from outside the region. As early as 775 CE newcomers were immigrating from the south, and by 850 we recognize that at least two and possibly three or four cultural groups were coexisting in certain villages. The large feasts and ceremonies associated with these villages might have helped ease social tensions and allowed leaders to show off their status. Other innovations of the time were immense, deep pit structures (up

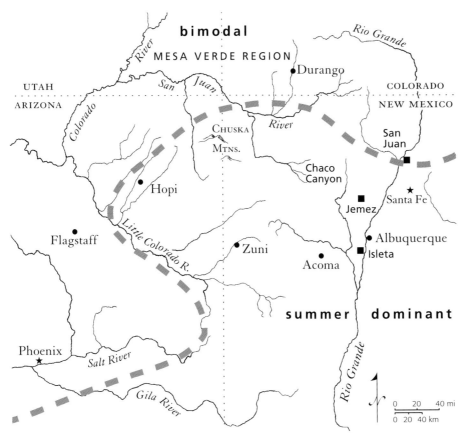

Figure 3.7. Seasonal precipitation patterns in the northern and southern San Juan regions.

period, I estimate that at least 8,000 people were living in the central Mesa Verde region by 860 CE—an amazing increase from late Basketmaker III times. Although population growth and the construction boom of the late Pueblo I period were impressive, they were also short-lived—the latest Pueblo I villages lasted fewer than 40 years. Barely had these villages made their mark on the landscape than they were gone.

The Breakup of the Early Villages and the Beginning of Chaco's Influence

By 880 CE most villages in the Mesa Verde region had begun to break up, and the next century witnessed a sharp drop in population. The archaeological record offers only a few clues to what happened. The fact that people left behind large quantities of household goods suggests that they moved a long distance away. They also appear to have ceremonially burned down the large pit structures where village rituals had taken place. We know they burned these structures intentionally because they set up ritual parapher-nalia such as altars and offerings before starting huge fires in the middle of the floors to ignite the immense roof timbers.

Where did the people go? Most archaeological evidence points to areas south of the San Juan River, where we think the pattern of summer rainfall (essential for growing corn) was more predictable than the annual winter-summer, or "bimodal," pattern of precipitation in the north (fig. 3.7).

In 850 the Mesa Verde region truly was the center of the ancient Pueblo world, but by 950 the center had shifted south to Chaco Canyon. Many

to 75 square meters, or 800 square feet, in area) with massive roofs, which were focal points for villagewide festivals. It is no coincidence that these distinctive pit structures are typically found in the plazas of the larger U- and double U-shaped roomblocks such as McPhee Pueblo. Tom Windes, Ruth Van Dyke, and I have all suggested that these Pueblo I centers of community power were the models for early Pueblo II Chacoan great houses.

The concentration of population and power evident in Mesa Verdean villages between 850 and 875 CE stands in marked contrast to the relative simplicity and small size of settlements 200 years before. Each large village appears to have controlled the natural resources in a surrounding area of some 15 to 30 square miles. In addition, villages rarely existed alone. Usually, three or more were clustered on the landscape only about a mile apart. Thus, a single locale must have had a population of 600 to 1,600 people. Combining the populations of both large villages and outlying hamlets for this village emigrants of the late ninth century must have remembered histories of this southern region, considering that their ancestors had moved north from there only 100 to 200 years earlier. Similarly, when immigrants returned to the Mesa Verde region later, during the Pueblo II period, they undoubtedly must have heard of the great villages of the century before.

Richard Wilshusen is an archaeologist who has worked in Central and South America and the American Southwest. His research interests include rapid population change and settlement shifts in the Basketmaker III and Pueblo I periods and Navajo settlement systems between 1500 and 1750. He lives in Boulder, Colorado.

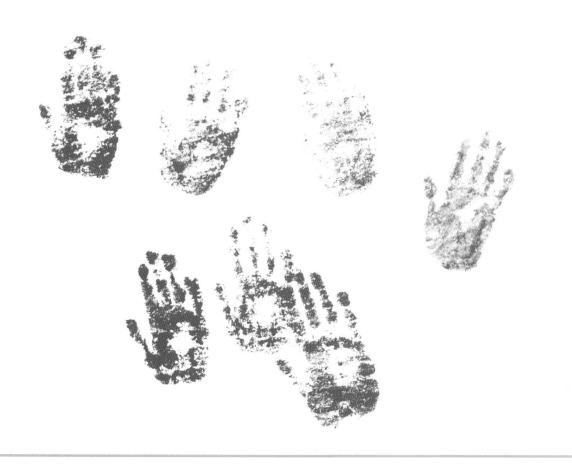

Figure 4.1. Looking west over the Great Sage Plain from a kiva in the Escalante great house, located at the Anasazi Heritage Center near Dolores, Colorado.

The Mesa Verde Region during Chaco Times

William D. Lipe

Although the communities of the Mesa Verde region were largely self-sufficient economically, they were never isolated from events taking place elsewhere in the Southwest. This was especially true in the Pueblo II period, from 900 to 1150 CE. The Mesa Verde people watched from a distance as complex communities dominated by monumental "great houses" developed in Chaco Canyon to the south. As time went on, they became increasingly involved with Chaco, and a small Chaco-style great house came to be a central feature of many Mesa Verde communities. Then, in the early 1100s a massive great-house complex was built at Aztec, in what is now northwestern New Mexico. It signaled that the seat of Chacoan influence and power had moved north to the Totah area, in the southern part of the Mesa Verde region (see map, p. viii). Despite being drawn into the large-scale Chacoan system, the Mesa Verde people maintained their distinctive culture, inventing new ways of doing things while continuing long-standing traditions.

Population Bust and Boom

As Richard Wilshusen noted in the preceding chapter, the boundary between the Pueblo I and Pueblo II periods, 900 CE, falls at a time when many people had moved out of the Mesa Verde region, probably following a southward shift in reliable summer rainfall. In the 900s and early 1000s, when population was sparse in the Mesa Verde region, it was booming south of the San Juan River, especially in and around Chaco Canyon. There, some families and lineages were accumulating land and status and

were beginning to construct impressive great houses as ostentatious symbols of their power. Wilshusen suggested that the first Chacoan great houses might have been modeled after prototypes built in the 800s in the Mesa Verde region, from which some of the Chacoan people may have come.

Although much of the Mesa Verde region was deserted in the 900s and early 1000s, people continued to live in agriculturally productive areas such as the Mesa Verde proper and on some of the other mesas farther west. Rather than spread out over the landscape in individual family farmsteads, they tended to cluster in a few hamlets and small villages.

The Mesa Verde region began to grow rapidly again in about 1050 because families were doing better and having more surviving children and probably because some people were moving back to an area their ancestors had left several generations earlier. People cleared new land and also planted fields that had lain fallow for many years. Both the new settlers and those whose families had stayed in the area tended to live in small, one- or two-family homesteads close to their fields, rather than in concentrated villages (fig. 4.2). Their communities are visible to archaeologists as clusters of these small homesteads, often spread over several square miles. Frequently, the members of a community built a great kiva in order to have a place for ceremonies and other gatherings.

After about 1075 some community leaders began to build small great houses designed to show their familiarity with things Chacoan. In a survey of 36 central Mesa Verde–region communities dating

Figure 4.2. Adapted from an artist's depiction of a typical ancestral Pueblo homestead in the Mesa Verde region around 1050 CE. One-story dwellings probably did not have hatchways on the roof.

to the period 1050–1150, Mark Varien found that nearly 60 percent had a small Chaco-style great house as a central building. Additional examples occur in the Totah and perhaps other parts of the Mesa Verde region, and still others undoubtedly remain to be recognized by archaeologists.

By the end of the Pueblo II period at 1150 CE, the region was in the grip of a severe drought, and people had stopped constructing new Chacoan-style great houses. Population may have remained fairly steady during the decades-long drought, but families built few new houses—the tree-ring record shows that not many trees were cut down for construction timbers. People seem to have "hunkered down," getting through the hard times as best they could.

Architecture Evolves

From around 750 to 1300 CE (the Pueblo I through Pueblo III periods), Mesa Verdean households hardly changed the basic pattern of their residences. These consisted of a few adjoined rooms on the ground surface, a pit structure to the south or southeast of these, and an ashy midden (trash mound) just beyond. Some families lived in single homesteads, others in clusters of such residences, and still others in small hamlets or villages where their homes were joined side by side (see fig. 3.5). Although families used this basic housing plan for centuries, from time to time they changed the way they built their homes, and the Pueblo II period was no exception.

Large, square pit structures, often called "proto-kivas," had become common in the late 700s (Pueblo I). These were usually 12 to 20 feet in diameter and 3 or 4 feet deep, with the walls and roof extending somewhat above the ground surface. In the middle 900s and early 1000s (early Pueblo II), these gave way to smaller, circular pit structures, usually called "kivas" (fig. 4.3). These tended to be 10 to 15 feet in diameter and often were deep enough that their roofs sat flush with the ground surface. Thus, the roof could be part of the outdoor living space in front (just to the south) of the sur-

Figure 4.3. A Mesa Verde–style circular kiva, looking south toward the recess over the ventilator tunnel.

face rooms. Initially, these early kivas were unlined; their walls consisted of the subsoil into which the pit had been dug. Fresh air came in through a vent shaft to the south that was linked to the main chamber by a short tunnel—the same scheme used in the earlier protokivas. Also carried over from earlier times was construction of a small pit in the floor north of the central firepit. This "sipapu" is thought to have symbolized the emergence of Pueblo people from worlds below this one. Four wooden posts, often recessed into the pit-structure wall, supported the roof.

By the mid-1000s some kivas had roof supports of short masonry pillars or "pilasters" resting on a low bench that encircled the periphery of the structure. In the late 1000s and early 1100s (late Pueblo II), kivas were more commonly lined with masonry and were more elaborately built, often with a deep recess over the southern ventilator tunnel, giving the structure a "keyhole" shape in plan view. By this time, most kivas had six masonry pilasters spaced equally around the bench, supporting several courses of short timbers "cribbed" around the periphery of

the structure, with the flat part of the roof resting on the cribbing.

The Mesa Verde people undoubtedly incorporated deep-rooted religious symbols into the design of their kivas. Their subterranean character, roof entries, and sipapus would constantly have reminded people of the belief that humans and other living things emerged from a world or worlds below the present one. The standard north-south orientation of the vent tunnel, central firepit, and sipapu, and of the residential unit itself, probably symbolized cosmological beliefs as well. Building kivas in an increasingly stylized and formal way is consistent with creating spaces appropriate for religious rituals. Scott Ortman (see chapter 12) makes a good case that people of the Mesa Verde region envisioned the earth as a bowl and the sky as a basket—beliefs that were represented by kiva architecture.

Abundant evidence exists that Mesa Verdeans used their kivas not just for occasional religious rituals but also for ordinary household activities. Artifacts left on some of the floors record corn

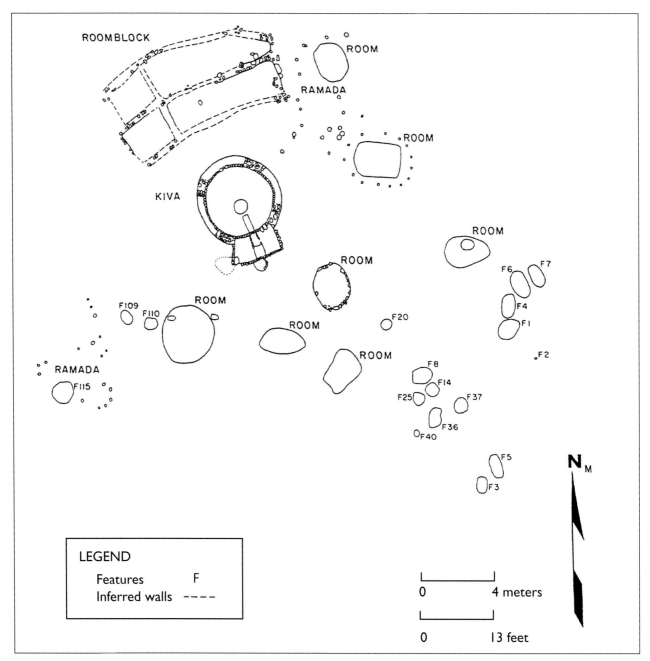

Figure 4.4. The Pueblo II site 5MT8943.

grinding, pottery making, and the manufacturing of stone tools. Food remains left in the hearths show that people cooked meals there, and they probably slept in the warm, underground kivas in the winter. Thus, these early Mesa Verde kivas differ considerably from those of the present-day Pueblos, which are used primarily for religious rituals by groups larger than individual families.

In the 900s and early 1000s (early Pueblo II), people continued to build surface rooms with post-and-mud (jacal) walls similar to those of the Pueblo I period. They built larger front rooms, sometimes with hearths, and used them as work and cooking areas and as sleeping places, especially in summer. They made the adjoining back rooms smaller and used them mostly to store dried corn. The Mesa Verdeans knew how to make stone masonry as early as the 700s, but in most places they did not use it in their houses consistently until the late 1000s or even the 1100s.

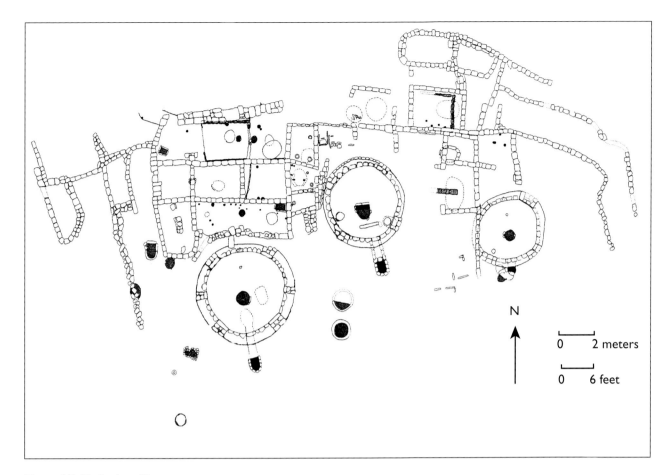

Figure 4.5. Big Juniper House.

These architectural changes did not occur in lockstep throughout the Mesa Verde region. Stone masonry appeared earlier and more consistently on the Mesa Verde proper than elsewhere. In some places, families were still building unlined kivas and pole-and-mud surface rooms until the early 1100s. In general, people seem to have invested more time and effort in their housing in places where farming was most productive and population density highest. Archaeologist Michael Adler has argued that in such situations, rules for land tenure develop and people tend to stay longer in one place. They need long-lasting buildings to show that they have rights to a certain piece of land, even if they are not using it that season or year. When roofs can be supported by masonry walls instead of wooden posts sunk into moist soil, the structures last longer and are easier to maintain.

Two nearly contemporaneous settlements from the late 1000s and early 1100s clearly show these contrasts in types of construction and amount of time invested in buildings. Site 5MT8943, located south of Ute Mountain, was occupied briefly sometime between 1050 and 1120 (fig. 4.4). Its residents probably relied on runoff from summer rains to water their crops, and they expected to have to move their farming locations—and often their homes—frequently. Big Juniper House was inhabited between about 1080 and 1130 on the Mesa Verde proper (fig. 4.5). There, deep soils and reliable annual rainfall made dry farming successful in most years. Big Juniper House residents used much more masonry and made their kivas more elaborate and formal than did the occupants of 5MT8943.

Conserving Water and Soil
The Mesa Verde people were primarily dry farmers of the mesas, dependent on the rain that fell directly on their fields, although those who lived at lower elevations also relied on runoff after rains or

Figure 4.6. Natural pools in the slickrock, southeastern Utah.

spring and from thunderstorms in the summer (see chapter 15). The reservoirs probably did not hold water year-round, but they would have reduced the times when domestic water was really scarce. They could also have been used for laborious "pot irrigation"— carrying water to individual corn plants during the dry early part of the growing season. Reservoirs became widespread over the larger Mesa Verde region during the Pueblo II period.

During the 1000s CE, farmers of the Mesa Verde region also began to conserve soil and water by building series of small check dams across ephemeral drainages and constructing low terraces at the bases of slopes (see fig. 1.2). In some places, they just laid rows of stones parallel to the slope contours. These devices slowed runoff after rains so that the water would soak into the soil, and they also helped control soil erosion— undoubtedly a problem in densely settled areas where much of the natural vegetation had been cleared for farming. These small, fertile plots might have provided some insurance against crop failure on the much larger dry-farmed fields, or they might just have been intensively cultivated "kitchen gardens" close to residences. Some of the check dams could also have helped recharge groundwater flow to nearby springs and seeps.

Chaco Moves North
By about 1075 CE (late Pueblo II), the political-religious leaders of many Mesa Verde communities were building structures that obviously imitated some of the architectural features of Chaco Canyon's ostentatious great houses and great kivas. Examples include Lowry Ruin (see pl. 6) and Chimney Rock Pueblo. Although large and architecturally impressive relative to the unpretentious houses that surrounded them, the Mesa Verdean great houses were quite small in comparison with

farmed in valley bottoms where water tables were high. They collected water for drinking, cooking, and other domestic uses from scattered springs and seeps in the canyons, supplemented during the wetter seasons by water from ephemeral pools and "water pockets" in exposed bedrock on the canyon rims (fig. 4.6). Hydrological engineer Ken Wright and archaeologists Jack Smith and David Breternitz have demonstrated that as early as the 800s, people on the Mesa Verde proper were organizing work parties to dig and maintain large earthen reservoirs that collected water from melting snow in the

Figure 4.7. This vessel, excavated at Lowry Ruin, may have been imported from the Chaco region to the south.

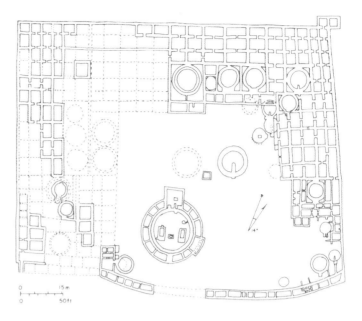

Figure 4.8. Plan view of Aztec West, Aztec National Monument.

the massive buildings in Chaco Canyon proper, such as Pueblo Bonito and Chetro Ketl.

In the very late 1000s and early 1100s, however, several great houses fully the equal of those at Chaco Canyon were built in the Totah—the part of the Mesa Verde region that includes the valleys of the Animas, La Plata, and San Juan rivers near Farmington and Aztec, New Mexico. During several bursts of activity in the 1090s, well-organized work parties rapidly built the Salmon site (Salmon Ruin) overlooking the San Juan River. It has at least 110 ground-story rooms, with another 50 to 60 estimated for its second story. Between 1110 and 1120, an even more impressive great house (with well over 400 rooms) was built at Aztec, in the Animas River valley. Over the past 25 years, National Park Service archaeologists have discovered that Aztec West (fig. 4.8) is just one building in a complex of great houses, great kivas, roads, and ordinary houses that extends for several miles along terraces bordering the Animas valley.

Like the major great houses at Chaco, Aztec and Salmon display evidence that strong leadership was at work. They were built rapidly, according to a plan, with individual construction projects consisting of large blocks of rooms. In the roofs, the builders frequently used ponderosa pine beams cut

to size in distant highland forests and carried to the Totah by work crews. Some of the smaller roof timbers were aspen, also imported from the mountains, even though cottonwood grew in abundance locally. These great houses and great kivas were built to be seen and to impress the viewer; the message was that great people must live in them. Steve Lekson has argued persuasively that the Aztec complex was located nearly due north of Pueblo Bonito in order to follow the north-south axis that looms large in Chacoan cosmology and religious symbolism and that is physically expressed in the "great north road," which can still be traced partway between Chaco and Aztec.

Although the Chaco great-house style developed over several hundred years and some buildings in Chaco Canyon (Pueblo Bonito, for example) have long histories, this was not the case for the principal Totah great houses. Buildings of this size and elaborate Chacoan architectural style had not previously been seen in the Mesa Verde region. Their construction must have been directed by leaders who had more centralized power and hierarchical status than was typical during most of the long sweep of Puebloan culture history, both before and after the Chacoan florescence. Many scholars interpret the Aztec complex as indicating that the seat of Chacoan religious and political power moved from Chaco Canyon to the Totah in the early 1100s. Several lines of evidence, from both the Totah and Chaco Canyon, support this conclusion.

But what about the many small Chaco-style great houses built in small communities throughout the central Mesa Verde area in the late 1000s and early 1100s? Were they administrative outposts of a conquering political system centered first at Chaco Canyon and then at Aztec? This view has been promoted by archaeologist David Wilcox and a few others. Or did they represent attempts by local leaders to enhance their rather modest status and power in their own communities by showing their connection to things Chacoan?

Like many of my colleagues, I think the bulk of the evidence favors the latter interpretation, at least for the great majority of the outlying communities that have Chaco-style great houses. Archaeologists Jim Judge and Wolcott Toll have proposed that local leaders gained status and religious influence by making pilgrimages to major ceremonies at Chaco or Aztec hosted by the politico-religious elites of those centers. The pilgrims might have contributed to the success of those elites by bringing food or by joining organized work parties to cut and deliver construction beams, build roads, or carry water, mud, and stones for additions to the major great houses. In turn, they might have brought Chacoan ceremonies, and perhaps tales of being honored and blessed, back to their home communities. Another mechanism for linking outlying communities with the major centers might have been arranged marriages that enabled Chacoan elites to create kin ties with leading families of communities in the Mesa Verdean "outback." Archaeological or biological evidence of such intermarriage would be hard to come by, but cross-culturally it is well documented as a way elites can extend their influence.

However the Chacoan system worked, it created conditions for the movement of goods—and probably people and ideas—around large parts of the northern Southwest. In the Mesa Verde region, more pottery from outside the area, as well as more exotic goods such as turquoise and shell

ornaments, appears in sites dating to the late 1000s and early 1100s (late Pueblo II) than in those dating earlier or later (fig. 4.7). The pilgrimage system just described would have given people opportunities to trade with and find marriage partners among members of other communities.

The years of maximum Chacoan influence seem also to have been generally peaceful ones. During that era, most people in both the Mesa Verde region and the Chacoan heartland south of the San Juan lived in dispersed homesteads and hamlets clustered loosely around a central place dominated by a great house and great kiva. This was not a settlement pattern designed for defense against raiding parties, either from the major centers or from neighboring communities.

The End of Chaco and Pueblo II

The onset of a severe drought in the mid-1100s coincided with the decline of Chacoan influence in the northern San Juan. The latest dates for construction of an outlying Chaco-style great house are in the 1130s, from Escalante Ruin, a small but impressive building situated on a hilltop near Dolores, Colorado. Although the Aztec and Salmon centers continued to be occupied and some new construction took place at both in the 1200s, there were no more massive building projects using beams imported from distant mountains. Long-distance trade in pottery, turquoise, and other desirable items had declined by the late 1100s, and as Mark Varien notes in the following chapter, isolation of the Mesa Verde region intensified in the 1200s.

Some scholars, including Steve Lekson and David Wilcox, argue that the main Chacoan centers, either at Chaco Canyon (Wilcox) or at Aztec (Lekson), continued to play leading roles in the political, economic, and religious lives of Pueblo people in the Mesa Verde region and elsewhere in the Southwest through the 1200s. I (and many of my colleagues) see an alternative scenario, in which the Chacoan developments represent a rather short-lived experiment with a hierarchical society. In this view, a newly powerful political and religious elite emerged at Chaco Canyon about 1040, and for most of the following century it was able to extend its influence widely over the northern Southwest, eventually including the Mesa Verde region between about 1075 and 1135. The religious authority that was one source of the elites' power was undermined when the rains began to fail in the mid-1100s. The hard-pressed farmers of the hinterland became less motivated to make pilgrimages and to contribute the food and labor on which the elites depended.

The mid-1100s are marked by evidence of violence and instances of cannibalism at sites in the central Mesa Verde area. Several scholars, notably the physical anthropologist Christy G. Turner, have suggested that these incidents reflected the Chacoan elites' policy of using selective terrorism to extend and maintain political control over far-flung Mesa Verdean communities. The timing of most of these events indicates to me, however, that they were products of social and economic disruption caused by the deepening drought, the related collapse of Chacoan religious influence, and the weakening of local community leaders' authority.

The people of the Mesa Verde region must have experienced new opportunities and challenges as they coped with the short-lived Chacoan expansion into the region. When all was said and done, however, daily life in their scattered small communities was probably little changed. Memories of the great Chaco centers undoubtedly endured, and they might have promoted attempts both to preserve and to expunge practices and ideas derived from the Chacoan experience. But as Mark Varien discusses in chapter 5, the Pueblo III period that followed (1150–1300) was not just a continuation of patterns established in the preceding two centuries. Rather, both the Pueblo II and Pueblo III periods represent distinctive and uniquely Mesa Verdean chapters in the long and rich history of Pueblo people in the northern Southwest.

William D. Lipe is a professor emeritus at Washington State University and a research associate and member of the board at Crow Canyon Archaeological Center. He has done archaeological research in the Glen Canyon and Cedar Mesa regions of southeastern Utah and in the Dolores and McElmo regions of southwestern Colorado. He was senior editor and author of *Colorado Prehistory: The Southern Colorado River Basin*, published in 1999.

Figure 5.1. Courtyard in Spruce Tree House, a cliff dwelling in Mesa Verde National Park.

Turbulent Times in the Mesa Verde World

Mark D. Varien

How could so many people have thrived in the Mesa Verde region in the mid-1200s CE only to have perished or emigrated by 1285? This paradox captures our imagination. In Pueblo III times (1150 to 1300), Mesa Verdean villages proliferated and reached their largest sizes. This was also when ancestral Puebloans fashioned multistory buildings with incredible precision and decorated pottery with the most elaborate designs. The remains of their villages and cliff dwellings are among the world's greatest archaeological treasures (see pls. 8, 11, 13, and fig. 13.1). Yet, their cultural florescence suddenly and perplexingly came to an end.

It was the remarkable preservation of Pueblo III dwellings, as well as the puzzle of their abandonment, that first drew researchers' attention. William Henry Holmes and W. H. Jackson wrote the earliest thorough scientific reports on the area in the 1870s, and their work stimulated new studies, journalistic accounts, and the public display of artifacts at the Columbian Exposition of 1893. Early reports described spectacular buildings containing a wide variety of craft items and tools—among them, expertly made pottery vessels, hafted stone axes, and sandals woven of yucca fibers—all left behind as if the occupants had only recently departed. The descriptions helped inspire a national consciousness about archaeological research and produced calls for the protection of these irreplaceable treasures. As a result, in 1889 Goodman Point Pueblo, in the center of the Mesa Verde region, became the first prehispanic archaeological site in the United States to be protected (fig. 5.2). Seventeen years later,

Congress passed the Antiquities Act and established Mesa Verde National Park.

Since the pioneering work of the late 1800s, archaeologists have continued to study Pueblo III settlement. They have come to recognize that the final 150 years of Pueblo occupation in the Mesa Verde region must have witnessed more changes over a shorter span than any previous era. The Mesa Verdeans adapted to environmental changes, moved to new locations, and created larger villages with more innovative layouts and architecture. They also experienced an escalation of conflict, a decline in long-distance trade, and rapid fluctuations in their population.

I want to examine each of these changes as it took place in the central Mesa Verde region, as well

Figure 5.2. Goodman Point Pueblo (lower left and center), a large thirteenth-century village on the Great Sage Plain. A spring and drainage, seen at the center, divide the site. Mesa Verde is visible on the horizon to the southeast.

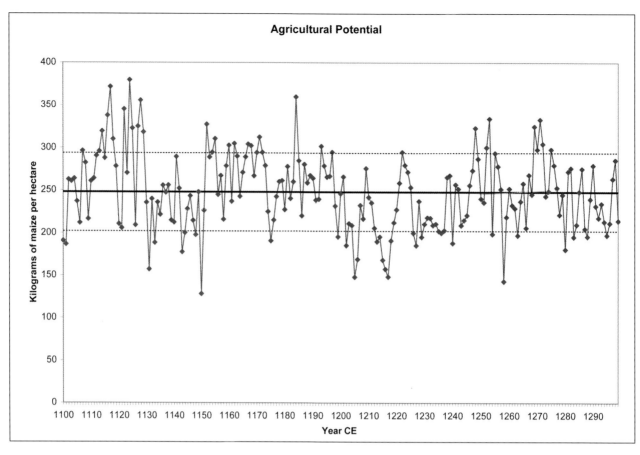

Figure 5.3. Estimated agricultural productivity in the Mesa Verde region, 1100–1300 CE, in average kilograms of maize per cultivated hectare.

as in the area to the west and in the "Totah" of northwestern New Mexico. Within the central Mesa Verde region, I distinguish between settlement on the Mesa Verde escarpment and in the area between McElmo Creek and Comb Ridge, which I call the "Great Sage Plain." (See map 2, p. ix.)

An Ever-Changing Environment

For Pueblo people living in the Mesa Verde region, coping with an ever-changing environment was a fact of life. Archaeologists are able to analyze data pertaining to the environment and identify years when change was most pronounced—when, for example, precipitation, seasonal temperatures, and the length of the growing season had the greatest effects on Pueblo farmers.

In the Village Ecodynamics Project, Timothy A. Kohler, of Washington State University, and his colleagues combined estimates of precipitation and temperature into a single measure, which they used

to calculate the amount of corn (maize) that Pueblo farmers were able to grow each year. In figure 5.3, part of Kohler's longer graph (see chapter 8), we can see the extent of annual variation and recognize that the years from 1131 to 1150, 1199 to 1219, 1226 to 1240, and 1280 to 1299 must have been especially challenging for Pueblo farmers. The 1200s as a whole had 69 below-average years and 31 that were above average. That Pueblo people continued to prosper during these difficult times makes the Pueblo III period even more remarkable.

From Mesa Tops to Canyons, from Farmsteads to Villages

Between 1150 and 1285, the locations and sizes of settlements in which Mesa Verdeans lived changed dramatically. In the mid- to late 1100s, most families lived in small, scattered farmsteads on mesa tops, situating their homes next to the best soils for farming. By the end of the period, they had moved

Figure 5.4. A tunnel connecting a kiva and tower at Mule Canyon Indian Ruins, west of Blanding, Utah.

into canyon settings or near springs (see pl. 3). For 600 years people had lived next to the areas they farmed and had walked to water, but during the thirteenth century people began living by their water source and walking to their fields. Why did this happen? Later I will offer some clues.

As the Puebloans moved to new locations, they also began building larger settlements. The mesa-top farmsteads, normally housing one or two families, typically consisted of an aboveground pueblo with 5 to 10 rooms and an underground chamber, or kiva. By 1260, however, for the first time in about 400 years, most of the population had moved into larger villages where family dwellings—individually still much the same as before—now sat side by side. The archaeologist Donna Glowacki inventoried 228 large Pueblo III villages in the Mesa Verde region, most of them in the Totah and central area. In the western area, families continued to live in small farmsteads. Almost no one lived in the eastern Mesa Verde region at this time.

Village architecture is best preserved in the cliff dwellings in Mesa Verde National Park. The largest site, Cliff Palace, contains 23 kivas and about 150 rooms. Impressive as these sites in alcoves are, they do not compare in size to some of the village sites on the Great Sage Plain north and west of Cortez. There, the largest village, Yellow Jacket Pueblo, had at least 195 kivas, 600 to 1,200 rooms, and about 20 towers. During its heyday in the 1200s, Yellow Jacket was home to some 700 people.

Larry Nordby, who has conducted extensive research at Cliff Palace, estimates its resident population at a relatively modest 125 people. He believes community leaders used this village for administrative purposes to integrate the activities of the many families who lived in the surrounding area. Roughly 60 smaller cliff dwellings lie nearby, with a total of about 45 kivas and 500 rooms. As a whole, then, this community housed around 625 people, equivalent to the populations of the largest villages of the Great Sage Plain.

Architectural Innovations
Remarkable architecture is a hallmark of the Pueblo III period. An important change during the last Pueblo II decades set the stage for architectural innovations during Pueblo III times: buildings

Figure 5.5. This ancient tower, perched on a boulder, was photographed by Gustav Nordenskiöld in 1891. The standing figure may be Richard Wetherill.

Figure 5.6. Square Tower in Hovenweep National Monument.

changed from earth-and-timber to stone masonry construction, extending the length of time that buildings and villages could be inhabited. In my research, I have found that, on average, families during the Pueblo II period occupied their timber-and-earth dwellings for about 20 years, in comparison with about 50 years for Pueblo III masonry dwellings. Pueblo III settlements possessed a permanence that was unmatched in earlier times.

Coincidental with stone masonry construction, new types of buildings proliferated, including towers and structures with multiple concentric walls. Pueblo builders first erected freestanding towers at their hamlets in the late 1100s. In most cases, they constructed a circular tower next to a kiva and built a tunnel connecting the two (fig. 5.4).

Later they built the first monumental towers, which sometimes served as central buildings in villages. Best known are the architectural wonders at Hovenweep National Monument, where Pueblo architects situated towers as if to defy gravity. So they still stand today, perched on a canyon rim or delicately balanced on a boulder in a canyon. These

towers display a wide range of shapes and rise two, three, and even four stories high. To me, they represent the height of the Mesa Verde Pueblo architectural aesthetic. One remarkable example, Square Tower at Hovenweep, exhibits a subtle twist as it reaches up from its base; I believe the Pueblo people deliberately designed it this way (figs. 5.5, 5.6, and pl. 4).

Pueblo people also built their first multiple-walled structures in the late 1100s, but this unusual form of architecture became more common in the next century. Most of these buildings were circular or D-shaped and had two or three concentric walls, with the spaces between them divided into rooms. Archaeologists refer to them as "biwall" and "tri-wall" structures (fig. 5.7). Glowacki plotted the locations of these structures and discovered that most of them were on the Great Sage Plain. Circular multiple-walled structures were most common in the eastern portion of that area, and D-shaped buildings were more common in the west. There were fewer in the Totah area, and they were absent in the western Mesa Verde region.

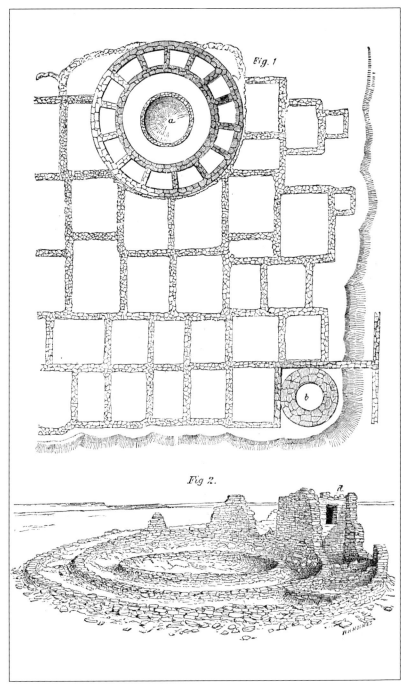

Figure 5.7. A triwall structure at a site (probably Mud Springs) in the central Mesa Verde region.

Multiwall structures with interior kivas might have been the homes of leaders, who hosted important, secret rituals in them.

The archaeologists William D. Lipe and Scott Ortman have documented the many characteristics common to Pueblo III villages, some of which can be seen in an artist's reconstruction of Sand Canyon Pueblo (pl. 13). Like Sand Canyon, most other villages had towers and an enclosing wall, and many had multiple-walled structures. Some had unroofed great kivas, large storage facilities, and plazas, all of which played a part in the communal life of the village and helped to integrate the community.

In the Pueblo III period, people often laid out their villages in two parts divided by a drainage and clustered their homes around or near a spring. Even the largest cliff dwellings were divided in half by a wall or row of rooms. This village design reminds one of present-day Taos Pueblo, which is divided by a stream. It also suggests that the dual division was an important feature of Pueblo III society (see chapter 13). Lipe and Ortman interpret all these shared characteristics as evidence for the intensification of warfare and ritual and for the appearance of distinct social groups.

Previous researchers have argued that Pueblo III villages were short-lived and lacked formal plazas, but recent work demonstrates this to be untrue. In fact, the occupation histories of Pueblo III villages range from

Archaeological investigations have revealed the presence of kivas in the centers of the D-shaped biwall structures at Sand Canyon and Hedley Pueblos, as well as evidence that the inhabitants used these buildings for both ceremonies and daily living. However, Mitchell Springs, another pueblo in the area, had no kiva in its triwall structure.

a few decades to more than two centuries, and almost all have distinct plazas. In addition, virtually all were built in places where an earlier community had existed. In many cases, the later inhabitants continued to use the earlier community's public buildings, creating a tangible link through time to the ancestral community. Each Pueblo III village had its own history, and I believe everyone knew that history and shared a strong sense of place that was rooted in the centuries-long habitation of the area by their ancestors.

Escalating Conflict

I want to address two questions regarding warfare: when did it occur, and who fought whom? As Kristin Kuckelman explains in chapter 16, conflict escalated in the Mesa Verde and entire Four Corners region during the thirteenth century. My interpretation of the evidence is that this conflict reached unprecedented levels between 1275 and 1285, the last decade before everyone left the region. Most researchers believe conflicts to have arisen among Pueblo people, but at Sand Canyon Pueblo Kuckelman has documented the presence of projectile points made outside the central Mesa Verde region—evidence for contact between that pueblo's residents and outsiders. Some of these points were found near people who died during the final years of the pueblo's occupation. Bone chemistry analysis of skeletons indicates that one person who died at Sand Canyon at this time had grown up outside the Mesa Verde region. Such contact with people from distant regions indicates to me that the question of who was fighting whom remains to be resolved.

Long-Distance Trade, Local Exchange, and Regional Organization

Several researchers have concluded that in the thirteenth century, Mesa Verdeans began to trade less over long distances and became increasingly isolated from the rest of the Pueblo world. Donna Glowacki recently found that at the same time, Mesa Verdean people increasingly exchanged pottery, especially bowls, within their own region. She and others have demonstrated that some of these exchanges took place during communal rituals.

Great Sage Plain residents were central to this exchange, as we infer from the fact that bowls from this area are found throughout the larger region. Glowacki concluded that the Great Sage Plain was the social and political center of the northern San Juan region, as well as its geographical center. She

believes that the inward focus on the Great Sage Plain explains why the region as a whole became increasingly insular and detached from the rest of the Pueblo world: connections with the central area took precedence over contacts with people in adjacent regions.

Glowacki's findings disagree with the assertion by the archaeologist Stephen H. Lekson that the Aztec Ruin Group, in the Totah area, replaced Chaco Canyon as the primary Pueblo center during the late Pueblo III period. She demonstrated that the number of vessels imported into Aztec was far smaller than the amount of pottery imported into Chaco Canyon and, in contrast with residents of the Great Sage Plain, Pueblo people in the Totah exchanged few vessels with people in the western Mesa Verde area. Many lines of evidence indicate that Aztec never exerted influence as far-reaching as its predecessor at Chaco. Instead, Glowacki sees competition and even conflict between people of the Totah and the Great Sage Plain as the latter area assumed its central role during the thirteenth century.

Population Growth and Decline

Many researchers have examined population dynamics in the Mesa Verde region. Their estimates of peak population range from about 10,000 to 30,000, but they disagree over when population peaked and declined. In 2005 Scott Ortman and other archaeologists at Crow Canyon completed a comprehensive analysis of population dynamics on the Great Sage Plain. They concluded that population remained stable during the persistent drought of the middle 1100s, increased modestly during the drought and colder-than-normal temperatures of the early 1200s, and then grew rapidly between 1225 and 1260. The growth rate during the middle 1200s suggests that people were moving to the central Mesa Verde region from other areas (fig. 5.8). Glowacki's assessment of population trends indicates that population in the Totah and western Mesa Verde areas, in comparison with the central region, was smaller and peaked earlier, during the early 1200s.

Reconstructing population dynamics is important because it shows that the depopulation of

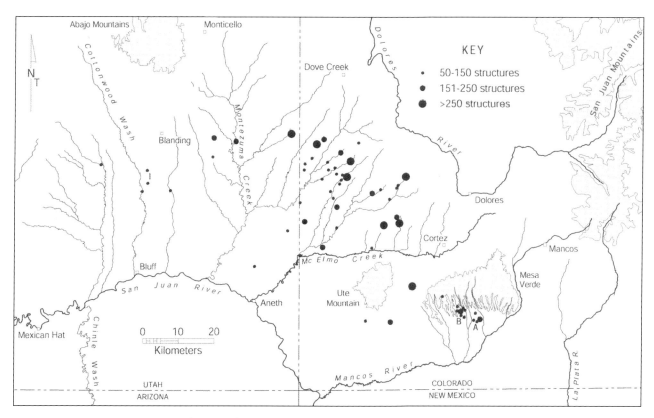

Figure 5.8. Community centers in the central Mesa Verde region in the thirteenth century.

the region was a complicated process. Migration from the peripheral parts of the Mesa Verde region began around 1200, but population increased in the central area at this time. Between 1260 and 1285, however, tens of thousands of people either died or emigrated to other parts of the Southwest.

The Final Migrations

Moving from one place to another was a common way in which ancestral Pueblo people responded to their changing environment. But emigration from the Mesa Verde region during the thirteenth century differed from earlier migrations in three ways: the larger number of people who moved, the completeness of the regional depopulation, and the fact that neither the emigrants nor their descendants ever returned to live there permanently.

Pueblo people had lived in the Mesa Verde region for more than seven centuries, overcoming difficult circumstances that included several episodes of drought and colder-than-normal temperatures. This tells us that during the 1200s something more than climate change caused them to leave.

The ancestral Pueblo migration from the Mesa Verde region is often viewed in isolation, but I believe we can understand it better by examining a larger area. Large portions of the Colorado Plateau were being depopulated during the thirteenth century, and this demographic instability likely meant that people from distant places moved through the Mesa Verde region near the end of its occupation. Contacts between local residents and people on the move may have taken many forms, but some of the interaction was violent, especially after 1270.

The population growth witnessed on the Great Sage Plain in the thirteenth century was unprecedented. It taxed the environment and increased people's competition over land, water, and game. Regional population declined rapidly after 1270, and by 1280 surviving villages may have been smaller and inhabited, in part, by people who were unable to move, perhaps because they were too old or infirm. By the time conflicts like those

Figure 5.9. A Hopi farmer planting corn in an arid field.

documented at Castle Rock and Sand Canyon Pueblo took place (chapter 16), the Mesa Verde region was a far different place from the one it had been even a decade earlier.

Beginning in the late 1270s, a severe drought and abnormally cold temperatures beset the Mesa Verde region. I believe the final migrations were completed soon thereafter. I base this belief on analyses of tree-ring cutting dates, which indicate that timbers were harvested almost every year during the centuries before depopulation. The latest tree-ring cutting date from the entire region is 1281, and it seems likely that all Pueblo people left the area within a few years after that. How did this sudden and complete depopulation come about?

Kristin Kuckelman presents evidence that the people at Sand Canyon Pueblo could not grow enough corn to feed themselves and that their turkey flocks were decimated during the final years of the site's history. Although food was scarce, I also think the turbulent times made it difficult or impossible for people to employ time-honored survival strategies. For example, as a means of insurance during dry periods, ancestral Pueblo people commonly planted fields in many scattered locations. But this strategy might have been too dangerous in a time of warfare. Likewise, sharing food helped people survive hard times, but a depleted population and the threat of conflict might have undermined their ability to trade.

Using the estimates of agricultural productivity given in figure 5.3, we can infer that 1280, 1283, and 1284 were especially meager years. I believe the food shortages that Kuckelman documents likely occurred then and the depopulation of the region was complete by 1285. These were extremely harsh times for Pueblo people, yet despite many hardships, they found a way to succeed. They moved away, formed new communities, and survived (fig. 5.9). Their courage, ingenuity, and devotion to their beliefs enable them to thrive to this day.

Acknowledgments

I am grateful to many colleagues who provided information that I used in this chapter, including Donna Glowacki, Dave Johnson, Tim Kohler, Kristin Kuckelman, Bill Lipe, Larry Nordby, and Scott Ortman. Several people, including Donna Glowacki, Chris Kantner, Tim Kohler, Jim Martin, and Scott Ortman, read an early draft, and their comments helped me improve the final essay. I thank David Noble for asking me to contribute to this book and for his editorial work on my chapter, and Jane Kepp for her copyediting.

Mark D. Varien, director of research at Crow Canyon Archaeological Center, has worked as an archaeologist in the Mesa Verde region since the late 1970s. His numerous articles and books include *Sedentism and Mobility in a Social Landscape: Mesa Verde and Beyond.*

Figure 6.1. The author's mother, Rose Naranjo (left); grandmother, Gia Khun (center); and uncle, Manuel Holcomb.

Plate 1. Winter evening view of Point Lookout on the northeastern rim of Mesa Verde in southwestern Colorado. The entrance road into Mesa Verde National Park winds up the mesa's escarpment. The Chuska Mountains can be seen in the distance.

Plate 2. Mesa Verde from the air, looking west-northwest. In the foreground, the sun reflects off the park headquarters buildings and Chapin Mesa Museum. Spruce Tree House lies in the shadowed canyon across from the sunlit rooftops, and Sleeping Ute Mountain is in the distance.

Plate 3. A complex of ruins surrounding a spring in Hovenweep National Monument.

Plate 4. Horseshoe Ruin, a Hovenweep-style tower, with Sleeping Ute Mountain in the distance.

Plate 5. Edge of the Cedars Pueblo at Edge of the Cedars State Park in Blanding, Utah. This site, which is open to the public, includes 6 residential complexes, 10 kivas, and a great kiva.

Plate 6. Lowry Ruin, the northernmost Chacoan great house, lies nine miles west of Pleasant View, Colorado. Constructed between 1089 and 1120, it was the dominant building in a large farming community.

Plate 7. Far View Ruin, a mesa-top pueblo in Mesa Verde National Park, with rabbitbrush in bloom.

Plate 8. Kodak House, a cliff dwelling of more than 70 rooms in Mesa Verde National Park.

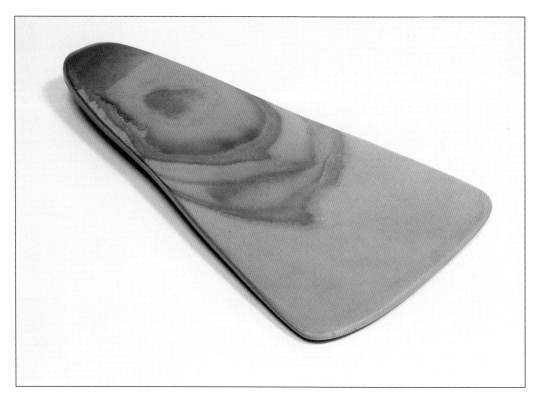

Plate 9. An outstanding example of a stone artifact known as a *tchamahia*, sometimes referred to as a "ceremonial hoe." Although archaeologists have found tchamahias at many sites in the Mesa Verde region, they do not know how ancient people used them. This one is made of tan hornstone, a coarse form of chert, and was quarried at a site in extreme southeastern Utah.

Plate 10. This unusual Mesa Verde Black-on-white double mug may have had a ceremonial use.

"We Came from the South, We Came from the North"

Some Tewa Origin Stories

Tessie Naranjo

As a young girl living at Santa Clara Pueblo in the early 1940s, I was surrounded by a large extended family that formed a community in which one called older men "uncle" (*meh-meh*) and older women "aunt" (*ko'o*). We took care of one another. We survived in this way. Our values to this day include respect, sharing, industriousness, interconnections, social courtesies, and the belief that there is life in all things.

I felt safe growing up in that environment. There was permanence and stability about the place, and I felt a sense of security. Storytelling was a weekly event: my extended family members would walk to my great-grandmother's house to hear stories from the elders about times past and present. Storytelling began to awaken in me thoughts beyond those of playing games, doing the small household chores I was assigned, and taking care of my younger brothers and sisters.

Storytelling as an extended family activity stopped in the early 1950s. My great-grandmother, Gia Khun, born at Santa Clara in 1870, died around that time. My mother, Rose Sisneros Naranjo, who was raised by my great-grandmother, continued the pattern of storytelling, but informally (fig. 6.1). She would tell me about Tewa Pueblo ways as we were driving somewhere, as we were going for clay to make pottery, or as we were engaged in household tasks.

It was from my mother that I first got the notion of the history and patterns of our people's geographical movements. She awakened in me an awareness that in the past our people had followed a trail of migration to new locations. We did not have the permanence I had envisioned as a child. Instead, our existence went far into the *opa nanungeh*, or beyond my childhood universe. For example, before Santa Clara Pueblo, there was Puje (Puyé), 10 miles away, and there were Galisteo Basin communities before Puje (fig. 6.2). I slowly began to understand that we had come from somewhere to where we were now.

Figure 6.2. The ancestral Santa Clara Pueblo site of Puyé.

Figure 6.3. The San Luis Valley with the Rio Grande in flood.

Tewa Stories of Origins and Migrations

As I was growing up, when I asked my mother about our Santa Clara Tewa origins, she would tell a story about how our ancestors had traveled from the direction of Santa Fe to our present location in the Española Valley of New Mexico. Here is my mother's story:

> We were coming from the direction of Santa Fe. Some were stopped. First they were going by Oga-P'oquin-geh. [Adolph F. Bandelier spelled this "Oga P'Hoge," and John Peabody Harrington spelled it "Ogapoge."] There they buried *kha-je* [sacred objects] that will bring soft rain. From there they traveled and got to Te'tsu-geh [cottonwood tree place]. Some were left at Te'tsu-geh. From there on they traveled and they traveled to Nambe [pueblo of the roundish earth]. They traveled again and stopped near P'osuweh-geh [drinking water place], and from there they went to P'owho-geh [where the water slides down]. From there they came to O-weneh, singing. Then the leaders

went to Tsi'kumu. There a *kha-je* was planted, and so if a cloud appears, a very heavy rainstorm will come, [and] make mean clouds. It's because the *kha-je* are angry. From there some of the people went to Ohkeh [San Juan Pueblo]. From there others went to Picuris and Taos. Taos is called "P'insuu" because the mountains are so tall in that area. They went to Blue Lake, and that became the place with the most *p'in-nung* [great power], because that's where the *kha-je* which have the most *p'in-nung* were left.

Another Santa Clara elder described our migration this way:

> We came from some place under the earth. When they came out from there, they started coming and moving and then they settled and then they stood up again and then they started moving again. When they started moving, they started moving to another location and then they stayed there for a few years. Most of the people that were migrating, they were coming

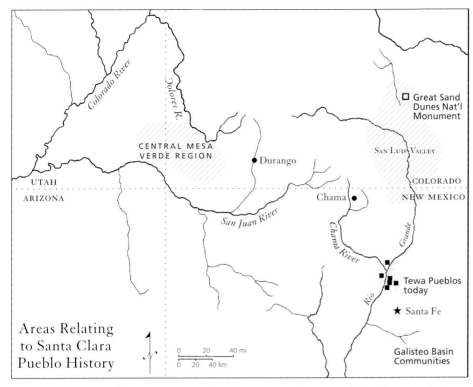

 (label on map)

CENTRAL MESA
VERDE REGION

UTAH
ARIZONA

Colorado River

Dolores R.

• Durango

San Juan River

Chama •

Chama River

Rio Grande

Great Sand
Dunes Nat'l
Monument

SAN LUIS VALLEY

COLORADO
NEW MEXICO

■ Tewa Pueblos
today

★ Santa Fe

Galisteo Basin
Communities

Areas Relating
to Santa Clara
Pueblo History

0   20   40 mi
0   20 40 km

Figure 6.4. Tewa Pueblo country in northern New Mexico (lower right) and areas relating to Santa Clara Pueblo history.

through the mountains mostly. Then later on the people started moving on down into the valley.

In 1995, when I interviewed six elderly Santa Clara people, ranging in age from 78 to 86, about Tewa migrations, I noticed differences in the way knowledge is understood and accepted by Pueblo people and archaeologists. The interviewees had one thing in common: they all said, "We came from P'oquin Owingeh [or P'oquingeh]," which translates not as a specific place but as "the village under the lake." Where is this lake? It is actually located in different places by different people. For instance, some Santa Clara people say that the lake of emergence lies north of San Juan Pueblo. Others say it is near Chama. Still others place it in the San Luis Valley of southern Colorado (figs. 6.3 and 6.4).

According to various writers on this subject, other Tewa communities have similar origin stories. (There are six upper Rio Grande Tewa pueblos in New Mexico—San Juan, Santa Clara, San Ildefonso, Nambe, Pojoaque, and Tesuque—as well as another on First Mesa on the Hopi reservation in Arizona.)

Elsie Clews Parsons, in her book *Pueblo Indian Religion*, recorded an interview with a San Juan Pueblo consultant who recounted the Tewa emergence story and named "Sand Lake" as the place of emergence. Alfonso Ortiz, the late San Juan Pueblo anthropologist, identified the northern site of emergence as "Sandy Lake…somewhere to the east of Alamosa [Colorado]." John P. Harrington located Sandy Lake in the eastern portion of the San Luis Valley, near Great Sand Dunes National Park. In his article "Ethnogeography of the Tewa Indians," he used linguistics to identify the locations of ancestral Tewa settlement sites.

In June 1892 the archaeologist Edgar Lee Hewett visited the San Luis Valley and in his diary described the landscape of the eastern area, noting that he occasionally encountered "quicksand-like" soil. He also observed a lake of black, brackish water, around which a number of cattle lay dead. Harrington quoted from portions of the diary in which Hewett described how he had received help from a "garrulous old man" who rescued him from an irrigation ditch by pulling his vehicle out with a team of oxen. The man lived on Sierra Blanca (Mount Blanca) and told Hewett that he "had seen the lake and claimed it never dried up: that many cattle died drinking the water every dry season." A friend of Hewett's from Florence, Colorado, told him that "this was a place around which some interesting legends centered."

Harrington's work with nearly all the pueblos of New Mexico yielded many different linguistic terms for Mount Blanca and other geographical features of the San Luis Valley, including "the lake." At the time of Harrington's research in the late 1880s, the

Figure 6.5. Mesa Verde from the north.

mountain and lake held significance in all eastern Tanoan Pueblo origin stories (from Taos in the north to Isleta Pueblo in the south, encompassing all the Tewas, as well as the Tiwas and Towas) and as far west as Zuni. I personally know only of the significance of "Sandy Lake" to the Tewas since time began.

Many generations of archaeologists working in the Southwest have tried hard to make firm connections between the Tewa Pueblo peoples of today and those who lived in the Mesa Verde area, west of the San Luis Valley. Yet, to date, they have found no direct proof that the Tewa ancestors migrated from there to the northern Rio Grande Valley (fig. 6.5). Indeed, many stories offer a different account. Archaeologists use evidence from material culture to make claims about people who are no longer available to tell their stories; indigenous cultural historians use stories that have been passed on for generations in order to understand the "facts of history" for their own and other people.

Some scholars talk or write about ancestral Tewa people and refer to our Tanoan ancestors, people who shared a common language before the languages used today became clearly separated from our larger family stock. They, like Harrington, use linguistic information to try to trace and prove our origins. Other scholars who write about our origins use archaeological "evidence" in order to theorize about how, when, and where our ancestors lived. But how do these writings fit with our own cultural understanding of where we came from, and when?

An Interview with an Elder

A Santa Clara Pueblo man recently sat down with me and talked at length about his understandings of our origin stories. In what follows, I quote at length from a 90-minute, tape-recorded session with him, because he explained with great clarity the complex details of our principal legend.

The Tewa mind, because of functional orality, isn't analytical or doesn't go around asking questions. [The Tewa people] take it that those are our supernaturals and…no questions asked, that we came from P'oquingeh. Since we didn't write our stories down, we live in a

Figure 6.6. Harvested corn and squash at Santa Clara Pueblo, 1935.

culture of primary orality. We adults pass the culture on and interpret it to our children the way we understand it and perceive it, and therefore we tell our children that we came from P'oquingeh, [the place that] the ritual dramas tell us about. *P'oquin* is a high-context word [that] simply means "lake" [in English]. But in Tewa that's not the case. *P'oquin* is a metaphor that means many things. [For example,] the *p'oquin* is a kiva, too, so it's a sacred place. Where there is a *kha-je*, there is a *p'oquin*, or sacred place. Therefore, those places that are *p'oquin* [include] not only the kiva but where you collect Douglas fir for ceremonial dances; where you bring the Douglas fir to is a prayer shrine, a *p'oquin*. If we came from P'oquingeh, it does not mean that we came from a body of water, literally, although that's

the way anthropologists and archaeologists have interpreted it. That's the only way they can interpret it if they don't know Tewa [and] they don't understand the many contexts and meanings of *p'oquin*. If you follow the many meanings and contexts of the metaphors and of the drama associated with the emergence legend, that you will read here and there, you [will] find that the non-Pueblo writers are misunderstanding the stories and meaning of the words and ceremonial activities.

In *Pueblo Indian Religion*, I read emergence legends of Nambe, San Juan, Santa Clara, and all of the Tewas. Elsie Clews Parsons went around collecting emergence legends, and all she writes about are variants of one basic story. The variants always mention the lake where we came from, and the *p'oquin* is always to the north. The *p'in piea* [toward the north], where we came from, is somewhere toward the mountains, and that was our original *p'oquin*. But that doesn't mean there was a lake there. If you carry the kind of thinking that we have just gone through in terms of [the lake's being] a metaphor and if you string several metaphors together, you can [get the idea]; so you have to change your thinking and say we came from these sacred places, but not from a body of water.

We came from a sacred place, somewhere to the north. But there are many sacred places that are scattered all throughout the north. [As I said,] a kiva is a sacred place, and so is a *tay* [the Douglas fir, which grows only at elevations of 9,500 feet or higher]. So we came from a very high place. Then we ran into corn; otherwise, why would we make corn our supernaturals? Our supernaturals are "corn mother close to winter" and "corn mother close to summer." (See figs 6.6 and 6.7.) So [referring to] our place of origin, we always point toward *p'in piea* [toward the northern mountains].

The rest of the directions are relatively unimportant, except that *than piea* [toward the sun] is also important, because with every song they're chasing the sun. Father Sun rises at that place [in the east], and even in the Bible, you know, the dawning has sacredness to it. Well, the Tewas made the dawning a sacred thing, too, so that it's mentioned in all the songs. *P'in piea* always takes precedence over *than-piea*, [because] we came from somewhere in the north. We say we came from P'oquingeh, and we came and went from there, the sacred places, several times. But we didn't have to come from a lake.

So that describes this sacred place that we live in. But we came from beyond this sacred place that's bounded by four mountains. *Opa nanungeh di piung gi powa:* We came from a place beyond our geographical knowing. We came from lakes but don't think of [the word] "lake" as a body of water [but rather as] a metaphor [for] sacred places.

Well, the north [is] where we found

corn...because corn is what the principal emergence legend seems to be about. We are seeking life in all our religious ceremonies. Our ancestors led us from the north to the places we call *p'oquin*, and we have to go revisit them still now at various times and on various occasions of need in order to learn more. Therefore, [in the past] we were going and coming to these [same] sacred places, which were being used and reused over again, according to how I understand what the legend seems to be saying. If those *p'oquin*, those sacred places, were built all along the way, then who is to say that we didn't at one time go by Chaco Canyon [or] by Aztec. We may have [been to] all of those [places] and even the one at Ojo [Caliente, the site of Posi owingeh]. It was a progression of sacred places that we came through.

The legend doesn't make a distinction of who people were, but as Tewa people, we know that we separated ourselves. Our story tells about other people who came and who were of a different mind than us. These ancestors also came out of the *p'oquin*, out of those sacred places. They also came from some sacred places in the north where corn was developed. We know that corn came into all that area around the Great Sage Plain [the area west and north of Mesa Verde] fairly early from Mexico. Somehow the trading went north and corn went north into southwestern Colorado, where the farming culture and the communities developed. Communities and kivas came into being when these [ancestors settled down] and did dry farming. Then we came to identify ourselves as the kind of people we were. If you put archaeology and legends together, then we didn't develop ideas about who we were or what we were until corn came into being.

There's such a complex of ruins in that area [southwestern Colorado] which, of course, are full of *p'oquin*. But we also believe *p'owaha*—water, wind, breath—still is up there where we left it. Every time we tell the story, it is a renewing. The oral legend is a renewing of

Figure 6.7. Corn Dance, Santa Clara Pueblo, date unknown.

ourselves. And we can only trace it that way to *p'owaha* and *p'oquin* and the songs that are sung. I have no idea where P'oquingeh is, but my guess [is that] Ts'in Ts'ina P'oquingeh was a pueblo, which is now a ruin. [This was] a long time ago, while it was dawning, and we subsequently heard [about] it. Little pieces of evidence like that gives us an idea that there were places that were made sacred, communities that were made sacred, kivas that were made sacred, where we lived and where we traveled from. It's always from the *p'in piea*, from the north.

We are constantly going back and forth between *pa-nyogeh* and *tehnyudi* [summer and winter], you know, and that tells us that all we were doing was living a subsistence lifestyle that was transformed from hunting and gathering. *Pa-nyogehdi* and *tehnyudi*—it was a natural way to organize ourselves from what we knew.

Those *p'oquin* that we built all along the way are still scattered up towards the north, you know, and if there were some persons from way back who could remember where Ts'in Ts'ina P'oquingeh was, they might take you to somewhere like Aztec Ruin [or] they might take you to Mesa Verde. As villages and pueblos were developing, then we built myths, and myths are all that we have to live by, what we choose to live by, and we can only build on that in the dramas we practice, [in the] songs we sing, and [in the] stories we tell, and from what our social organization tells us. Only a Pueblo person who has lived in the culture from times past might have a better inkling of where these places were, but to us [that] time has passed, so that we have forgotten. One thing that we have to start breaking apart is origin myths that [say] we came out from a lake. No one can understand that high-context language and the multiple references to *p'oquin* in Tewa. The only thing we can remember is that at the dawning of change we became Pueblo people. Before that we were whoever we were, prehistoric Indians. Somewhere in

our distant past, it's just my guess, we were clan-type people, before we became [divided into two groups] *kwe-de* [winter people] and *kha-je* [summer people].

We have become a literate people. As we became literate, we [came to] know both cultures. It was the nature of Tewa people to accept what was passed on orally and not to analyze it. [Today] if you understand the Tewa world, you have to ask critical questions [about] what *p'oquin* means, because of heightened literacy. Tewa people constantly lived in a metaphorical world and a world of drama. We performed the dramas to remind ourselves, because that's one way that we could teach. When you became an elder, then you had the right to interpret all of these [stories]. Well, you add literacy to that and you can say that we have the right to say to anthropologists and archaeologists that we came out of a [metaphorical] lake, with all these things that we talked about, including certain places [where we once lived]. It's the prayer shrines, it's those [sacred] locations, those high mountains and the *opa nanungeh*, which is beyond that place that we described, beyond those mountains, beyond that territory [where we lived before] we moved into the Rio Grande Valley. We did come from the *opa nanungeh*. We arose from there and then we came into this place [where] we now live. What we left behind and what we made sacred were those prayer bundles, and we sanctified [those places] by both living there and leaving things there. And remember, *p'owaha*—water, wind, breath—never dies, so our *p'owaha* are still at those places.

As much as we might want to believe that the sacred stories tell empirical truths about our place of beginning (Sandy Lake, an underground lake in the San Luis Valley of Colorado, or elsewhere), it seems much more practical to accept that we Tewas probably use metaphors for our physical origins in the same way that we use metaphors for explaining our other beliefs. The stories that we tell in our songs, dances, and other dramas, and to our children orally, contain the historical knowledge of how we came to be and how we now live our simultaneous realities of past and present. This chapter is an example of our storytelling.

Tessie Naranjo grew up in Santa Clara Pueblo and continues to live there. She has a master's degree in health education and a Ph.D. in sociology from the University of New Mexico. She has consulted with tribal and other museums around the country, in addition to her ongoing work in indigenous language preservation and revitalization. Her primary focus is cultural preservation at both the family and community levels.

Figure 7.1. Classic Mesa Verde Black-on-white kiva jar.

Craft Arts of the Mesa Verde

Richard W. Lang

There is a quality of Eden-lost in this space. A sanctity peculiar to high places and their quietudes hangs on the breezes of the Mesa Verde, and in the scale of its narrow, pine-sheltered canyons and small, scattered ruins, modern man finds an unusual intimacy with the past. The Green Mesa draws us to it by these and other qualities, through our sometimes paradoxical veneration of the ancient and by our wonderfully unquenchable curiosity.

In their mysterious, hallowed vacancy, the stone villages whisper uneasily of life's fragility, of those dark bogies of chance and the unpredictable that haunt our progress and erase our labors and our loves with alarming regularity. In the unadorned, almost stark beauty of rock and mud transformed by mind and hand, these little towns and farmsteads speak praise for common works and qualitative thought, for the pursuit of art in all our undertak-

ings. Their compact and ordered aspect, their rustic artistry, are true reflections of the lives and attitudes of their builders. Among the people of the Mesa Verde, knowledge was largely practical and spiritual and was transmitted with little personal modification over short generations and long centuries.

Figure 7.2. Pottery ladle.

Figure 7.3. Black-on-white mugs.

Figure 7.4. Flaked stone points.

Change came slowly, great changes developing progressively out of earlier, minor ones. Invention and creativity were expressed in subtle ways within a framework of traditional modes. Art was everywhere, and the most utilitarian of objects was often deftly created with the greatest care (figs. 7.1, 7.2, and 7.3).

Care, quality, and a sound understanding of the properties and potentials of the raw materials at hand are written broadly on the artifacts of Mesa Verde (see pls. 9, 10). Such aspirations and knowledge remain embodied in the finely flaked knives of gray flint and the carved and polished bone of flesher and awl (fig. 7.4). These and other tools were made well and made to work. The ongoingness of humankind depended on it. Stone hoes and wooden digging sticks prodded and cut the earth for planting and tending the all-important crops of corn, beans, and squash. Stone axes bit the tough wood of juniper or the softer wood of pine in the procurement of the stuff from which roof beams and cradles are made. Serviceable coiled, twilled, and plaited baskets of willow, oak, yucca, and rabbitbrush may have held the day's laundry or the meal fresh from the metate (fig. 7.5). Blankets of cotton, fur, feathers, and twine kept off winter's

chill (fig. 7.6). The list of objects and functions goes on and on, in correspondence with the many needs of a people whose daily existence and survival necessarily centered on the ability of each individual to glean from field and woodland the sustenance that each required, while contributing to the buffering surpluses of their communities. Given moisture-bearing winter snows, timely rains, fertile soil, and the successful husbandry of domestic turkeys, the Mesa Verdeans were a people self-sufficient in all that was necessary for the good life.

Science and history provide us with the only time machines we possess. Were we to be allowed a day on Mesa Verde, however, in that time when Cliff Palace and Long House echoed with the voices of their inhabitants, our minds would boggle at the range and depth of knowledge of practical things held by each of those inhabitants. To them, a field of cactus, yucca, and grasses was not a barren place but a storehouse and a garden that would, with the passing of seasons, yield fiber for cordage, footwear, baskets, and more, as well as fruits, seeds, tubers, and dyes. A graceful and magnificent buck mule deer was far more than a fellow creature to be admired from the roadside. He was a source of much-needed protein, hide, sinew, oil, bone, and

Figure 7.5. Large coiled basket.

Figure 7.6. Cloth fragment.

antler. From the body of that deer came human energy, stitching materials, the tools of the weaver and tanner, shoes, shirts, blankets, and the hard tine used to flake flint.

Of all that the Mesa Verdeans left in their passing, the most impressive is certainly their architecture, but perhaps the most appealing is their pottery. For the modern Pueblos and, presumably, for their Puebloan ancestors, both clay and the knowledge of pottery making were gifts from the gods, who enjoined them never to forget this skill so important to their well-being.

The fundamental techniques of the potter's art first filtered into the Southwest from Mexico around 300 CE. Gradually, over the following 800 years, these techniques diffused to most of the peoples of the Southwestern culture area. The idea of pottery making came to these northern peoples not as an isolated trait but as part of a developed Mexican complex that included agriculture and the concepts and elements of settled village life. Earlier Southwestern hunter-gatherers, with their mobile lifestyle, had no reason either to use or to want the rather fragile tool that is pottery. But during the last millennium before the common era, the northern bands began to experiment with rudimentary farming, working it into the fabric of their cultures, and generation to generation saw agriculture change

their lives. Farming both required and facilitated a more sedentary lifestyle, just as the processing of corn led to the modification of old tools and the adoption of new ones, such as pottery.

When this ceramic craft appeared in the Mesa Verde region, it was full-blown and formed part of the cultural baggage of farmers settling the Colorado highlands in the late sixth century. The pottery these early settlers brought with them from the valleys of the San Juan River drainage was in most ways typical of that found among their brethren scattered across the northern Southwest in hundreds of unimposing pithouse villages. It was a gray ware, open fired, without free access of oxygen, so that carbonaceous matter in the clay remained unburned. The result was pottery of a gray color, which is emblematic of most northern Pueblo ceramics.

The clay most used in the Mesa Verde region may have been mined from the Mancos shale, deposited by a stagnant sea that had slowly advanced over southwestern Colorado more than 65 million years before. To counteract shrinkage of the vessel walls and lessen the risk of cracking during the drying and firing process, the clay was tempered with minute fragments of even older igneous rock, formed when the crust of the planet was first in the making. Mixed with water, these vestiges of a poisonous,

Figure 7.7. Corrugated jar with spiral decoration.

and red washes went out of style. Corrugations formed of unobliterated coils appeared as a decorative zone on the necks of jars by the late 700s, and by the 1000s such corrugations often covered the entire exterior surfaces of storage and cooking jars with wide, belled mouths (fig. 7.7). The corrugations were manipulated for decorative effect in a number of ways, the most common of which was uniform indenting with the fingertip to provide a crimped effect. This extensive exterior texturing made these jars easier to grip and may have had other functions as well. With time, polishing of painted surfaces became more common, and painted designs more elaborate and complex. Although local and individual variations in forms, surface finishes, and designs are apparent, many of the changes seen in Mesa Verde pottery over its long span reflect broad shifts in function and style that periodically swept across the Pueblo world. Many of these seem to have been of ultimate Mexican origin, whereas others mark Southwestern innovations. Both passed from one group to another through trade and other contacts. The potters of each region drew selectively from these idea pools, not only adopting but also adapting forms, motifs, and complexes of designs in a manner distinctive to their own people.

Many of the ceramic works of the Mesa Verdeans of the Pueblo II and III periods—about 900 to 1300 CE—are true masterpieces in clay. Although some contemporary Pueblo potters have attempted to revive indented-corrugated pottery, none has yet achieved the fineness of surface texturing or the thinness of wall regularly seen in this prehistoric gray ware. But without doubt, the highest ceramic accomplishments of the Mesa Verde potters are found in a black-painted, white-slipped pottery termed "Mesa Verde Black-on-white" (figs. 7.1, 7.2, and 7.3).

Pueblo potters have traditionally given "life" to their pots through their own breath, and in the strength and beauty of Mesa Verde Black-on-white

fiery Earth and ancient oceans were transformed into malleable ropes of tempered clay, coiled concentrically, then pressed, pulled, scraped, and rubbed into desired shapes. And of shapes there were many: pitchers and bowls; small, globe-shaped, neckless jars and large ones with long, slender necks; canteens, dippers, and ladles patterned after the familiar gourd vessels, unembellished or adorned with lugs and given handles for holding and hanging. These varied forms reflect the range of needs for storage, transport, cooking, and service—all the many everyday tasks that pottery facilitated.

Most vessels were left undecorated, but some were painted with a red earthy wash, and others, with simple, appealing geometrics, suggestive of basketry designs, fired black to reddish brown against the open gray field of the container's surface. For these, iron-bearing mineral paints or carbon-based paints made from plant extracts were used.

Over the next 700 years, many changes occurred in Mesa Verde pottery. Between 700 and 1000 CE, oxidized, red-fired pottery saw some use,

Figure 7.8. Pottery bowl, Mesa Verde Black-on-white.

Figure 7.9. Kokopelli figure, Mesa Verde Black-on-white bowl.

that life clearly lingers. The designs and finish of this pottery exhibit a bold perfection. Even in vessel wall thickness and the density of white to gray slips, there is an implication of delicate solidity. There is a strong balance of light and dark in the largely abstract, geometric designs arranged with a high consciousness of symmetry. In looking at this pottery, one cannot help but suspect that the potters of the thirteenth century lived in a tightly organized society and, further, that they saw the decorating of ceramics as one of its high arts. Long gone are the truly whimsical qualities that characterized much earlier design and that continued into the 1100s. Here, structure and detail are paramount (fig. 7.8).

Rarely do we see biomorphic forms incorporated into the design of Mesa Verde pottery, but they do occur. Among them are wonderfully stylized representations of the macaw, the sacred bird of the sun; a racing herd of deer or sheep; a dancing hermaphrodite; a flock of feeding ducks, entranced, awaiting the arrows of a hunter graced through ritual; a dancer, half man, half bighorn sheep, leaping across the exterior of a painted bowl; and the ubiquitous humpback, playing out the tune of life upon his flute, urging, Panlike, increase of man, plant, and beast (fig. 7.9).

These depictions are tangible expressions of a society in which human action was central to the course of natural events, in which all was bound by a shared understanding of life and its ultimate purpose, by the linkages of man, nature, and spirit. Even the hunter and the ducks possess a shared view of rightness in the world of the Mesa Verde towns, communities that sustained a moral order in which the guiding focus of everyday activities was continuity, balance, and fecundity in all things. Here, religion had the power to call the deer and draw goodness from an invisible world that was everywhere, that literally invested art with spirit and gave life to the very stones (fig. 7.10).

In the surviving arts and crafts of Mesa Verde, we are privileged to have contact with one of the many adaptations that triumphed for a little while on the timeline of human experiment. Through these remains, we find appreciation for the Mesa Verdean accomplishment, for its creative simplicity and down-to-earth practicalities. Certainly theirs was a far from perfect society. Life made hard demands on these people. Old age came quickly, and children and adults often met death prematurely. Food was not always plentiful, and the harsh environment was ultimately unforgiving. It is also safe to guess that this was a culture of

Figure 7.10. Carved stone lion effigy.

relatively narrow vision, in which the social bond overrode reason and both reason and action existed largely within a sometimes uncompromising traditional and corporate structure.

Nonetheless, there are aspects of this culture that are worthy of our contemplation, that can perhaps speak to us in useful ways about our dwindling self-reliance; our voids in understanding of place and environment; about human-centered processes in which organization serves the concrete needs of people; about the virtues of quality, community, smallness, harmony, and simplicity. Perhaps among the ashes, sherds, and crumbling walls, we may find a strange and unexpected sort of wisdom.

Richard W. Lang was formerly director of the Wheelwright Museum of the American Indian in Santa Fe and a staff member of the School of American Research. He is an anthropologist and artist and the author of many works on the archaeology and native cultures of the American Southwest.

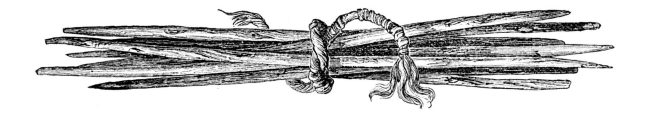

Figure 8.1. Computers have become essential tools in archaeology for recording and storing data and developing simulations.

Simulation and Imagination Fistfight in the Mesa Verde

Timothy A. Kohler

The year after the summer of no corn, nearly everyone left the river valley. Weeds took over the fields, and eventually the shrubs and trees started to grow back. A few deer ventured down from the highlands to the north. It was a long time before Mitsha, now of age, could find a husband among the few families left in the neighborhood. Okoya was two years her junior, from one of the families that had stayed on down by big bend. Together they settled outside the valley in the direction of the high mesa and farmed a plot of land near a spring, an hour's walk from his parents. Soon she had a child.

Why do we do archaeology? Perhaps for the same reasons we read biographies or novels: to learn something about the experience of others and, perhaps, to benefit from their experience. I wonder what southwestern Colorado was like 1,000 years ago. Would we have enjoyed living there? Would we even have survived?

One way to try to address such questions is by doing archaeological or ethnographic research and then applying our imaginations. Adolf Bandelier attempted this in *The Delight Makers*, a novel about life in what is now Bandelier National Monument in New Mexico before the arrival of the Spaniard Coronado. His story inspired my fictional passage about Mitsha and Okoya. Some contemporary archaeologists follow this literary path, using everything they know and can imagine to try to put flesh on the bones of the archaeological record. In this way, they hope to learn something about the values and goals of people long dead, their concerns, and what they found meaningful.

When I read these accounts, however, I often wonder how far I can trust their narratives. If some details are wrong, does that spoil the whole picture? How do I choose among *different* imagined pasts?

One problem with our imaginations is that they have evolved to help us live lives lasting a few score years at best. But archaeologists grapple with processes that unroll across many generations and spaces larger than individual lived experience. When we are fortunate, we have too much data to keep in our heads; then our imaginations want a helper.

A colleague of mine who also works in archaeological simulation (fig. 8.1) likes to call his project "a prosthesis for the imagination." I think he means that simulation helps him visualize the way many different interacting processes play out over long periods of time. He might also mean that our imaginations need concrete notions to bump up against —to constrain them—if we are to move forward rather than go in circles.

For the past decade, I have been working on a project that keeps expanding. It started when I had the good fortune to spend a sabbatical at the Santa Fe Institute in New Mexico in 1992–93. At that time, Chris Langton and other computer scientists there were beginning work on a new sort of computer program designed to study how systems composed of many interacting and potentially different "agents" would behave over time. Some of these systems displayed fascinating tendencies toward self-organization. (A recent example of self-organization is the growth of the internet, which has, for the most part, been dictated by local

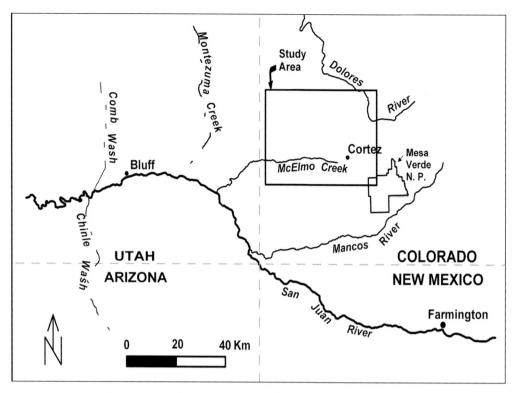

Figure 8.2. The study area in southwestern Colorado for the computer simulation project.

conditions and needs, giving rise on the global level to the network's current architecture.)

At the Santa Fe Institute, I became interested in seeing whether we could program the processes by which ancient households in the Southwest (the "agents" in our models) sometimes organized themselves into large villages and sometimes disbanded into little hamlets scattered across the countryside. Maybe, I thought, we could even get the perplexing late-1200s depopulation of the Mesa Verde to "emerge."

As I write this in 2005, we are still working, and some of our original goals are at least within sight. Now that we think we know what we're doing, others of our goals seem naïve. But even the process of learning why some goals were naïve has taught us much about the archaeological record in the central Mesa Verde region that we did not understand when we began this project.

How to Program a Household
In our model, the agent households may run in the thousands in our 726-square-mile study area just northwest of Mesa Verde (fig. 8.2). The households

have their unique histories and fortunes, but they live and die according to the same rules. They farm corn, gather fuelwood, haul water, and seek better places to live when conditions demand. They may trade, too, exchanging maize with other households. And we allow them to hunt deer, cottontail, and jackrabbits and to exchange the meat among themselves.

One of the first questions most people ask about our simulation work is how we determine realistic values for the many variables we put into our model. The answer depends on the variable. Some, such as probabilities of birth and death, we take from tables compiled for "natural fertility" societies (those without modern birth control) around the world. Others we derive from the landscape we are studying: for example, the topography, the soils, the distribution of water, and certain plant and animal species today resemble those of the distant past. In still other cases, we draw on data from the archaeological record. For example, we assume that corn (maize) was essential, making up 60 percent of the calories in the prehistoric Puebloan diet (figs. 8.3 and 8.4).

Figure 8.3. The maize harvest at San Juan Pueblo, New Mexico, in 1935 attests to the centuries-old importance of corn in the Pueblo diet.

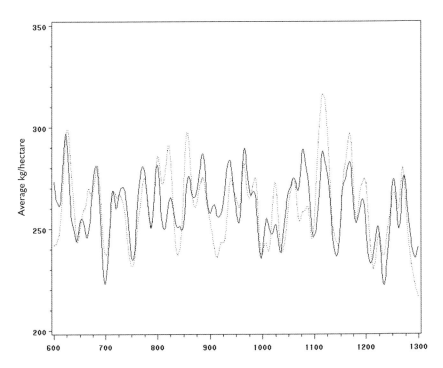

Figure 8.4. Two reconstructions of average annual maize production in the study area from 600 to 1300 CE, using slightly different tree-ring data to estimate temperatures. Both data plots have been smoothed to bring out variation on the order of a decade or more and to suppress year-to-year variability.

on the landscape the households should live, for example. Instead, we want to watch the way settlement patterns develop when we give households fundamental rules. One set of rules we are studying intensely says that households should attempt to find and live in places that minimize their caloric costs (labor) for obtaining the food, water, and fuel they need to survive on this landscape.

This may sound like an easy assignment for those households, but the weather in the Southwest varies greatly from year to year, which affects harvests. We are fortunate to have a detailed tree-ring record that allows us to estimate precipitation and temperature and therefore the potential yields for maize in any year back to 600 CE. Our current reconstructions of maize production are shown in figure 8.4. The same factors affecting maize also determine the growth of other plants and animals, though less dramatically.

Of course, we have to be careful not to program in archaeological data that we would like to see emerge. We prescribe nothing about precisely where

Figure 8.5. A Hopi cornfield on a sand dune demonstrates how Pueblo farmers adapted their cultivation methods to local landscapes and soils.

was now eight and could help in the fields and in gathering wood and getting water; with this extra pair of hands, Okoya brought another field into production. Mitsha's sister's family lived in a higher area with short summers and some years had to ask Mitsha for corn to get through till the next harvest. Mitsha was always able to help; it was their custom to give what they could to relatives, knowing that they would receive the same. But this was not always true for their neighbors. Mitsha had helped out Shotaye three years ago, when harvests were poor in their neighborhood, and had yet to be paid back. She would not make that mistake again.

As commonly happened, a household's farm plots might produce well one year but not the next. Also, soil fertility slowly diminishes, weeds take hold, and erosion removes topsoil. People use up all the convenient deadwood for fuel and then start to chop down living trees for fuel and construction material. They may overhunt game near larger settlements. And households situated in a desirable location are soon joined by others, causing competition for fuel and game. Finally, local springs respond to wet and dry periods lasting several years.

Our agent households must cope with a landscape that is constantly changing in response to weather, history of use, and local population densities. As our simulations run, it is fascinating to watch the households move about on the landscape, trying to adapt to circumstances.

Yet we know that in the real world, people are not pushed around like leaves before a storm. Households can buffer changes in agricultural production by storing food and exchanging it with kin or neighbors. We can observe the effects of these actions in the simulation as well.

Mitsha and Okoya prospered. Three more children arrived, though one died in his first winter. The oldest

What We Are Learning

What we learn by modeling is different from what we learn when we excavate a site. The model shows us what households *ought* to do, if they follow the specific rules we give them. When we look at the archaeological record, we learn something about what people *actually* did. No matter how good our simulations are, we can never hope to faithfully reproduce any specific aspect of a society's behaviors, let alone all of them.

This limitation is not as serious as it might seem. Take the example of population size in our project area. Except at the start of the simulation, when we put some households randomly on the landscape, households do not come into our area through immigration during a model run. And the only way they can leave is by dying out: no emigration is possible. Clearly, in the "real world," people and communities were always evaluating whether they should move out; most people in the late 1200s evidently decided they should. On one hand, our model tells us how many households could make it in our area, given our assumptions about their rates of resource use, the condition and productivity of the landscape, and so forth. The archaeological record, on the other hand, tells us, within the limits of our ability to decipher it correctly, how many households actually were there.

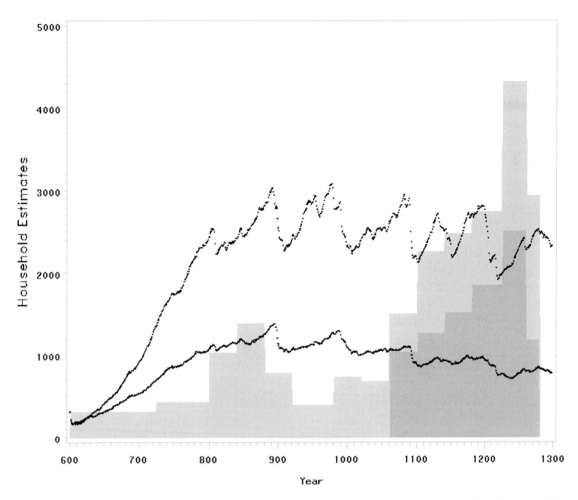

Figure 8.6. Estimates of the numbers of households in the study area between 600 and 1300 CE (gray bars), along with population histories generated by two simulations.

Figure 8.6 illustrates this difference. The two gray zones show our estimates of the number of households in our study area between 600 and 1300 CE, based on archaeological data organized by Scott Ortman of Crow Canyon Archaeological Center. (For the mid-1000s through the late 1200s, we have a maximum and a minimum estimate; before that, we have only one estimate.) The wiggly lines are based on simulation runs with different settings for two key variables: how fast population can grow and how much productivity fields lose when they are continuously cropped. The upper line is from a simulation with high population growth and small losses of productivity; the lower line shows a simulation with slower growth and greater productivity decreases due to soil nutrient depletion, erosion, weed growth, and other factors. Most of our runs produce popula-

tions somewhere between these two extremes, depending on the exact choices for the variables we did not change in these two runs.

Neither run produced populations as high we think might have existed in our study area in the mid-1200s. Because our simulations give estimates of the carrying capacity for this area under the assumptions we make, then either some of our assumptions about how much people could produce are wrong, or the population in the mid-1200s was larger than could be viably maintained in this area.

We acknowledge that many of our assumptions might be a little wrong. For example, we assume that over 700 years, people made no improvements in productivity by adopting new varieties of maize, new ways of growing maize, or new ways of controlling maize pests. In truth, new varieties of maize were coming in from Mesoamerica and being refined locally throughout this sequence. Beginning in the 1000s people began to build terraces and check dams on slopes and across small drainages, and these ways of managing surface water and topsoil became more important over the next two centuries. Finally, if the Mesa Verdeans were depleting deer, then they were managing one of their major maize pests.

Quite likely, the most important difference between what simulated households do for food and what the real households did arises only after the 900 CE (Pueblo I) population peak. In the 1000s people began to raise turkeys as a regular part of their diet, and by the 1200s turkeys had become extremely important, completely displacing deer in some sites. We know from our simulations that when more than about 1,000 households reside in our area, they begin to kill more deer through hunting than can be replaced, even when we assume that they needed to hunt for only a small part of their protein requirements.

So it is no surprise to find that turkeys started to replace deer in the diet in the mid-1000s, when local populations began to exceed 1,000 households and continued to grow. Even though raising turkeys is a lot of work, it became easier than hunting for ever scarcer and more distant deer. But this strategy concealed a danger. In addition to gleaning whatever they could around the pueblo, turkeys probably ate some corn. If so, then people began to depend on corn not only for their calories but increasingly for their protein as well.

The Social Fabric
One contrast between our models and the real world lies in the degree of people's sociality. For most purposes, our households are completely independent and make their own choices. True, they can build up exchange relationships with other households and depend on their assistance in bad times to a certain extent. Even so, in the end each is independent and can move on when the need arises (so long as they stay in the study area).

Members of the real societies that lived here, however, probably made many important decisions at the level of the community, not the household.

These might have included decisions on where to live, when to leave, whether to hunt together for distant deer, and whether to wage war against, or trade with, neighboring communities. At this point, we have no *collective action* in our model, though we hope to in future work. This surely explains some of the differences between the model results and the real world.

For example, notice how the simulated populations tend to cycle in size less drastically than the real population (fig. 8.6). Part of this is probably because, on the model side, our households can't leave except by dying, which is, after all, a last resort. But on the archaeological side, part of the difference is probably due to community-level decisions to immigrate or emigrate that affected many people. These decisions could therefore result in large population swings, like the two large cycles of population size we see for this area. We can infer that these decisions were not very finely tuned and might indeed have been somewhat inaccurate. The fact that many communities seem to have made similar decisions at the same time also suggests that communities were somewhat conformist in their decisions: they tended to do what other communities nearby were doing—in the same way households within a community apparently followed the group's decisions.

Thirty Ways to Leave Mesa Verde
In his short story "The Lone Ranger and Tonto Fistfight in Heaven," the novelist Sherman Alexie tells the story of two lovers—one white, one Indian—who become estranged yet still need each other. It is the same with simulation and imagination. Neither alone is complete; we need both in our attempts to solve one of the classic problems in North American archaeology. I exaggerate only a little when I suggest that archaeologists have come up with 30 different explanations for the depopulation of the northern San Juan region (of which Mesa Verde is just a part) in the late 1200s.

If Mitsha and Okoya really had lived in our study area in the early to mid-1200s—instead of being names I assigned to anonymous agents in our simulations—they would have seen unprecedented events that we are still trying to under-

Figure 8.7. Part of the Painted Hand Site, at the center of one of the small communities founded in the western half of the simulation study area in the mid-1200s.

stand. The first 35 years or so of that century were generally very cold and quite dry. This may have provoked a wave of immigration into our area from less favorable places, pushing population to its prehistoric maximum in the mid-1200s. The new arrivals tended to settle in small communities in the western part of the study area. We know from simulation that populations this large make significant inroads on fuelwood and deer. Moreover, our simulations almost never generate populations as large as the maximum estimate for the mid-1200s shown in figure 8.6, and only a few combinations of the variables will result in populations as high as our minimum archaeological estimate for this period. This many people probably strained the productive capacity of the landscape at a time when its productivity was already declining through climate change (fig. 8.4).

It's a bit of a mystery why the eastern portions of our study area were not more densely occupied at this time. Indeed, a large swath of territory known to archaeologists as the "Piedra" district—from a little east of Cortez west to beyond Durango and down toward the present border with New Mexico—was also vacant, depopulated in the mid-1100s. One possibility is that distant clusters of communities were essentially at war with one another. If raiding from the cluster of Pueblo III communities near Farmington and Aztec was a threat, for example, then a predictable response would be for a no-man's-land to develop in this area and for communities in our study area to pull together spatially and politically.

As Mark Varien relates in chapter 5, we do not know the precise combination of factors leading to the decision to emigrate. From the archaeological record, we know that violence contributed to these decisions and that some residents did not make it out alive. The simulations help us put these data in context by showing that population in the 1200s was very large relative to the productive capacity and condition of the landscape.

The rest is left to our imagination and to the patient labors of future archaeologists to sort out. I cannot help wondering what the pioneers of Southwestern archaeology—the likes of Fewkes, Kidder, and Hewett—would think of our attempts to harness computers to help us finish what they began.

Timothy A. Kohler is a professor of archaeology at Washington State University. A former resident scholar at the School of American Research and a current external faculty member at the Santa Fe Institute, Kohler is author of the book *Archaeology of Bandelier National Monument: Village Formation on the Pajarito Plateau, New Mexico*, published in 2004.

Figure 9.1. Late evening view of Yucca House, an unexcavated ancestral Pueblo village southwest of Cortez, Colorado. Mesa Verde lies on the center-right horizon, and the La Plata Mountains can be seen in the distance. Both the upper and lower house mounds are visible in the foreground.

Mesa Verdean Sacred Landscapes

Winston Hurst and Jonathan Till

From the north edge of the Mesa Verde, one reels at the vastness and majesty of the landscape. We humans are tiny specks lost in this immensity, and even the great mesa itself seems small. Stretching our minds to include the dimension of time, our significance dwindles further, and we catch a glimpse of the awe that the landscape must have inspired in its ancient inhabitants.

We will never know exactly how the ancestral Pueblos thought about this land. Like certain other aspects of their experience—personal names, place names, myths, and rituals, for instance—their cultural views of the landscape are veiled from the prying eyes of archaeologists by time and the limitations of science. Yet hard clues do exist—"tussocks of empirical certainty," the archaeologist Earl Morris called them, "to guide our speculation across the fen of time." They take two major forms: physical evidence left on the land by the ancients (the archaeological record) and information preserved in the cultural behaviors and memories of their living descendants, the Pueblo peoples of Arizona and New Mexico (the ethnographic record). Weaving together the archaeological and ethnographic clues offers some glimpses into what the sacred Mesa Verdean landscape might have looked like to its Puebloan inhabitants.

Sacred Landscapes

We use the term *sacred* loosely, to refer to anything that inspires a sense of spiritual awe, reverence, prayerfulness, or transcendence; to anything that is perceived as having a connection to things spiritual —to ancestors, deities, spiritual beings, or times or places of mythical or religious importance; or to anything that is the site or focus of ritualistic, religious activity. A sacred *place* is one that invokes a sense of transcendence in the mind of a visitor. A sacred *landscape* is a set of such places that together constitute a layer of sacred meaning mapped onto a piece of geography.

Sacredness is not implicit in the landscape. Rather, it is a purely subjective property that exists only in the eye or heart of the beholder. In that sense, sacred sites and landscapes always are manmade: human viewers respond to or manipulate the meaning and significance of places and natural features. Their manipulations can range from massive constructions to a simple mark on a rock where someone went to meditate or pray. Inherently striking geographic features such as caves, bedrock holes, pinnacles, and springs may be left unmodified.

Because families, clans, communities, and larger cultural or ethnic groups commonly share many perceptions of the landscape, it is possible to speak generally about *the* sacred landscape of a particular people at a certain time. Such perceptions, however, change over time and vary to some degree among communities, families, and even individuals within a family. Any sacred landscape is really a kaleidoscope of overlapping or layered sacred landscapes unique to the experience, understanding, and viewpoint of each person. The real sacred landscape of the ancient Mesa Verdeans was actually much more intricate and complicated than can be represented here.

Figure 9.2. Centuries ago, indigenous people inscribed this boulder overlooking the San Juan River valley below Cedar Mesa in southeastern Utah.

The Sacred Landscape of the Mesa Verdeans

In their attitudes toward landscapes, Pueblo people and anthropologists share an important concept: the landscape is a rich repository of historical and cultural information (see chapter 6). Also, they often recognize ancient sacred sites in much the same way, by looking for attention-demanding natural features and certain types of cultural sites, such as ancient ruins, cairns, rock enclosures, formal trails ("roads"), rock art, and constructed alignments that might have archaeoastronomical significance. All these kinds of features can be found in the Mesa Verde region, sometimes joined in one location.

Natural Features of Likely Significance

Traditional Pueblo people utilize a complex array of shrines, some constructed and some unmarked, situated on the landscape in and around their villages. They often place their shrines on mountain peaks, hills, and pinnacles; by water sources, including lakes, springs, and rivers; in caves or rock clefts; or in association with unusual natural features.

We assume that ancestral Pueblos had similar traditions. High points that might have been significant to them in the Mesa Verde region include Hesperus Peak in the La Plata Mountains, the cone of Sleeping Ute Mountain, Abajo Peak, and the

Bears Ears. Locally, hills and impressive geologic anomalies were probably important too. The sandstone bridges of Natural Bridges National Monument and the arches of Sand Canyon, Arch Canyon, and Butler Wash, for example, might have triggered spiritual responses. Striking features such as the Twin Rocks pinnacles at Bluff in southeastern Utah surely commanded attention in a spiritual landscape. The frequent presence of carved or painted images at or near sites like these attests to their significance (fig. 9.2). Permanent sources of water—seeps, springs, and permanent streams such as the Dolores and San Juan rivers and some of their tributaries—might also have been held sacred. In addition, the Mesa Verde country harbors thousands of more intimate places that today trigger a sense of awe and wonder in many of us and might have inspired similar feelings in ancient people.

Ritual Architecture

Certain buildings in prehistoric Mesa Verdean villages stand out for their inordinate size and formal design. Such structures, commonly identified as "great houses" and "great kivas," are interpreted by most archaeologists as ceremonial centers that helped integrate the members of a community.

Great houses were multistory, massive, masonry buildings, commonly with large rooms and interior, aboveground kivas (see pl. 6). They were bigger and more solidly constructed than other buildings in their community. Although great houses are commonly associated with the Chacoan community pattern, many are found in the northern San Juan region at long distances from Chaco Canyon (see chapter 4). In the Mesa Verde region, recognized great houses appeared in the late eleventh and early twelfth centuries, though some archaeologists see evidence for possible great houses in sites dating as early as the ninth century CE.

Researchers have identified great houses throughout much of the Mesa Verde region, from

Figure 9.3. Twin Rocks, a prominent landscape feature in Bluff, Utah, is aligned with a nearby Chaco-style great house.

the Grand Gulch plateau in the west to the Animas River in the east and from the San Juan River in the south to the Dolores River and the foothills of the Abajo Mountains in the north. Typically, builders sited their great house on a hill or ridge, visually dominating a surrounding Puebloan community or overlooking an outstanding feature in the natural landscape. The Bluff Great House, for example, was erected on a prominent terrace commanding the San Juan River and a community of smaller sites, with a clear view of both an unusual pair of cliff alcoves and the strikingly paired pinnacles known as the "Twin Rocks" or the "Navajo Twins" (fig. 9.3).

Mesa Verdeans commonly built their great houses on or near the remains of substantial, ninth-century Puebloan villages. Pueblo people today hold ancestral sites to be sacred and often treat them as shrines, so this practice in the past might have been a way to sanctify or legitimate the new great house in the eyes of the community.

Although no great-house site has been identified as a paramount ritual center for the entire Mesa Verde region, it is possible that certain major sites exerted ritual influence over a relatively large area. The region appears not to have been strongly integrated, however, and most archaeologists view it as a patchwork of autonomous community territories, each with a dominant central site and a hierarchy of smaller settlements. In actuality, the ritual integration of communities probably varied over time. Chaco Canyon may have asserted paramount ceremonial influence over much of the southern Colorado Plateau during the late eleventh and early twelfth centuries, but any such status was apparently short-lived. By the thirteenth century, the Mesa Verde world seems to have been broken up into smaller, "Balkanized" community territories, each with its own ceremonial sites and sacred landscape. Nevertheless, communities likely shared certain shrines and ceremonial locations, and certain large

Figure 9.4. Circular and square towers in Hovenweep National Monument.

communities (Yellow Jacket Pueblo, for example) probably exerted far-reaching ritual influence.

Great kivas have a history going all the way back to the sixth century CE and may represent the earliest form of true public architecture in the Mesa Verde region. These extraordinarily large, circular, subterranean or semisubterranean structures appear to have served as ritual gathering places that brought the members of communities together during the communities' formative stages. As communities matured, their residents tended to let these buildings fall into disuse. This pattern demonstrates the way sacred landscapes can evolve and change in the course of a community's life cycle.

The thirteenth century, a time of increasing drought and stress, saw two interesting developments in settlement patterns and architecture that reflect changes in people's perceptions of the sacred landscape. The first was that populations reorganized themselves across the terrain, aggregating into more massive and concentrated pueblos built close to springs (see pl. 3). In previous times, Mesa

Verdeans had generally kept their settlements discretely away from springs, which we believe were shrine sites whose water was considered to be a free and public commodity. In the thirteenth century, people became much more possessive of their water, concentrating their settlements closely around their water sources. They thus assumed direct control of the springs both as places of supernatural power and, more pragmatically, as resources critical to survival.

The second development was that at about the same time the Pueblo III communities were wrapping themselves around their springs, they also began building stone towers. Hovenweep National Monument displays the best-known examples of these structures (fig. 9.4). Towers vary interestingly in ground plan, from circular to rectangular to mixtures of circularity and squareness (**D**-shaped, for example). The mixing of circularity and squareness has a conscious, formal quality that suggests symbolic significance, perhaps related to balance between male and female principles or similar

Figure 9.5. Ancient Indian trail along the San Juan River, southeastern Utah.

opposites in the universe. Towers appear both in the new aggregated villages (Sand Canyon Pueblo alone has 14) and in isolated locations, but almost always close to water sources. At some level, they might represent the architectural formalization or incorporation of spring-related shrines.

Roads and Trails

Trails assume an aura of sacredness in many cultures, particularly when they lead to places of mythical or ritual significance. In the Puebloan Southwest, large, formally constructed trails (commonly referred to as "roads") appeared as early as the ninth century CE but proliferated during the eleventh and twelfth centuries. Although these features are commonly associated with relatively complex organizational and architectural developments in the Chaco region to the south, examples have been identified in various parts of the Mesa Verde region as well.

Roads in the Mesa Verde region generally appear as subtle linear swales, 15 to 45 feet wide, bordered by low, earthen berms (fig. 9.5). They can be difficult to date, but most appear to have been contemporaneous with the great-house communities (late 1000s and early 1100s) or with later, more aggregated, twelfth- and thirteenth-century pueblo communities. Some connect such communities, others lead to evident shrines, and still others have no obvious destination. Several "belt loop" roads have been identified, partially or completely encircling great houses at a radius of several hundred feet.

Most of the known road sections consist of excavated swales across landscapes where travel was easy. They are only minimally developed in rough places where they might actually have eased transport or travel. This observation has led a growing number of archaeologists to believe that the roads served a symbolic or ritual function, physically marking linkages between important places, rather than as conventional roads built mainly for travel or transporting goods.

Another fascinating aspect of roads is that they sometimes connect settlements that were not occupied at the same time. John Stein, Stephen Lekson, and others who have researched roads in the Chaco region have dubbed such features "roads through time." In such cases, inhabitants of the later sites probably treated the earlier sites as ancestral shrines.

Although some roads remain clearly visible to the trained eye today, others are only faintly recognizable or have large gaps where erosion has obliterated all traces. In some areas where they are better preserved, or at least better studied, the roads appear to link great houses and shrine features into networks. Whether these were local networks or parts of a sprawling but largely undetected system that reached all the way to Chaco Canyon and beyond is unclear, but no roads have yet been discovered that link any site in the Mesa Verde region with Chaco Canyon.

Figure 9.6. A circular feature in the Mesa Verde landscape, thought to be an ancient shrine.

fied features like these along roads and in pueblo sites. The enclosures typically have low walls of roughly stacked stones several courses high (fig. 9.6), although a few have mortared walls several feet high. Shrines in ancient Mesa Verdean sites generally sit atop architectural rubble mounds or in kiva depressions, indicating that they were built or at least maintained long after the sites were vacated, perhaps by the Puebloan descendants of the ancient inhabitants.

Stone enclosures located along roads —called *herraduras* (Spanish for "horse-shoes") in the archaeological literature —were probably road-related shrines. Although most currently known examples are found west of Blanding, their full distribution (like that of the roads themselves) is yet unknown.

Scott Ortman, of Crow Canyon Archaeological Center, recently reported a series of apparent directional shrines in McElmo Canyon, associated with the substantial Castle Rock Pueblo. Ranging from bermed depressions to rock enclosures, some opening toward Castle Rock, they suggest a landscape of directional shrines similar to those maintained to the present day around some of the living pueblos in New Mexico and Arizona. Archaeologists have barely begun to identify such features, so we do not yet know how common or uncommon they were or how their form and distribution might have changed over time.

Little is known about the shrines and shrine-like features in the Mesa Verde region beyond what is evident at the surface, because few of them have been excavated. The only excavated examples are shallow, C-shaped rock alignments in kiva depressions that yielded no clearly associated artifacts.

If the locally linked sets of sites in the Mesa Verde region do represent discrete local networks, they may differ in scale from east to west. For example, in the western portion of the region, an extensive network of roads and great features extends in a loop nearly 60 miles long, linking four recognized great houses and a prominent shrine. No such network has yet been documented in southwestern Colorado, though a number of substantial road segments have been identified there. The largest network documented in that area so far is a single road less than three miles long, connecting two nodes, the Casa Negra and Shields Pueblo great houses.

Cairns and Rock Enclosures
Rock cairns ranging from a few crudely stacked stones to tall, carefully erected monuments can be found across the Four Corners country, including the Mesa Verde region. Some of these were probably left by the Mesa Verde Puebloan people, but their precise age and origin are difficult to determine.

Many Native American cultures constructed C-shaped or ovoid shrine enclosures of stacked rocks, from several feet to more than 30 feet in diameter. In the Mesa Verde area, archaeologists have identi-

Rock Art Sites
The term *rock art* encompasses a great variety of designs and figures that Native Americans inscribed or painted on cliff faces, boulders, and stone masonry (fig. 9.7). Examples include pecked or incised petroglyphs and painted pictographs. How can we twentieth-century researchers and observers

Figure 9.7. Late Basketmaker panel of petroglyphs near the San Juan River in southeastern Utah.

know the meanings of these ancient images? Not easily, and sometimes not at all, but we can make some educated guesses.

In order to understand the importance of rock art to ancient people, it is crucial to recognize that many traditional people believe that images have the power to affect nature, that art invokes reality, that art can *make things happen*. Creating art, therefore, is a potentially powerful and sometimes dangerous act. Ancient Puebloan people likely made most of their rock art as a way to supplicate or manipulate supernatural powers to provide protection and healing, bring rainfall, grant hunting success and fertility, bring harm to an enemy, and the like. Some images appear to depict prowess in combat or to commemorate historical or mythical events. Unfortunately, many sites are so esoteric or abstract that we probably will never understand their original significance. Present-day Pueblo people visiting rock art sites commonly interpret the motifs as clan symbols or symbols related to esoteric ceremonial societies, but their stated interpretations often vary from person to person, clan to clan, and village to village. This makes it hard for us to know with any certainty what the art meant to its makers centuries ago.

Mesa Verdean rock art is not uniformly distributed across either space or time. It is abundant in some areas and sparse in others, and it varies over

time in abundance, style, and degree of formality. This suggests that the importance of rock art as an element of the sacred landscape varied from group to group and changed through time.

Perhaps the greatest concentration of rock art in the Mesa Verde region is found along the middle stretches of the San Juan River and its tributaries. This concentration suggests a degree of ritual focus on the San Juan River, possibly because of its status as a major water source or travel corridor. In the Mesa Verde core area of southwestern Colorado, where the best-known, large, late pueblos cluster, rock art is less common.

Throughout the American Southwest, including the Mesa Verde region, traditional people often made rock art close to where they lived and along the trails they used. They also placed rock art near sources of water—close to springs and at the confluences of rivers and streams. The placement is not always intuitively logical, however. Rock art often appears in isolated, unexpected places, but prominent, patinated faces that would seem to have been natural canvases were left unadorned.

Panels placed in clearly visible spots along major trails or overlooking fields would have been seen by people going about their daily activities, as well as by approaching visitors. Some such panels may overlook ancient ceremonial gathering sites or dance grounds. Such public displays of rock art presumably held instructional significance for communities or other social groups, reminding viewers of group identity, ownership of resources or territories, or proper behavior. More hidden, less public sites presumably were related more to personal activities.

The content of rock art is too complexly variable over space and time to be itemized here. Some frequently recurring motifs that must have held widespread iconic or symbolic significance include—to name just a few—processions of human figures (see fig. 3.4), human figures holding various objects or assuming certain postures, handprints, sandal tracks, animal tracks, spirals, concentric circles, snakelike wavy lines, bighorn sheep and other animals, hunting scenes, images of copulation and childbirth, and large circular images that appear to represent shields.

Human processions appear in two common varieties: apparent dancers, sometimes holding hands or playing flutes, and lines of "humpbacks," probably representing travelers with packs. The latter are sometimes depicted on a horizontal or meandering line, presumably representing a mythical or historical trail or journey.

Humans are depicted with various postures and adornments. Examples include lizardlike forms, front-facing forms with one raised hand, figures holding crook-necked staffs, figures with bird-shaped heads or headdresses, figures playing flutes, and figures holding what appear to be human heads or scalps.

Track depictions include human sandal forms and tracks of a variety of animals—canines, cats, bears, badgers, rabbits, deer, sheep, elk, and others less easily identifiable. Tracks of large carnivores (lion, wolf, bear) associated with defensive sites and trails may represent power imagery related to defense or hunting.

Handprints are associated with coming-of-age rituals in some Native cultures. They seem not to be important in the living Pueblo communities, however, and their significance for the Mesa Verde Pueblo people is unclear.

Spirals and concentric circles have been variously interpreted as representing the sun and migration journeys. Some are clearly placed to interact meaningfully with patterns of light and shadow in calendrical monitoring sites (more on this subject later).

Hunting scenes commonly depict humans with either bows and arrows or atlatls and darts, as well as animals with protruding arrows or darts (fig. 9.7). They presumably represent hunting-related rituals.

Wavy lines may represent snakes, lightning, or the bounding motion of running deer or bighorn sheep, all of which are directly or indirectly related to water in many Southwestern cultures (water and lightning both travel in a snakelike zigzag, so snakes and other things that move in wavelike or zigzag fashion are related symbolically and spiritually to water).

Scenes depicting human copulation or childbirth occur occasionally but widely. They are presumably related to fertility rituals. Shield-size circular motifs with widely varying internal design organizations probably represent actual shields. These images occur almost exclusively on defensive walls or on cliffs directly above defensive walls, in sites constructed during the thirteenth century. In the far west of the Mesa Verde region, shield representations sometimes depict a human standing behind a shield. The various shield figures were likely created as emblems of protective magic —as invocations or expressions of defensive power. Their appearance in association with late defensive structures reflects rising militarism and defensive posturing during the stressful decades leading up to the great abandonment of the late 1200s.

Rock art motifs tend to cluster—certain sites contain concentrations of certain motifs. One site, for example, might be dominated by animal tracks, while another consists largely of handprints or ceremonial processions. Some sites are dominated by incised grooves and cupules that appear to be the result of the removal of sandstone, likely for some ritual usage, from places of power.

Archaeoastronomical Sites

Archaeological evidence suggests that the ancient Mesa Verdeans used the land and the sky as a vast and intricate calendar to guide them in their scheduling of ceremonies and to remind them of the proper times for planting, harvesting, and hunting. Like their Puebloan descendants, they did this by observing the way patterns of sunlight and shadow moved across the surfaces of rocks, walls, or floors as the sun's pathway changed with the seasons (see fig. 10.6). They carefully observed the changing location of the rising and setting of the sun and certain stars along the horizon (or through doorways, windows, or hatches). The interplay of astronomical events with the natural and constructed landscape formed an important component of the sacred landscape. Places from which calendrical observations were made were probably treated as shrines.

Almost any room, pithouse, or kiva had the potential to serve as a clock or an astronomical calendar. Sunlight angling through an opening would move across the floor and walls, illuminating different features at different times of the day or year.

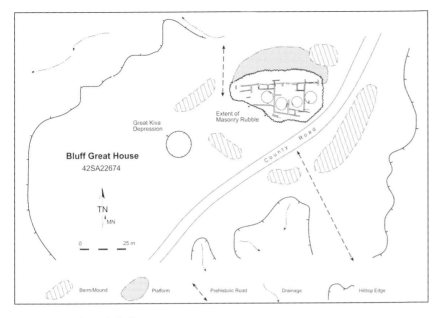

Figure 9.8. Plan of Bluff Great House.

At night, a person sitting inside a room or kiva could have observed changing star patterns through a hatch, doorway, or smoke hole. Certain buildings, such as Sun Temple on Mesa Verde, may have been intentionally designed to function as observatories (see chapter 10). Many great houses in the Mesa Verde region appear to have been constructed with at least one major wall carefully oriented to a cardinal direction, suggesting that they were intentionally designed with a certain relationship to the cosmos. For example, the back wall of Bluff Great House (fig. 9.8)—the thickest wall in the site and the structural backbone for the building—is aligned due east-west, in line with the Twin Rocks pinnacles and the equinox sunrise.

The Sacred Mundane

Traditional Pueblo people hold as sacred certain things that western Europeans and modern Americans normally view as mundane or even unclean. We have already mentioned the sacredness with which Pueblo people view their abandoned ancestral homes, but most Pueblos also traditionally regard as sacred all material that passed through the household or the community—everything from worn-out stone and bone tools

and broken pots to ash, charcoal, and floor sweepings. In other words, Puebloan middens (trash dumps) are sacred. It is therefore not surprising that Pueblo people have traditionally used their middens as cemeteries, a custom that archaeologists have traced in the Mesa Verde region as far back as the Basketmaker III period, the seventh century CE.

Conclusion

Although we will probably never fully reconstruct the sacred landscape of the ancient Mesa Verdeans, careful attention to the archaeological record and the cultural traditions of living Pueblo people can provide many insights. Those insights remind us that the landscape is a vast repository of cultural and historical knowledge, marked and imprinted with a fragile record of past cultures and communities. For the members of those ancient communities, the land was infused with sacred meaning. Although landscape has lost much of its spiritual dimension for most modern Americans, it remains as sacred to those who value historical knowledge and cultural understanding as it was to the ancient peoples whose records it contains. Just as the landscape offered them interface with their spiritual universe and their cultural history, so it allows them to speak to us across time. It is our bridge to their world, about which we still have much to learn. It is a rich and eloquent record that can teach us important things if we can teach ourselves to pay respectful attention.

Winston Hurst is an independent consulting archaeologist who lives and works in his hometown of Blanding, Utah. Jonathan Till is the laboratory analysis manager at Crow Canyon Archaeological Center. His archaeological research interests include monumental architecture and cultural landscapes of the Chaco period in the Four Corners region.

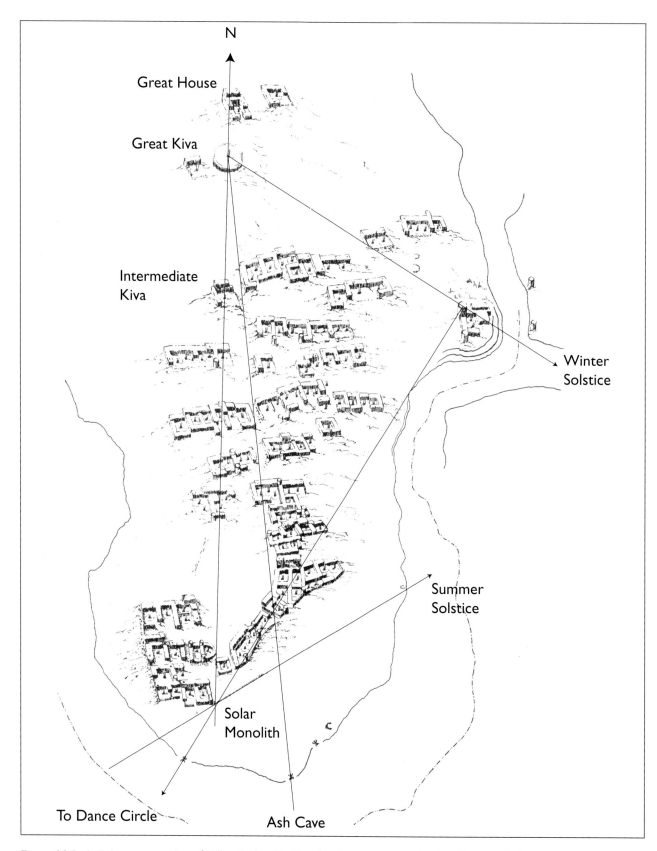

N

Great House

Great Kiva

Intermediate
Kiva

Winter
Solstice

Summer
Solstice

Solar
Monolith

To Dance Circle

Ash Cave

Figure 10.1. Artist's reconstruction of Yellow Jacket Pueblo, showing astronomical and architectural alignments.

The Cosmic and the Sacred at Yellow Jacket Pueblo and Mesa Verde

J. McKim Malville

Throughout the land north of the San Juan River, the ancestors of the modern Pueblos devised ingenious ways to mark the positions of the sun at the solstices. At places such as Hovenweep National Monument, Mancos Canyon, Grand Gulch, and Cottonwood Canyon, the play of light and shadow across rocks and buildings identified the extreme positions of the sun in June and December. Plazas, cliff alcoves, and ceremonial structures may have been used as places for public gatherings to honor the sun and celebrate these nodes of cyclical and sacred time. At sunset on the summer solstice, a beam of light enters a porthole at Hovenweep Castle. The winter solstice sun sets precisely on top of the toe of Sleeping Ute Mountain as seen from the great house called "Yucca House." The Perfect Kiva enclosure of Grand Gulch might have been the site of winter solstice celebrations. There, bedrock metates point toward the rising sun, which may have been greeted by a chorus of manos grinding on metates.

In these periodic activities, the ancient Puebloans shared with people of all continents and all ages the celebration of the cycles of nature. In Ireland the sun illuminated the dark corridor of the ancient tomb of New Grange on the winter solstice beginning around 3200 BCE. Sometime later in Great Britain, the sun began to rise close to the heel stone of Stonehenge at summer solstice. The solstice sun entered the Egyptian temple of Amon-Ra at Karnak near Luxor and touched the golden walls of the Temple of the Sun, known as the "Coricancha," in Cuzco, Peru.

Two areas north of the San Juan River stand out for the complexity of their astronomy: Yellow Jacket Pueblo (fig. 10.1) and Mesa Verde. Yellow Jacket Pueblo lies on a 100-acre peninsula at the head of Yellow Jacket Canyon, north of Cortez in southwestern Colorado. During the Pueblo III period, it may have contained as many as 1,200 rooms and 195 kivas, with a population estimated by Kristin Kuckelman to lie between 850 and 1,360 persons. For a time, it was the largest settlement of the ancient Pueblo world.

In Pueblo III times, the combined populations of the famous cliff dwellings of Mesa Verde appear to have been significantly smaller than that of Yellow Jacket. Cliff Palace, for example, the largest of the cliff dwellings, contained 150 rooms, 23 kivas, and a resident population of between 150 and 250. Although archaeologists have interpreted the movement of people into cliff dwellings as a defensive measure at a time of social unrest, the suitability of a place for ceremonies and devotional activities was also important in their choice of a building site. On the southwestern horizon of Cliff Palace, for example, Sun Temple, one of the largest exclusively ceremonial structures of the ancient Pueblos, marked the setting of the winter solstice sun and the major standstill moon.

Cosmic Centers and Sacred Centers

The astronomy that is imprinted on the landscape of Yellow Jacket appears to have been initially influenced during the late Pueblo II period by Chacoan cosmology. In Pueblo III times, the symbolic landscape was apparently transformed by more local influences. The Chacoan imprint on Yellow Jacket is similar in design to that of other "cosmic" cities of the world, whereas post-Chacoan influences appear to have converted Yellow Jacket into a sacred place with a unique location and special meaning. A similar quality of sacredness and uniqueness is found in Cliff Palace, Sun Temple, and other sites on Mesa Verde.

The archaeologist Colin Renfrew has proposed that Chaco Canyon qualifies as a "location of high devotional expression (LHDE)," one of many places in the ancient world that were products of powerful symbolic systems and complex mythologies. Visited periodically by celebrants to participate in rituals, festivals, and astronomical observations, these sites supported and promoted ceremony, trade, and social integration. In many of them, public plazas and architectural features were designed to guide the eye to devotional objects such as significant mountains or positions of the sun or moon.

Locations of high devotional expression were "cosmic" when they emphasized connections to the heavens, often by establishing alignments to the north or to all four cardinal directions. In Chaco Canyon, the eye and mind were guided northward by devices such as the dividing wall of Pueblo Bonito, the North Road, Casa Rinconada, and the north-south line connecting Tsin Kletzin and Pueblo Alto. These LHDEs might have been "sacred" if they drew upon the power of a sacred local landscape and its mytho-history. Both types of places, the cosmic and the sacred, had theaterlike settings for pomp, ceremony, and ritual processions. Whereas cosmic centers might have been established by powerful elites, sacred centers often grew spontaneously, inspired by local events, pilgrimages, and traditions. After the decline of the power of Chaco Canyon around 1125–50 CE, the residents of Yellow Jacket and parts of Mesa Verde may have lost interest in symbolic connections to a larger cosmos and begun to honor more the sacredness of the local landscape.

Yellow Jacket Pueblo (5MT5)

It is ironic that one of the greatest settlements of the ancient Pueblos is a little-known site now set among bean fields. In the thirteenth century, Yellow Jacket Pueblo became a huge and complex community. Its fertile neighborhood may have been the breadbasket for the ancient Mesa Verde world and beyond. Today the region is known as the "Pinto Bean Capital of the World." The red soil at Yellow Jacket is fertile loess blown in from the Kayenta region around Monument Valley, Arizona. According to the late archaeologist Joe Ben Wheat, Yellow Jacket hay has been shipped to dairy farmers as far away as California, who value its high protein content.

I first visited Yellow Jacket Pueblo, 5MT5, in the summer of 1986 with Mark Neupert, who was then a student in one of my introductory astronomy courses. Mark had told me about a marvelous monolith still standing at the southern end of the site and had speculated that it might have astronomical meaning (fig. 10.2). He had spent the previous summer at the University of Colorado field school working under Joe Ben Wheat, who had been excavating sites just to the west of 5MT5 since 1955.

During that summer of 1986, Mark and I established that the carved top of the monolith was oriented approximately toward summer solstice sunrise, which occurred on the distant shoulder of the 14,000-foot snow peak of El Diente. We also discovered in the deep sagebrush along the solstice line three fallen monoliths, a wall, and a small shrine at the edge of the mesa. A line established by 20 points—including the bases of the monoliths, blocks in the wall, and the center of the shrine—was within one-tenth of a degree of our estimate of the sun's first gleam on the summer solstice in 1200 CE (figs. 10.3 and 10.4). Also on that line, just below the shrine, sat a large cave open to the east, as well as a tower and kiva. Adjacent, sheltered terraces might have been used for early ritual plantings.

Even though it had been one of his dreams, Joe Ben Wheat never got to excavate 5MT5, but his knowledge of the site from surface inspection and the accuracy of his interpretations were legendary. During the next two summers, I mapped Yellow Jacket Pueblo with a crew of students from the University of Colorado, looking for additional astronomical alignments. A few years later, Crow

Figure 10.2. Standing monolith, Yellow Jacket Pueblo.

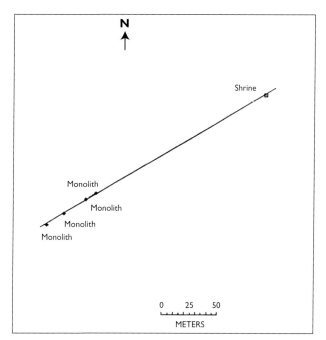

Figure 10.3. Solstice axis through the Yellow Jacket monoliths and shrine.

Figure 10.4. Summer solstice sunrise, Yellow Jacket Pueblo.

Canyon Archaeological Center also mapped the site and, with permission of the Archaeological Conservancy, which owns the eastern half of Yellow Jacket, excavated more than 100 test pits. Crow Canyon Archaeological Center has created an extensive website on the archaeology of Yellow Jacket Pueblo, documenting much of its complexity and many transformations. The history of the site can be divided into four phases.

Phase I: Pre-Chaco Populations

Basketmaker III people first settled the Yellow Jacket area. To the west of 5MT5, at the Stevenson Site, 5MT1, Wheat had excavated pithouses dating back to 519 CE. A neighboring site, 5MT3, had a long history of occupation, from Basketmaker III until the abandonment of the area in late Pueblo III. Wheat's thorough excavation of these sites revealed some fascinating and unusual features, such as a carved kokopelli on the floor of a kiva, a formal

burial of an eagle, many tunnels, and a carefully constructed dance circle.

In Pueblo I times, people had migrated out of the area to the Dolores River valley, but they moved back during Pueblo II, partly because of cold air pooling in the Dolores canyon. At that time, two streams of people may have entered the area, from Dolores and from Chaco Canyon. The result may have been social stratification. The "poor" folks, who suffered bad nutrition, lived across the draw at 5MT3, and higher-status people, who controlled resources and had Chacoan traditions, lived at Yellow Jacket, 5MT5.

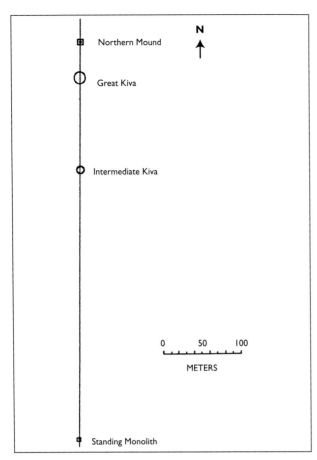

Figure 10.5. Yellow Jacket's north-south axis, from the northern mound (great house) to the standing monolith.

Phase II: Chacoan Occupation

Around 1080 CE, people built a three-story great house in a prominent place at the northern edge of Yellow Jacket Pueblo. At this time or later, other ceremonial and nonresidential structures—a great kiva, an isolated medium-size kiva, and the standing solstice monolith—were placed along a line extending southward from the great-house mound (fig. 10.5). Over a distance of some 1,700 feet, this line of structures departs from true north by less than half a degree. The centers of the medium-size kiva and the great kiva depart from true north-south by only one-sixtieth of a degree. At the southern end of this line, a small plaza next to the standing monolith would have been an excellent place for ceremonies associated with the June solstice sunrise, utilizing the alignments of monoliths, walls, and shrine.

Between the great kiva and the monolith, the

inhabitants of Yellow Jacket constructed two rows of kivas at right angles to the north-south axis. The archaeologist John Fritz has convincingly argued that such an axis is a hallmark of Chacoan influence. Three open areas might have been public plazas. The largest, about 300 feet in diameter, was initially identified as a reservoir, but studies of pottery by Crow Canyon Archaeological Center show that it probably served as a plaza instead. The great house, great kiva, and public plazas, together with the north-south alignment and the orientation to solstice sunrise, convey the style of a planned Chacoan "cosmic" settlement.

Phase III: Pueblo III Transformation

Beginning around 1180, Yellow Jacket Pueblo saw major changes in population and landscape design. For one, the Chacoan features of the site appear to have decreased in prominence, to be replaced by a greater interest in the local landscape. For another, the population rose to 10 times that of the Chacoan phase.

The resulting community was dominated by kiva rows that were rotated out of cardinality by an average of 5.4 degrees. A new form of ceremonialism appears to have replaced the previous emphasis on an accurate north-south organization of space. The kiva rows and architectural blocks built during this phase established a new axis for the pueblo, formed by the line connecting the great kiva to a cave at the southern edge of the peninsula. Over the entrance to the cave is one of three petroglyphs found at the site that perhaps depict "lizard man."

The cave floor contains a fine gray ash, which Wheat speculated might have originated in the many ceremonial fires that burned in the community's nearly 200 kivas. He proposed that people used slow-burning piñon and juniper in kiva fires to produce fine ash. Instead of unceremoniously discarding the ashes, they might have carried them to the cave and placed them there. A similar tradition has been found among the Hopis, members of whose Fire Clan gathered the ashes of kiva fires and deposited them in a suitable location. The Rio Grande Pueblos had a similar tradition involving the mischievous Ash Boy, one of whose duties was to collect the fine hearth ash, considered sacred, and deposit it in a special place. This cave of ashes at Yellow Jacket might have been understood as a sipapu, a symbolic entry to the underworld. The new geometry of the place might have been part of an elaborate symbolism integrating fire and ash, life and death, cosmos and underworld.

A road extends southward from the great kiva toward the ash cave, marked on its western edge by a swale that runs for some 1,000 feet toward the large plaza. It is uncertain whether this road was associated with the Chacoan occupation or the Pueblo III transformation, but its perpendicularity to the Pueblo III roomblocks and its orientation toward the cave of ashes suggest that it was post-Chacoan.

Another noncardinal line, nearly 2,500 feet long, may also have been conceived during this phase. It runs from the dance circle of 5MT3 across the intervening canyon, over the standing monolith, and on to the Great Tower. Oriented 33 degrees east of north, the line crosses the second "lizard man" petroglyph and a number of other important features of Yellow Jacket Pueblo. It connected Yellow Jacket with the subsidiary site 5MT3 and might have been a symbolic link between ceremonial features of the two sites. It might also have been a "line across time," connecting the new features of Yellow Jacket Pueblo with one of the earliest settlements in the area.

It thus appears that local topography had trumped the cosmos. The transformation of the symbolic landscape from cosmic to sacred might have been accelerated by an influx of former neighbors, some of whom had been marginalized during the previous Chacoan occupation. At the end of the peaceful period that Steve Lekson has called "Pax Chaco," people began moving into more defensive living spaces, such as the cliff enclosures of Mesa Verde. Yellow Jacket Pueblo offered safety in numbers, as well as the security provided by the cliffs on two sides of the peninsula.

Phase IV: Construction of Towers

In the decades from 1240 to 1280, a new phenomenon arose as ancestral Pueblo people built towers north of the San Juan River at Hovenweep, Sand Canyon, Goodman Point, Yellow Jacket, and many

other places. The most famous groups of towers are found near springs at the heads of canyons and along the canyon rims in Hovenweep National Monument. At Hovenweep Castle on summer solstice, the light of the setting sun falls on the doorway of an interior room. On a rock panel near Holly House, the summer solstice sun creates two horizontal spears of light that cut through a pair of spiral petroglyphs (fig. 10.6).

Yellow Jacket Pueblo contains the remnants of at least 18 towers ranging from 8 feet to 19.5 feet in diameter. Concerns for defense cannot account for all of them. Some may have been connected to kivas by tunnels, like those found on Mesa Verde at Cedar Tree Tower and Badger House. Four towers were placed around the important spring in the northeast sector of Yellow Jacket. Like the other towers, their purposes may have been both practical and ideological: to protect the spring, honor sacred water and the world beneath, and ascend toward the skies from the symbolic underworld of the kiva.

The largest tower at Yellow Jacket is a remarkable biwall structure near the northeastern spring. Consisting of a kiva enclosed by a two-story ring of rooms, the Great Tower of Yellow Jacket is larger than any tower at Hovenweep. It lies on the line to the winter solstice sunrise as viewed from the great kiva. Unfortunately, the decayed condition of the tower prevents a more detailed comparison with the towers and buildings of Hovenweep. A tree-ring date of 1254 CE may establish its date of construction. Another beam with a cutting date of 1101, found in the vicinity of the Great Tower, indicates that this area was also used during the Chacoan occupation and might have been paired at that time with the great kiva in a winter solstice alignment. Analysis of faunal remains has shown that the Great Tower complex probably had special significance in the community. The high percentage of bones of large game animals found near the towers suggests ritual feasting or special access to large game by elites living among the towers.

Mesa Verde

It appears that the inhabitants of Mesa Verde had knowledge of the complex cycles of the sun and

Figure 10.6. At summer solstice, a beam of light enters a cave at Holly House in Hovenweep National Monument to intersect spiral petroglyphs on the wall.

Figure 10.7. View of winter solstice sunset over Sun Temple from the pecked basin in Cliff Palace.

moon. In a display of serendipitous wisdom, J. W. Fewkes so named Sun Temple because of a sunlike image on a rock at its southwest corner. That rock may reveal the essence of the site and be the key to its understanding. In 1916 Fewkes commented, "The shape of the figure on the rock suggests a symbol of the sun, and if this suggestion be correct there can hardly be a doubt that solar rites were performed about it long before the Sun Temple was built."

The southern end of the Cliff Palace alcove contains a pecked basin on a smoothed platform. From this spot, one can observe the winter solstice sun setting over Sun Temple and the adjacent sun rock (fig. 10.7). From the sun rock itself, celebrants could have watched the summer solstice sun rise over the Cliff Palace enclosure. As Fewkes suggested, the sun rock could have been the site of solar ceremonies before the construction of Sun Temple and perhaps even before the construction of Cliff Palace.

In its **D** shape, Sun Temple is reminiscent of Pueblo Bonito, and its design might have been intended to simulate that largest of the great houses of Chaco Canyon. But whereas Pueblo Bonito contains a number of carefully established cardinal alignments, the flat southern wall of Sun Temple is rotated away from true east-west by 10.7 degrees. The noncardinal alignment of Sun Temple may be another example of local sacred landscape playing

a more important role than abstract cosmic design. The intentionality and importance of this alignment are suggested by a pecked basin in bedrock just north of Sun Temple. The perpendicular drawn from the prominent alcove that is set into its southern wall crosses the basin and extends to another pecked basin in the center of Cedar Tree Tower, 2.4 miles away.

The line continues another 5.4 miles north to a third basin at Battleship Rock in Soda Canyon. The co-linearity of these three basins is remarkable; the basin of Cedar Tree Tower is less than 50 feet from the line connecting Sun Temple to the high basin of Battleship Rock. During the late Pueblo II period, the area near Battleship Rock may have housed one of the densest concentrations of people on Mesa Verde, besides serving as a pan–Mesa Verde ceremonial center. The Battleship Rock community contained some 41 dwellings, 16 kivas, and a great kiva. The nearby broad canyon bottom provided excellent farming. The line connecting Sun Temple and Battleship Rock might have been another "line across time" connecting Pueblo III and Pueblo II ceremonial centers.

Another remarkable feature of Sun Temple is its alignment to the major southern standstill of the moon, which occurs every 18.6 years. A line tangent to its two interior circular rooms aligns with the major southern standstill of the moon in one direction and with the four-story square tower

Figure 10.8. Sun Temple, with Cliff Palace in the distance.

large firepit at the moment it was first touched by the light of the morning sun, perhaps similar to the ceremony of New Fire at Zuni.

Summing Up

Time, space, and people are intertwined in Pueblo traditions. Space establishes a platform for experiencing and celebrating the natural rhythms of heaven and earth. The need for accurate timing of festivals in Chaco Canyon might have motivated ancient sun watchers to become careful astronomical observers, a tradition that continued into Pueblo III times north of the San Juan River. At Mesa Verde and Yellow Jacket, we find evidence of astronomies as complex as those of Chaco Canyon. For these ancient Puebloans, observations of the changing positions of the sun and moon on the horizon would have been useful for establishing a calendar. Perhaps more significantly, the sun and moon generated patterns in the natural and built environments that must have contributed meaning to the cultural landscape of each place.

of Cliff Palace in the other (fig. 10.8). The interior of this tower contains four painted lines with tick marks, averaging 18.5 marks per line, suggesting the possibility that people recorded four standstill cycles at this location. Another pictograph in the tower may represent the changing positions of the moon throughout the year.

Beneath Sun Temple, deep in Fewkes Canyon, the rising sun at winter solstice illuminates the firepit of Fire Temple. A winter solstice celebration might have included the lighting of a fire in the

J. McKim Malville is emeritus pro-fessor and former chair of the Department of Astrophysical and Planetary Sciences and director of the Honors Program at the University of Colorado. He has long been interested in archaeoastronomy and is the author of *Prehistoric Astronomy in the Southwest* and other books and articles.

Figure 11.1. Kiva A of the Lowry Pueblo great house, with its famous murals, during Paul Martin's excavations. The bowl (inset), also excavated from Lowry, has a similar stepped design. Lowry Pueblo is located near Pleasant View, Colorado.

Imagery and Tradition
Murals of the Mesa Verde Region

Sally J. Cole

In the shadows of cliff dwellings, one easily envisions the importance of Mesa Verde culture and its contributions to Pueblo history and traditions. There, multistory buildings, kivas, tunnels, and plazas are preserved, and masonry and jacal structures are finished with earthen plasters in many colors. Painted auras outline windows and doors; bold and intricately drawn murals appear on the exteriors of houses and inside rooms.

Although fragile and often fragmentary, the murals are rich sources of information, enabling us to see how Pueblo people identified themselves and the places they occupied. We can infer whether icons and symbols were public (openly displayed on building façades and visible from plazas and walkways) or relatively private (displayed inside houses, multistory buildings, and kivas). From the distribution of images and patterns, we can study the way people exchanged ideas. Most significantly, the imagery and patterns of use point to relationships within villages and across the landscape during times of migration. The lines of evidence lead into the historic period and to Pueblo communities in Arizona and New Mexico.

Plaster murals appeared at late Pueblo II and Pueblo III sites north of the San Juan River between approximately 1020 and 1300 CE. We find them at open sites (on mesa tops and valley floors) and in cliff dwellings, but much of the information from open sites has been lost to the elements. Pueblo people periodically renewed the plaster on their buildings and painted murals on the plaster. We see evidence of this on eroded surfaces, and during excavations investigators remove multiple layers of plaster to expose the murals. Paul S. Martin, of the Field Museum of Natural History in Chicago, excavated at the Lowry Pueblo great house, in what is now Canyons of the Ancients National Monument, during the 1930s. He described four murals in Kiva A and reported finding 25 coats of plaster to a thickness of five inches.

A few examples of early murals, dating from 1020 to 1150 CE, have been found at sites in Utah, Colorado, and New Mexico. Later examples, from 1150 to 1300, are more plentiful and appear throughout the northern San Juan region and at culturally affiliated sites in the Chaco Canyon and Canyon de Chelly areas to the south. I presume these were made by immigrants. During the early period, people of the Mesa Verde region were influenced by Chaco culture, and they painted murals at their Chaco-related great-house communities. But although Chacoan culture shaped the development of mural art, its origins probably lay in Mesa Verde culture. Murals of the types I describe here are not evident at pre-1020 Chaco Canyon sites, and embellished architecture has a long history in the northern San Juan. In 1954, Earl Morris and Robert Burgh, of the Carnegie Institution, described petroglyphs on mud structures built between 200 and 500 CE near Durango, Colorado. In addition, petroglyphs and rock paintings of the Basketmaker II to Pueblo III periods (approximately 400 BCE to 1300 CE) are commonly associated with cliff architecture.

Two types of plaster murals offer an interesting view of iconography and its creators in the Mesa

Figure 11.2. Examples of textile- and potterylike designs from kiva murals dating between 1150 and 1300 CE.

Verde region during the eleventh, twelfth, and thirteenth centuries. Both include painted and incised imagery. One type shows horizontal bands of geometric designs resembling those of textiles and pottery, and the other shows sets and rows of triangles or mounds. The Pueblos made both types of murals (continuously, I assume) across much of the region, but the two expressions are visually, spatially, and socially distinct. I have found that they do not occur in the same rooms and rarely at the same sites. Most murals of both types are in private, exclusionary locations (rooms and kivas), indicating that the iconographies and activities associated with those structures were shared within select groups rather than by the population at large. Collectively, the Pueblos upheld the two mural traditions for more than 200 years, and their wide distribution and longevity suggest that they were tied not to specific kinship groups (clans, for example) but to larger, ritual societies.

Textile- and Potterylike Designs
I have identified murals with horizontal bands of textile- and potterylike designs at 13 sites scattered from Mesa Verde to Cedar Mesa (fig. 11.2). The designs are similar to textile patterns that began in Basketmaker III times or earlier (500 CE) and closely resemble those of Pueblo II and Pueblo III pot-

tery types, including Mancos Black-on-white, McElmo Black-on-white, and Mesa Verde Black-on-white. All but one of the murals are in kivas; the exception is on the outside of a Cedar Mesa granary.

In kivas, the designs, usually fragmentary, are typically found on the faces of benches and probably encircled the rooms. Sometimes, horizontal framing lines or rows of dots appear on the pilasters above. Murals with textile- and potterylike designs are typically painted and show only continuous geometric patterns, although there are exceptions—including one mural on Mesa Verde that depicts, above a painted geometric band, animals with long, sweeping horns. Well-known early murals are from three kivas at the Lowry Pueblo great house. These were exposed during Martin's excavations and are estimated to date between 1080 and 1150 CE. The Lowry murals feature "steps" in contrasting plaster and pigment colors of white or cream and brown; the designs range from a continuous pattern of linear "steps" to solid forms and checkerboards.

During the later mural period (1150 to 1300), Pueblo people continued to depict "steps," along with a variety of fret patterns. In some instances, the two are incorporated into interlocking designs. Zigzags and lines with tick marks, resembling textile stitches, were also added to the mix. The range of colors in the later murals is greater than that of the early ones and includes shades of green and greenblue, yellow, red and red-black, white, and brown.

Over time, murals with textile- and potterylike designs remained remarkably consistent in both appearance and setting. The uniformity extends even to a kiva mural at Mummy House in the Canyon de Chelly area. Only the Cedar Mesa granary design suggests a shift from private to public use of the imagery during the later period. Despite major changes in Pueblo mural art after 1300, the long association between kivas and textile- and potterylike designs seems to have survived all the way to fifteenth- and sixteenth-century kiva murals in the Hopi area.

Triangles and Mounds
Gustav Nordenskiöld published the first descriptions of murals with triangle or mound designs in an 1893 account of his explorations on Mesa Verde.

Figure 11.3. An example of a triangle design (top) and a mound design.

He analyzed the nearly complete mural in Kiva A at Painted Kiva House and recorded room murals at Spruce Tree House and Cliff Palace. I know of 17

sites in the northern San Juan region that display this type of imagery (fig. 11.3). The triangular and mounded forms are usually incorporated into dados—decorated lower portions of walls—projecting upward from a band painted around the base of the wall (fig. 11.4). Others sit on discrete lines, and a few are simply linked at the base and have no obvious base bands. These occur on the upper portions of walls and on kiva pilasters, as well as on the lower walls.

From early to late, differences exist between examples located in the central and eastern Mesa Verde region and those in the western part of the region—that is, on either side of a vague north-south line formed by Comb Ridge in Utah. The central and eastern ones are overwhelmingly private, appearing inside kivas and first-, second-, and third-story rooms. The triangles or mounds are typically upright and range from tall and slender to low and broad. They appear as sets (twos, threes, fours, and sixes) and in multiple and continuous sawtooth

Figure 11.4. Kiva A, Painted Kiva House, Mesa Verde National Park, showing triangles and dots as part of a dado.

patterns. Colors in this area are predominantly red, reddish-brown, white, and cream. Incised designs occur only in the central and eastern Mesa Verde region.

In the west, the forms are generally broad and triangular, occurring in sets (twos and fours) and as sawtooth patterns. Some examples are upright, but others point downward (pendant) or sideways. The western murals have a public component—they were painted not only in kivas but also on the exteriors of buildings, bordering walkways and plazas. In the west, the colors are green, white, red, reddish-brown, and tan-brown.

The earliest example of a triangle-mound mural comes from a Pueblo II kiva in the western area. It is estimated to date between 1020 and 1060 CE and displays pendant and sideways triangles. Other early examples are from the central-eastern area and generally date between 1123 and 1150. They include a mural in Kiva B at the Ida Jean site, a Chacoan outlier north of Mesa Verde in the Montezuma Valley, and room murals in the West Wing at Aztec Ruin National Monument. Later murals (1150–1300) are found throughout the northern San Juan region and appear at remote sites in the Chaco Canyon and Canyon de Chelly areas. Twelve sites at Mesa Verde exhibit the later murals, dating from 1190 to 1300. The tower at Cliff Palace has one of the finest examples, shown in plate 18.

I suspect that triangle-mound murals in the central and eastern part of the region originated with Chaco-related great-house culture and generally adhered to that norm over time. Meanwhile, in the west, people blended local traditions with the new great-house ideas. This might explain the timing of the murals, the overall privacy and uniformity of eastern iconography, and the mixed iconographies and settings of the west.

In kivas, triangle-mound designs appear on bench faces (near the floor and higher) and on the pilasters above. In kivas, rooms, and open areas, triangles or mounds are frequently attached to dados, and at Mesa Verde they also appear as discrete motifs within larger mural schemes. A variety of other elements show up in the later murals, including fingerprint dots, Ts resembling T-shaped doorways, parallel lines, blanketlike designs, a "string"

of projectile points, animals (a snake, birds, and a variety of animals with horns or long ears—possibly pronghorn, bighorn sheep, or deer), handprints, a bearlike paw print, and humans. The last group includes humpback figures (two wear "horn" headdresses and carry bows) and flute players (fig. 11.5).

Dots are the elements most commonly associated with triangle-mound imagery throughout the region. The other subjects appear at sites on Mesa Verde itself and signify a change in the way northern San Juan murals were conceptualized after 1150. These were not new subjects—most occurred widely in rock art and on pottery—but until then the Pueblos had not displayed them on architecture. In his search for precursors of fifteenth- and sixteenth-century murals in the Hopi and Rio Grande Pueblo areas, Watson Smith, of the Peabody Museum at Harvard University, observed in 1952 that the addition of animals and humans to Mesa Verde murals marked the genesis of a new style. The later murals are more realistic and more artistically complex. They illustrate a great variety of ceremonial and religious subjects, including corn, ritual objects, birds, katsinas, priests, dancers, and warriors.

Chaco Canyon and Canyon de Chelly murals with triangle-mound imagery are closely related to those in the northern San Juan, particularly those on Mesa Verde. All of the imagery is private (inside kivas and upper-story rooms), and the plaster and pigments are red, white, and cream. A Chaco-area kiva, for example, shows sets of upright red triangles and mounds projecting from a dado, accompanied by flute players and incised "handprints." A Canyon de Chelly kiva has cream-colored, upright triangles projecting from a dado and representations of animals above. Room murals show sawtooth rows of upright and pendant triangles, hinting at links with the northern San Juan's western section.

Meaning and Continuities

With the advent of plaster murals, icons and symbols merged with architecture and became integral parts of buildings and communities. When we study the imagery, we see these relationships and can track them over time and space. The northern San Juan murals came from ancient traditions influenced by Chacoan culture and were foundations of

Figure 11.5. Portion of a kiva mural in the Chaco Canyon area dating between 1150 and 1300, showing mounds, flute players, and incised "handprints."

art and ideologies extending beyond 1300 into historic times. The archaeological interpretations are enhanced by those of modern-day Pueblos, who perceive the murals as parts of identifiable legacies. These people's knowledge of history, practices, and symbolism enhances outsiders' understanding of the murals and the societies that produced them.

Scott Ortman, at Crow Canyon Archaeological Center, has studied murals with textile- and pottery-like designs at length and puts them in a broader category, "pottery band murals." He sees a "container" metaphor at work in ancestral Pueblo culture that involves textiles, basketry, pottery, and buildings (see chapter 12), and he proposes that this way of thinking distinguished certain populations. In a 2004 paper, he observed that the metaphor was not evident at Chaco Canyon sites, indicating that Chacoan culture was not the source of this type of mural.

The container metaphor and the close association between the murals and kivas raise interesting questions about the artists and, by extension, the societies in which they lived. Were the murals made by women, who, we presume, made baskets and pottery, or by men, who are likely to have woven cloth, or by both? Were kivas and kiva societies open to both genders? The use of plaster and murals by the Rio Grande Pueblos and the Hopis and Zunis suggests that a variety of situations and restrictions existed in the past. Historically, either

women or men renewed wall and floor plaster in their villages; men painted kiva murals at some villages, and men or women painted them at others.

As part of a 2003 study by researchers at Canyons of the Ancients National Monument, Laguna and Hopi traditionalists interpreted step designs in Lowry Pueblo kivas as representing altars or shrines used by Medicine People for an autumn ceremony (Laguna) and as representing moving clouds (Hopi). In 2001, Hopi consultants participated in interpreting rock art and murals at Mesa Verde National Park. They studied a mural showing an intricate geometric design and animals with long horns; they identified the design as instructive and the kiva as *pavasiwki*, a place for ritual supplication.

Researchers commonly describe triangle-mound murals as abstracted landscapes, and Scott Ortman included them in a 2004 analysis of "horizon scene murals." This characterization is well suited for places such as Mesa Verde, where mountain peaks and ranges are visible in all directions. They are prominent landmarks, integral to the cardinal directions and the movements of the sun and moon. I assume they were sacred—named in oral traditions and observed to chart seasonal changes and set ritual calendars. A related idea is expressed in a Hopi interpretation of a painted triangle-mound design at Mesa Verde: it describes *tuawi*, history.

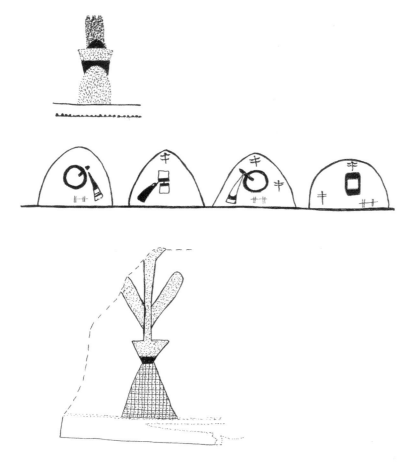

Figure 11.6. Schematic adaptations of details from fifteenth- and sixteenth-century kiva murals at Awat'ovi and Kawàyka'a in the Hopi area, showing "corn mountains" with attached prayer feathers and other embellishments.

The landscape analogy is most convincing with regard to dados in which triangular or rounded "mountains" sit on floor-band "horizons." Correlations exist with natural landscapes. For example, the sets of "peaks" and sawtooth patterns in Mesa Verde murals could be schematic representations of the nearby San Juan and La Plata mountains. In a 1982 analysis of a late-period mural in the Chaco Canyon area, Patricia McAnany described flute players above a horizon line interrupted by mountains resembling Cabezon Peak and Mount Taylor in northwestern New Mexico.

A kiva mural dating between 1350 and 1360 at Homol'ovi II, an ancestral Hopi site in the middle Little Colorado River valley, supports the possibility that landscapes and mountains were represented in earlier murals. In 2002, E. Charles Adams, of

Arizona State Museum, identified paintings in this mural as depicting the San Francisco Peaks, prominent features on the horizon of northeastern Arizona. The depictions at Homol'ovi II are more realistic than "mountains" in northern San Juan murals, but the layout is similar to the dado and floor-band "scenes."

Clouds, also parts of horizon views, are another explanation for triangle-mound imagery. They are suggested by white and gray mounds and "lightning sticks" in a fifteenth-century Rio Grande Pueblo mural at the Pottery Mound site. The clouds "sit" on a base band (or line), as illustrated in 1975 by Frank C. Hibben, of the University of New Mexico.

My research suggests that in addition to mountains and skies, triangle-mound imagery represented ears of corn and mounds of soil in which corn was planted. It shared the symbolism of late Pueblo II and Pueblo III stone artifacts from Mesa Verde that Jesse Walter Fewkes, an anthropologist with the Smithsonian Institution in the late 1800s and early 1900s, interpreted as representing the end of an ear of corn and "corn hills" symbolic of fertility.

In fifteenth- and sixteenth-century murals in the Hopi area, Watson Smith identified conical and mounded forms as "corn mountains." These are items of stone, wood, or clay (sometimes marked with corn kernels) that support prayer sticks (with feathers) during ceremonies. In the murals, the corn mountains sit on base bands and are marked by feathers, "corn plant leaves," sticklike forms, and other images (fig. 11.6). Some triangle-mound designs, particularly those from Mesa Verde sites, resemble corn mountains. A mural from Fire Temple at Mesa Verde shows mounds with dots (corn kernels?) attached, and a fragmentary mural at Cliff Palace includes a triangle with attachments on the sides and top that could represent sticks, leaves, or feathers (see fig. 11.3, top).

"Horizon views" and "corn" are interestingly intertwined with the concept of abstracted landscapes. For the Pueblos, corn ears, corn hills, and corn mountains are visually and ideologically congruent with landforms, as is demonstrated by To'wa Yäl'länně (Corn Mountain) near Zuni Pueblo and Qa'ötukwi (Corn Rock) near the Hopi village of Mishongnovi. The symbology of clouds fits easily with both mountains and corn—clouds hang above the mountains and are synonymous with rain and, by extension, corn. All of these are related to the earth and to the concept of a sacred landscape where food is grown.

Acknowledgments

I thank Chuck Adams, Joel Brisbin, Gary Brown, Winston Hurst, and Scott Ortman for sharing information about murals, and I acknowledge Mesa Verde National Park and Canyons of the Ancients National Monument for assisting my research.

Sally J. Cole, an archaeologist specializing in rock art studies, is the author of *Legacy on Stone: Rock Art of the Colorado Plateau and Four Corners Region* and many articles and papers. She lives in Dolores, Colorado.

Figure 12.1. This large spherical jar is a fine example of the technical mastery and aesthetic brilliance achieved by Mesa Verdean potters.

Ancient Pottery of the Mesa Verde Country

twelve

How Ancestral Pueblo People Made It, Used It, and Thought about It

Scott Ortman

The Mesa Verde country is justifiably famous for the bright white pottery with black geometric designs that adorns the surfaces of archaeological sites and the shelves of museums. Many first-time visitors are amazed to learn that people who lived in comparatively simple circumstances had the time and motivation to create everyday objects exhibiting such artistic and technical mastery (fig. 12.1; see also chapter 7). The pottery of the Mesa Verde country is also famous among archaeologists, who, after more than a century of careful study, have accumulated a wealth of knowledge about its evolution, its uses in household and community life, and its symbolic role in ancestral Pueblo culture.

The Earliest Pottery

Whether pottery was actually invented in the Four Corners area or imported from the south is still a matter of mystery. In the 1920s, the pioneer Southwestern archaeologist Earl Morris found some unfired, shallow bowls made of clay mixed with juniper bark in protected alcove sites near Canyon de Chelly in northeastern Arizona. Several of these vessels preserved impressions on their exterior surfaces of the baskets in which they had been molded. Morris developed a theory whereby pottery was invented as a by-product of using these shallow, unfired clay bowls as parching trays. People discovered that heated clay became hard and eventually impervious to water when repeatedly used to toast seeds. An alternative view, espoused by C. Dean Wilson and Eric Blinman, is that true pottery making was introduced to the Four Corners area from the south. This view is based on the fact that brown-paste pottery was common in the Mogollon Rim country to the south during the first few centuries CE but appeared only sporadically in the Four Corners at that time.

Regardless of whether pottery making was introduced or invented, two facts stand out. First, the earliest unfired clay bowls were associated with coiled basketry, a craft that people of the Southwest had possessed for millennia. Second, the forms of early pottery containers (other than bowls) imitated dried squash or bottle-gourd vessels (fig. 12.2). These two facts indicate that, by and large, early experimentation with pottery was an attempt to improve upon existing containers of the time.

Figure 12.2. An eighth-century canteen illustrates how early artisans conceived of pottery as an improvement over perishable containers such as baskets and hollowed-out gourds.

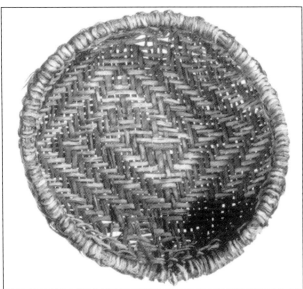

Figure 12.3. Woven basketry patterns often inspired painted pottery designs, as exemplified by this plaited basket and black-on-white seed jar.

The earliest true pottery of the Four Corners area dates to around 400 CE. Potters made basket-inspired bowls and gourd-inspired jars and dippers by building up coils of clay (fig. 12.3). They smoothed and sometimes polished the interiors of bowls and exteriors of jars. The new technology offered several benefits. Whereas earlier people had to rely on pitch-lined baskets, dried gourds, and tightly sewn skins to store water, people could now make more permanent water-storage containers rel-

atively easily. In addition, storing agricultural seeds inside sealed pottery vessels provided much better protection from dampness, insects, and rodents than did containers of organic materials or storage bins resting on the ground.

By 600 CE, Four Corners potters had begun using harder-firing, shale-based clays and had added crushed sandstone or igneous rock to the ground, moistened clay. These inclusions, known as *temper*, create more "flexible" pots that were better able to withstand the thermal shock experienced during cooking. In addition, the wide-mouthed jar forms that began to be made at this time appear to have been designed specifically as cooking pots. It is clear that by 600 CE, Pueblo cooks were boiling soups and stews in clay pots set directly on an open fire.

The development of cooking pottery was revolutionary. Before, food was roasted, baked in a pit oven, parched in a basket (clay lined or not), or boiled by dropping heated rocks into a watertight basket. Squash was easily baked whole, and both fresh and dried corn cooked relatively quickly in boiling water. Beans, however, must be boiled for an hour or more before they are edible, and the hot-rock method of cooking them must have been laborious, if even possible. It is perhaps no coincidence that the earliest well-dated beans in the Four Corners area come from sites that also contain hard-fired cooking pottery, of the type archaeologists call "Chapin" or "Lino Gray."

Beans made two important contributions to the ancestral Pueblo economy. First, as a source of high-quality protein, they allowed people to rely less on hunting for this nutritional need. Second, beans are legumes, which actually add nutrients to the soil that other crops, such as corn, use as they grow. Thus, growing beans along with corn probably improved the productivity of corn, the caloric staple, over the long term. All of this was made possible by the new technology of cooking pottery.

Beans grow exceptionally well in the deep aeolian loess soils of the Mesa Verde country. Indeed, Euroamerican farmers have grown a variety known as "Anasazi beans" using dryland (rainfall-dependent) methods ever since the area was homesteaded in the late nineteenth century. I point this out because sites dating to the Basketmaker II period,

Figure 12.4. From left to right, these vessels illustrate the development of cooking pottery technology between 600 and 1300 CE in the Mesa Verde country. Note the increasing use of surface texturing over time, the way corrugated vessels mimic the construction and appearance of coiled baskets, and the constriction of vessel throats that followed the adoption of corrugation.

which lacked cooking pottery and beans, are rare in the Mesa Verde country whereas literally thousands of sites date to the subsequent Basketmaker III period, which had both. Large numbers of people must have immigrated to the Mesa Verde country soon after the introduction of beans and cooking pottery. Perhaps these innovations made the area a more attractive place to farm and live.

The decoration of serving vessels, especially bowls, accompanied the development of cooking pottery. As one might expect, the earliest painted pottery designs mimicked those sewn into the walls of coiled baskets using colored stitching materials since at least 1500 BCE. It is also unsurprising that the earliest decoration graced primarily serving vessels, because meals are perhaps the most common and important setting in which social interaction takes place among family and friends in all cultures. Over the subsequent seven centuries, serving ware and cooking ware would follow somewhat different trajectories, but the fundamental unity of all pottery was maintained in some interesting ways, as we shall see.

The Evolution of Pottery Technology
A number of innovations in pottery technology arose over the centuries following the initial settlement of the Mesa Verde country (fig. 12.4). The first was the development of specific paste recipes for decorated serving and storage ware versus cooking ware. Early potters had used the same paste to

make decorated bowls, cooking pots, ollas (water jars), and seed jars. But through careful observation of the performance of pottery made with different batches of paste, potters eventually recognized that larger and more abundant temper particles of tough rock produced more resilient cooking pots. They also recognized that old potsherds could be ground up and used as temper in new decorated vessels. Sherd temper still protected these vessels from cracking as they dried and were fired, but it also made them easier to smooth and polish. This allowed potters to create smoother and more lustrous surfaces on which more precise designs could be painted using a yucca-leaf brush and paint of ground iron or manganese or of boiled beeplant or tansy mustard.

Potters also discovered that they could control the color of decorated pottery by selecting among various raw materials and by altering the atmosphere during firing. For example, pottery made of Mancos shale clays and fired in a neutral atmosphere turned out gray, but clays from the underlying Morrison Formation fired white under the same conditions. Clays from the deeper geologic layers exposed in southeastern Utah fired red in an oxygen-rich atmosphere. Over time, potters began to apply slips (clays thinned by water) made from certain clays to the surfaces of their decorated vessels; when fired in the appropriate way, they achieved the bright white or red that is characteristic of Pueblo pottery to the present day.

Another innovation was the development of texture on the exteriors of cooking pots. The earliest cooking pots were smoothed from rim to base. But for some reason, in the ninth century CE potters started leaving the junctions between clay bands exposed and unobliterated on the exterior necks of cooking pots. Over time these "neck bands" evolved from broad and flat to shorter and rounder and from stacked bands to one continuous, spiraling coil. Then potters began making patterned indentations on the neck coils, using a bone awl or their fingers. Finally, they began using this indented neck-coiling method to create entire cooking pots, from base to rim (see fig. 7.7).

The new "corrugated" variety of cooking pot replaced the older, neck-coiled variety virtually overnight throughout the ancestral Pueblo world around 1000 CE. Why did potters change the style of their cooking pots? I do not think it was because they were easier to make, stronger, or more durable. Instead, I think it was because corrugated pots worked better than the neck-coiled variety. The exterior surface area of a corrugated vessel is greater than that of its interior, and as a result, such vessels dissipate heat from their contents faster than smooth-surfaced vessels. Experiments by Chris Pierce using replica cooking pots indicate that this effect is real.

The somewhat counterintuitive advantage of this "radiator" effect is that corrugated pots full of bubbling posole, cornmeal, or beans would have been less prone to boiling over, so more of the contents found their way into satisfied bellies. Additional evidence that corrugated pots produce this radiator effect is that the "throats" of cooking pots got smaller, relative to the overall volume of the vessel, in the years after corrugation was invented. Corrugation seems to have solved the boil-over problem of neck-coiled cooking pots, and as a result, potters could design vessels with smaller throats and flared rims to further reduce spillage.

The Production and Exchange of Pottery

Who made pottery, and how did people obtain it? The answers are somewhat different for decorated pottery and cooking pottery. Over the years, archaeologists have excavated in the homes of many ancestral Pueblo families and have routinely found polishing stones and remains of unfired decorated vessels. From this we know that at least one person made decorated pottery in nearly every household; it was the ancestral Pueblo equivalent of Amish quilting. Donna Glowacki and I have each studied decorated pottery exchange by identifying the raw materials from which black-on-white bowls were made and comparing the sources of these materials vis-à-vis the sites where the bowls ended up. We have found good evidence that friends and relatives exchanged pottery regularly, even if they lived in different villages, but we have found no evidence of market-based trading like that which takes place in the traditional Indian markets of Mexico.

Although it appears that each household had at least one potter in it, groups of potters might have fired their work together in certain times and places (fig. 12.5). During the last few centuries of Pueblo occupation in the Mesa Verde region, potters fired black-on-white pottery in kilns made by digging a trench and lining the base and sides with sandstone slabs. They built a "pre-fire" in the trench, and after it burned down, they placed the clay pots on top of the coals and built a wooden "tent" over the pots. The tent ignited and in the process sucked hot air up from the coals over the pots, raising the temperature sufficiently to transform the clay into pottery. When the upper fire burned down, they covered the entire setting with dirt to keep out excess oxygen that would turn the vessels pink. After the smothered fire cooled, they had brilliant black-on-white pottery ready for use.

Potters located trench kilns in settings where natural airflow patterns would have encouraged a hot fire. Interestingly, most lie a mile or more from settlements and farming areas. The availability of large pieces of dry wood, which was needed for firing and would have been more abundant away from villages, might account for this pattern. It might have been easier to carry pots to the wood than the wood to the pots. In addition to being far from villages and fields, trench kilns varied greatly in length and thus in the number of vessels that could be fired at once. The largest trench kilns are an amazing 24 feet long and could have fired the work of many potters from many households at the same

Figure 12.5. Bringing an excavated thirteenth-century trench kiln back to life, Clint Swink and Lee Lacy load replica vessels for an experimental firing in 1995. The Pueblo potters who originally used this huge kiln located it away from their settlements, probably for more convenient communal use.

time. It might be that large firings used less fuel and helped to conserve diminishing wood supplies.

The production and exchange of cooking pottery were quite different from those of decorated pottery. An important difference between the two types is that cooking pots had to withstand thermal, as well as mechanical, stresses after they were fired. Recent studies by Kathy Hensler and Lori Reed indicate that crushed igneous rock temper helps cooking pots withstand thermal stress better than crushed sedimentary rock temper. Potters who lived close to sources of igneous rock could have produced better-functioning cooking pots that people elsewhere would have prized.

There is some evidence that potters who lived close to sources of igneous rock made cooking pots specifically for exchange with people in their own village and in other villages. For example, unfired cooking pottery is absent from most sites but is common at Shields Pueblo, a village within walking distance of Ute Mountain, the best local source of igneous rock temper. Most of these unfired vessels were tempered with igneous rock, and igneous-tempered cooking pots are indeed more widespread in the Mesa Verde country than igneous-tempered serving bowls. All of this suggests that a lively trade took place in cooking pottery made of the best raw materials.

Pottery in Community Life

Pottery was obviously an important part of everyday family life in the ancestral Pueblo world, but it was also used in the social and ceremonial life of communities. One advantage of living in a village is that after a poor harvest, families can more easily share food as a simple insurance policy. The anthropologist Richard Ford has shown that such food sharing has been codified in the rich ceremonial life of the historic Rio Grande Pueblos.

Archaeologists Eric Blinman and Michelle Hegmon have identified ceremonial feasting in the Mesa Verde country by examining the sizes of cooking pots, the painted designs on serving bowls, and the locations in which both types of vessels are found. They discovered that households in ninth-century villages typically had a few "fiesta" pots that were larger than everyday cooking pots (fig. 12.6). In addition, the designs painted on serving bowls were more diverse in trash associated with feasting locations than in trash associated with households. This might be because feasting trash contained bowls painted by more potters than did household trash. Or perhaps the large populations and intensive social interactions in villages encouraged potters to paint more distinctive, personalized designs. A variety of anthropological studies of living people indicate that manners,

etiquette, and an interest in social distinction usually develop in situations in which people who are neither friends nor relatives interact frequently. Perhaps the increasingly diverse decoration of serving bowls reflects this phenomenon.

In my own studies, I have found that "potluck" feasting had an even greater effect on pottery produced in larger, thirteenth-century villages. As these villages grew, potters began painting designs on the exteriors of serving bowls, probably to enhance their appearance when viewed from the side as food was presented to the community and consumed in the great kiva or plaza. Potters also began to make bowls of two distinct sizes: small ones for individual servings and large ones to feed five or more people. Households that participated in potluck ceremonialism also possessed a few large fiesta pots in which to cook extra-large batches of food for feasts.

Pottery as a Source of Knowledge

Because pottery making was clearly an essential technology for life in the high desert of the Mesa Verde country, it should come as no surprise that ancestral Pueblo Indians imbued pottery with symbolic meaning. One way they did this was by using olla necks or mugs with their bases removed to line the hole in kiva floors representing the emergence path, or sipapu. Ollas and mugs are containers for liquids, and in this light it is intriguing that even today the most likely descendants of Mesa Verde people in the Rio Grande conceptualize the emergence place as an underground lake (see chapter 6).

Mesa Verde people also imbued pottery with meaning through painted designs. Some of the first archaeologists to study ancient Mesa Verde pottery, including William Henry Holmes, Gustav Nordenskiöld, and J. O. Brew, noted that most elements of painted designs derived from specific forms of weaving. In my own research, I have discovered that this relationship was due to more than mere copying. Mesa Verde people viewed pottery as the conceptual mirror image of woven objects, including basketry and fabrics. I know this because the ways ancient potters translated weaving patterns and textures (fig. 12.6) into painted pottery

Figure 12.6. Paired overhead and side views of a small and a large serving bowl from Sand Canyon Pueblo. These vessels, decorated both inside and outside, were likely used in "potluck" feasting, the smaller one serving a single person and the larger one an entire family. The exterior design of the large bowl represents a loom-woven cotton blanket.

designs follow generalizations from experimental cognitive research into the ways humans "manipulate" cultural imagery and express it in figurative speech. For example, contemporary Americans often think about life using the metaphor of a journey and express the idea using concrete imagery of planes, trains, boats, and cars, as in "his career got derailed." In the same way, Mesa Verde people thought about pottery as textiles and used the concrete imagery of coiled basketry, plaited basketry, and loom-based fabrics to express this idea in their painted pottery designs.

The existence of a symbolic connection between pottery and weaving should come as no surprise. The earliest pottery improved on the functionality of existing containers, including baskets. Corrugation, which mimics coiled basketry, produced better-functioning cooking pots. Moreover, indigenous agricultural people throughout the Americas have viewed people as corn and corn

as people ever since they became dependent on maize agriculture. In the Mesa Verde country, corn was stored in seed jars and granaries, cooked in corrugated pots in the home, and consumed in a bowl either inside the home or in public spaces of the village. People, in parallel fashion, wrapped themselves in blankets and lived and grew inside homes and villages. In short, both corn and people were protected, nourished, and transformed through containers of various kinds. To view pottery, basketry, fabrics, and even architecture as complementary was a natural extension of their lived experience.

There is, indeed, substantial evidence that people included architecture in the list of items they considered "containers." I have identified a number of decorated buildings in the Mesa Verde country in which the circular interior walls of kivas are depicted as pottery bowls and the exteriors of granaries as seed jars. In addition, the cribbed roofs of

Figure 12.7. This kiva, in a cliff dwelling in southeastern Utah, is presented as a pottery bowl below and a coiled basket above. Because kivas were microcosmic structures, this imagery suggests that ancient Mesa Verde people conceived of the entire world as paired bowls, the lower, earthen half of pottery, and the upper, woven half as basketry.

Figure 12.8. Cannonball Ruin, in Canyon of the Ancients National Monument, illustrates the way thirteenth-century villages exhibit communal serving-bowl imagery. The houses were terraced down the sides of the canyon, facing inward toward the low, central area containing a spring, in the same way terraces decorate the interior of the large serving bowl in figure 12.6.

Figure 12.9. Maria Martínez and Santana firing pottery at San Ildefonso Pueblo, New Mexico, in 1933. The art of pottery making continues in an unbroken tradition to today.

kivas mimic the form and construction of an over-turned basket, thus forming a natural pairing with the pottery bowl image below (fig. 12.7). Finally, during the thirteenth century, Mesa Verde people constructed entire villages around canyon heads and surrounding springs, with inward-facing hous-es and central plazas in which they held communal feasts. It is as if the community viewed the entire village as a giant serving bowl, a container from which all received sustenance (fig. 12.8).

For Mesa Verde people, then, pottery was more than just a central technology for life—it was also a central symbol of life. It is incredibly interesting to me, at least, to learn that ancient Pueblo people developed what we might call, in English, religious concepts from their everyday experiences in mak-ing and using pottery. But, in fact, I view these concepts as more akin to the theories of scientists or the rhetorical devices of politicians. To concep-tualize a cooking pot as a basket or a village as a

communal serving bowl was to create knowledge based on parallels among diverse realms of experi-ence. These theories had practical benefits for Mesa Verde people: cooking pots made like coiled bas-kets worked better, and generalized food sharing in a "village bowl" reduced the threat of hunger in an environment where harvests varied from year to year and from field to field. Conceptual metaphors involving pottery were therefore every bit as use-ful to Mesa Verde people as "string theory" is to physicists or the "war" on drugs is to our elected officials.

Scott Ortman is director of the research laboratory and database manager at Crow Canyon Archaeological Center. He has studied ancestral Pueblo material culture since 1993 and has published reports on the artifacts from several major villages on the Crow Canyon website (http://www.crowcanyon.org/Research/publications.html).

Figure 13.1. Cliff Palace, one of the largest cliff dwellings in the Southwest, retains evidence of about 150 rooms and more than 20 kivas.

Understanding Mesa Verde's Cliff Dwelling Architecture

Larry V. Nordby

During the 1200s in what is now Mesa Verde National Park, ancestral Pueblo people lived mostly in shallow caves, or alcoves. Over the course of that century, they erected more than 600 buildings in alcoves, from individual storage rooms to villages such as Cliff Palace (fig. 13.1) and Long House with as many as 150 rooms and more than 20 kivas. Archaeologists call such buildings "cliff dwellings," though, of course, the term accurately describes only the ones that housed full-time residents; most of the smaller ones did not. The architecture of cliff dwellings—the way the Mesa Verdeans arranged their living, storage, and ceremonial spaces—can tell us much about their inhabitants' social lives.

Relying mostly on buildings to unravel the story of how people lived, without much recourse to their artifacts, admittedly has its shortcomings. But many of the excavations carried out at Mesa Verde were done early in the history of Southwestern archaeology, when—by modern standards—researchers inadequately recorded the associations between artifacts and the individual structures they came from. For many sites, all we will ever know must be either extracted from the walled or used spaces the ancient Puebloans left behind or learned by talking with their descendants.

Mesa Verde's well-preserved cliff dwellings attracted the interest of many early archaeologists, notably J. W. Fewkes, who excavated a good number of them between 1908 and 1922 as the new park was opened to the public. Since then, work on the cliff dwellings has been oriented largely toward preservation, with the exception of the Wetherill

Mesa Project of the 1950s and 1960s, which involved excavations at Long House and Mug House. Since 1995, Mesa Verde National Park staff have developed the Archeological Site Conservation Program to revisit research issues associated with the cliff dwellings: how spaces were planned, built, remodeled, and used.

Since Fewkes's work and the Wetherill Mesa Project, archaeologists have learned much about ancient Pueblo society by studying and listening to the views of modern Pueblo people, who are connected by oral traditions to Mesa Verde and its sites, where they believe the spirits of their ancestors still dwell. Ethnographic knowledge of modern Pueblo groups tells us that all aspects of their lives are permeated by social organization and its ritual and ceremonial associations. Most archaeologists share the view of Pueblo people that their fundamental social and ceremonial structure extends back into antiquity, even if some details have changed because of Euroamerican contact. Mesa Verde is one of the places where these traditions and the prehistoric families who lived them can be effectively studied.

A person living in a cliff dwelling recognized the importance of family and kinship. He or she was a member of a household, which, judging from most anthropological studies that involve discussions with modern Pueblos, was probably organized matrilineally—that is, in the female line. Most houses were likely owned by the wife or mother, and the children were part of her clan (a named group claiming descent from a common ancestor), with close ties to their maternal grandmother.

When a man and woman married, the husband moved into the buildings of the wife's clan, or nearby. A mother's brothers often forged a close bond with her male children and helped transmit to them oral traditions and techniques such as tool making. The father, although resident in his wife's household, remained part of the clan into which he was born—his mother's clan— with slightly different allegiances and responsibilities.

Although we cannot say definitively that people lived matrilineally in cliff dwellings, I believe we can recognize architectural units that most likely housed members of increasingly inclusive groups: nuclear families, extended families, lineages, clans, and even larger groups that integrated the smaller ones into a cohesive, cooperatively functioning community.

Figure 13.2. Courtyard Complex M at Cliff Palace has doorways opening onto what once was a kiva rooftop courtyard. The **T**-shaped doorway leads to a living space, and the rectangular doorways lead to storage rooms. The courtyard was once plastered and painted with red handprints and geometrical motifs.

The Family and the Clan

At major residential villages such as Cliff Palace, Spruce Tree House, Long House, and Mug House, there appear to have been two common kinds of homes, although we remain unsure about the scale of the social units—nuclear families, multigenerational families, or clans—that lived in them. Regardless of which scale we choose, the circular or keyhole-shaped kiva (see fig. 4.3), excavated into the ground and topped with a flat roof that doubled as a plaza, formed the hub of the household.

Among the Pueblos today, kivas serve as ceremonial and social epicenters. Most of them served that purpose at least partly in the past, although some of them, if not all, were probably used as residences too. The positioning of certain features such as wall niches and the sipapu in Mesa Verdean kivas may have been guided by social or religious conventions or by utilitarian function, but the style of construction may reflect ancient social traditions and group identity. For example, one group might have used masonry to build the deflector that protected its kiva's hearth from air drafts, whereas another

group placed a stone slab upright to serve as the deflector. This choice might have been related to construction methods passed down over generations and viewed as clan-based techniques.

The number of kivas in ancient Pueblo sites is usually much larger than in modern pueblos, perhaps reflecting a greater number of clans or complexity of other social units in the past. The abundance of kivas underscores how important they and their rooftop plazas were for larger social and ritual gatherings in cliff dwellings (fig. 13.2). There is no doubt that both helped to create group identity for the extended family household or clan.

Opening onto the kiva rooftops and plazas are rooms and "room suites"—linked rooms that may have been lived in or used exclusively by nuclear families of mother, father, and children. The doorways of living rooms could be closed from the inside by suspending a mat or hide over them. Often, additional rooms lie behind these front rooms, and together the rooms in a set form a suite. Each suite consists of at least one living room, which is most easily recognized by the presence of a hearth, a **T**-shaped doorway, or both. Often, a living room also has a ventilation port, which resembles a small window. In floor area these rooms tend to be larger than other rooms, though not always, and not all of

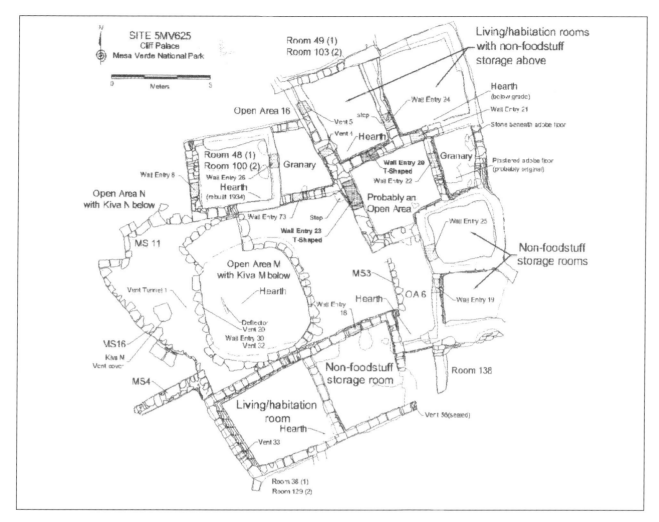

Figure 13.3. Plan of Courtyard Complex M at Cliff Palace, showing how the living and storage rooms partially encircle Kiva M and its rooftop plaza.

them have **T**-shaped doorways. It is the presence of the hearth, coupled with the room's placement fronting the courtyard, that is the key indicator of a living room.

Rooms situated behind the living room probably served for storage, something we infer from their doorways. These rectangular openings with elevated sills, much smaller than we would consider suitable for access, resemble what we would call windows. Virtually all of them were closed from the exterior so that the room's contents could be sealed inside. Although it is possible to squeeze into these rooms, it is likely that people usually leaned through the doorway to get to the contents, probably the family's food stores.

By any measure, the Mesa Verde room suites

were much smaller than we would consider adequate for living today. The most typical combination of structures was the required living room plus a single food-storage room or granary. The largest room suite consisted of only five rooms. Floor areas ranged from less than 65 square feet to a little more than 160 square feet. I doubt that even the members of a small nuclear family spent much time inside such quarters. The kiva and its rooftop plaza probably saw a good deal more of family living.

The kiva, with its rooftop plaza, and the surrounding room suites are together termed a "courtyard complex," something archaeologists interpret as having been a shared group space (fig. 13.3). In a Mesa Verde cliff dwelling, the courtyard, or plaza, is roofed by the overhanging bedrock of the alcove, so people normally could have carried out daily tasks there unhampered by rain or snow. Consequently, even if nuclear families lived in the room suites, the plaza and the kiva below it were probably shared as common social space by members of an extended family, a matrilineage (a multigenerational group based on the maternal line), or a clan. For this reason, many archaeologists use the number of kivas as a rough estimate of the number of households at a given site and then extend that figure to estimate the residential population. Courtyard complexes seem usually to have been composed of one to four room suites, along with other rooms that were not parts of suites.

Among the latter kinds of rooms, courtyard complexes included storage rooms that opened directly onto the plaza. These were often larger than other storerooms, but like the others, they lacked hearths and their doorways were sealed from the outside. It seems likely that such rooms once contained food stores for the extended family or clan; they might also have been places where people kept important ritual objects.

The walls surrounding the plaza and its underground kiva were plastered and painted with geometric designs or images of animals, perhaps clan totems. An additional decorative technique was to dip one's hand in paint and "stamp" it on the wall. Perhaps this latter decoration represented some sort of clan membership tally or was produced during initiations. Sadly for us, only vestiges of these decorations remain, even in the best preserved cases.

One issue that archaeologists have debated is whether prehistoric kivas actually served as residences. Traditionally, many researchers have viewed them not only as ceremonial places but also, much of the time, men's clubs—buildings where male-oriented craft work such as weaving and tool manufacturing took place. This inference, too, is based on modern uses of kivas, but it is supported to some degree by archaeological findings of certain kinds of manufacturing tools in kivas—for example, leatherworking implements such as fleshing tools, awls, needles, and reamers, all made of animal bone. Moreover, in larger cliff dwellings, kiva walls are heavily sooted, indicating heavier use than one would expect for a building that served only for

occasional rituals. When the walls became blackened by soot, villagers refurbished them with new plaster and paint. Taken together, these factors strongly suggest that the Mesa Verdeans used kivas as residences, at least in winter. Experiments indicate that even a small fire in the hearth will heat a kiva effectively and the warmth is retained much longer than in surface rooms.

Many smaller cliff dwellings follow architectural patterns similar to those of the large ones such as Cliff Palace. A small site might consist of a single ledge with a plaza, a kiva, and one room suite, with food storage rooms on separate small ledges or in pocket alcoves (fig. 13.4). Even if the ledges they occupy are too narrow to house the typical courtyard complex, these small sites still display living rooms, storage rooms, and kivas. They normally have at least one non-food-storage unit as well, although poor preservation may make it difficult to identify these.

At Cliff Palace, about 75 percent of the site consists of courtyard complexes. It is easy to imagine that most of them housed the members of a particular clan. Clans are important in modern Pueblo villages and often hold responsibility for certain social and ceremonial events in the yearly calendar. Rituals performed by a single clan, using paraphernalia imbued with power reinforced by centuries of oral tradition, affect the welfare of the entire village. Ritual information is passed down through the clan, and a clan mother may be responsible for it. Thus, a village with several clans offers a complex picture of clan interactions, and the village flourishes with the involvement of all clans. To see the unification of clans in a prehistoric village architecturally, we must turn to some buildings in the cliff dwellings that were based on organizational principles other than those inherent in the courtyard complex.

Civic Architecture and Village Identity
Larger cliff dwellings such as Cliff Palace and Long House feature specialized buildings that were not parts of courtyard complexes. They might be kivas without surrounding rooms; rooms without a kiva either adjacent to or near them; specialized rooms where women ground corn in mealing bins; circular towers; great kivas; or unique or "unusual" build-

Figure 13.4. This small cliff dwelling in a Mesa Verde canyon probably housed a single extended family. The relationship between such small alcove pueblos and large villages like Cliff Palace is the subject of ongoing research at Mesa Verde National Park.

ings. Logically, these buildings must have served as places of special use for collaboration among clans or even by residents of the entire village.

Approaches for interpreting such buildings are poorly developed, even if it is possible to identify the architecture as "out of the ordinary" or not based on clan identity. If clans were ceremonially and socially important to the welfare of the village, then what overriding group benefits might have been gained by allocating a portion of the finite dry space in an alcove to other kinds of buildings? I believe that just as a courtyard complex represented a lineage or clan, so these special buildings represented the identity of a group of clans or a whole village. The activities that took place in them—and perhaps even their very existence as symbols of the larger entity—helped to integrate the component groups of the cliff dwelling. Their use might have

encouraged cooperation, mutual aid, and civility; perhaps it even ensured the effectiveness of village-wide rituals. These were potent benefits indeed.

One way in which special structures might have helped to integrate clans was through their use by what anthropologists call "moieties." A moiety (from the Latin *medius*, or "middle"), is one of two complementary groups of clans, each of which has ceremonial responsibilities throughout a portion of the year—on top of the individual responsibilities of its component clans. Some modern Rio Grande pueblos, for example, are organized on the principles of moieties or show some level of dual division.

I believe moieties can be recognized architecturally in some Mesa Verde cliff dwellings through features such as symmetry in the placement or decoration of buildings and the division of buildings into two segments. For example, in what was probably the integrative kiva at Cliff Palace, people applied plaster to the walls in two colors, each color covering half the kiva (fig. 13.5). This kiva had no adjacent residential rooms and sat adjacent to another special building, Speaker Chief Tower. To me, this placement and the two-color decoration suggest that ceremonies held in this kiva brought together members of moieties or two major social groups at Cliff Palace.

I believe that each of the two social groups had its own two-room building, different from all other rooms at Cliff Palace, located near this kiva. One room in each unit is large, with a large rectangular doorway and elevated sill. The other room resembles a kiva but apparently was unroofed, so it formed a partially enclosed space. None of the four rooms contains a hearth. Tree rings show that the buildings were constructed between 1275 and 1280 CE, late in the history of Cliff Palace. The placement of the buildings separated the traffic pattern of the village into two parts, a pattern similar to that observed for Spruce Tree House and by Arthur Rohn for Mug House.

At Cliff Palace, then, it appears that each of two social divisions—whether their basis was clan membership or something else—had space allocated specifically to it and enjoyed access to a portion of the village that the other did not. Yet these dual divisions were organized into a single village. I think certain other structures in some of the cliff dwellings served to promote or symbolize village-wide integration and identity.

One such structure was the central building at Spruce Tree House, which I believe helped to unify the social groups who lived on either side of it and promoted their identity as members of a single community (fig. 13.6). Entered by **T**-shaped doorways from plazas on either side, this building formed the central leg of an **E**-shaped building at Spruce Tree House, a full-time residential site of some 15 to 18 households and about 135 rooms. The building, once three stories tall, was also linked by tunnels to kivas. Its walls were plastered in two colors and its interior adorned with painted and incised decorations. This building was once

Figure 13.5. Symmetrical application of two shades of plaster in a kiva at Cliff Palace; the dark and light plaster meet in a vertical line above the wall niche. Such decoration might reflect use of the kiva by clan-based moieties.

the most imposing part of Spruce Tree House. At Cliff Palace, this sort of integrating role was probably fulfilled by the structure that J. W. Fewkes, the site's excavator, called the "Speaker Chief Complex." Similar but less elaborate buildings are found at sites of as few as 30 to 40 rooms.

Cliff dwelling architecture offers many clues to the social life of the ancient Mesa Verdeans, helping to define the different scales at which people must have experienced their social and ritual responsibilities—from the nuclear or extended family to the clan, the moiety, and the village. The character, placement, and details of the buildings are tangible evidence of kinship relations, if only we can learn to read them. Archaeologists have just begun to ask questions about the social meaning of cliff dwelling architecture, especially about things

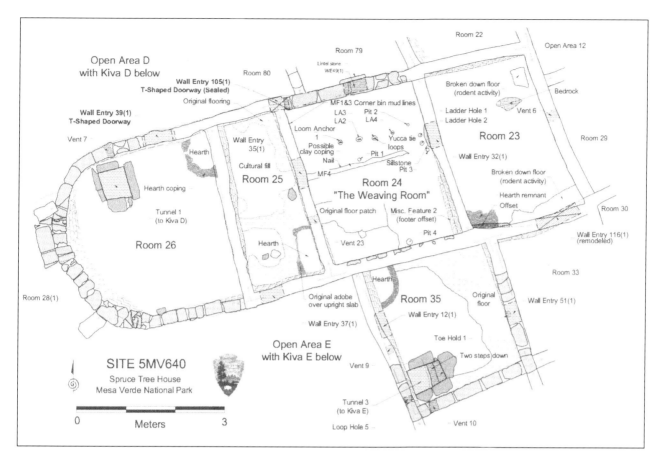

Figure 13.6. Plan of the first floor of the central building at Spruce Tree House, which served as the village's "group identity" building.

that fail to fit observed patterns. Further efforts to decode the cliff dwellings promise to reveal much more about the way people lived in them—which is why, after all, we study architecture in the first place.

Larry Nordby was formerly a research archaeologist and field director of the Archeological Site Conservation Program at Mesa Verde National Park. He lives in Placitas, New Mexico.

Figure 14.1. A 2002 wildfire in Mesa Verde National Park, shown here, threatened the research facility and other government buildings. Between 1998 and 2003, five wildfires swept over more than 50 percent of the park, burning 28,340 acres and exposing and damaging many archaeological sites.

Fire and Archaeology on Mesa Verde

Julie Bell

Mesa Verde holds one of the largest concentrations of archaeological sites in North America. Ancestral Pueblo people lived on this great escarpment for more than seven centuries, from approximately 550 to 1300 CE, and left everything from scattered pot-sherds and stone flakes to large, well-preserved pueblos and cliff dwellings. Although the cliff dwellings, sheltered in natural alcoves, are the most visible ruins, they represent only a fraction of all the archaeological sites recorded in Mesa Verde National Park—and people lived in them for only 75 to 100 years in the thirteenth century. Many more people lived on the mesa tops and in the canyon bottoms than in the cliff dwellings, and for much longer times. Paradoxically, wildfires—though archaeologists dread them as much as any-one else—have revealed many mesa-top sites that had lain invisible to researchers for decades.

Wildfires on the Mesa

Between 1996 and 2003, five wildfires swept over more than 50 percent of Mesa Verde National Park, burning 28,340 acres (fig. 14.1). These fires threat-ened buildings and human lives, burned extensive wooded areas, and damaged archaeological sites. We give fires names: Chapin V burned in 1996, the Bircher and Pony fires in 2000, Long Mesa in 2002, and the Balcony House Complex fires in 2003. The last was a series of five fires that began on the same day. Lightning strikes accompanying dry thunder-storms in a time of drought started all of them.

Fire can hurt archaeological sites in many ways. Direct effects cause rock to spall (break off in slabs)

and building stone and cliff faces to oxidize. The Chapin V and Pony fires severely damaged two significant areas containing rock art when nearby trees and shrubs ignited, raising temperatures high enough to crack and break off sandstone surfaces. Some of the ancient images were obliterated (fig. 14.2). Luckily, archaeologists had already thoroughly documented both sites. Although the direct effects of fire can be devastating to archaeological sites, the greatest damage can take place during fire suppres-sion itself or be caused by accelerated erosion from flooding during the first few months following a fire (fig. 14.3).

Visitors to Mesa Verde National Park cannot help noticing the results of the Long Mesa fire of 2002, which burned more than 2,600 acres near headquarters. It erupted quickly into a fast-moving crown fire, burned through the thick piñon and juniper forest, and threatened offices and employee residences. It destroyed telephone lines and even contaminated drinking water when the roof of the water-storage tank caught fire and collapsed into the tank.

Later that evening, the fire nearly reached the museum (built in 1921, the first in the National Park Service), the administration building, and Spruce Tree House, the third largest cliff dwelling in the park. Firefighters called in air tankers to drop retardant, a reddish biodegradable substance. Their planes flew so low overhead that we could count the rivets in their fusilages. Fortunately, when a spot fire started on the slope just below Spruce Tree House, firefighters detected it in time to contain it

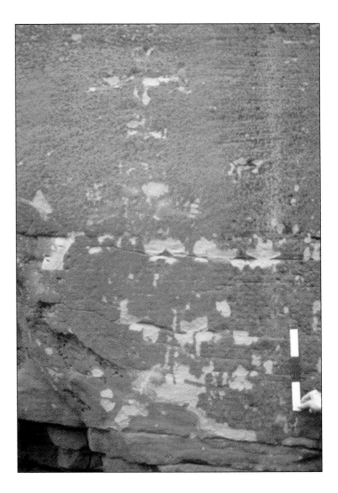

Figure 14.2. A petroglyph at Battleship Rock, photographed before the Chapin V fire (left) and after the fire damaged its surface (right).

to a single tree—saving this invaluable archaeological treasure.

Following the fire, park personnel took immediate action to prevent damage from water erosion to cliff dwellings in Fewkes Canyon, including Oak Tree House, Fire Temple, and New Fire House, all of which can be viewed from overlooks along the road. Workers laid excelsior matting and log diverters along gently sloping hillsides above these sites to slow runoff, accumulate topsoil, and encourage vegetation growth. Had these steps not been taken, erosion from rains would have carried ash and mud onto standing walls, causing mortar to disintegrate from wall joints and, ultimately, architectural collapse.

Archaeological Discoveries after the Fires

The deforestation and increased ground visibility resulting from the fires have allowed archaeologists to conduct more thorough and accurate surveys of the park's burned areas than ever before. Since 1929, approximately 90 percent of the park had

been surveyed, but dense vegetation had hampered investigators' ability to see sites, which are often subtle even when exposed. Since the 1996–2003 fires, two new surveys of more than 10,000 acres have brought to light many previously unrecorded sites. For example, archaeologists found 593 "new" sites in the scorched landscapes left by the Chapin V, Bircher, and Pony fires. Many of these dated to the Basketmaker III and Pueblo I time periods.

These surveys have contributed significantly to our understanding of Mesa Verde's prehistory. By opening up sweeping vistas across mesas and canyons, the fires have enabled us to see how sites were distributed and to understand more holistically how communities were organized and how they interacted with one another, especially during the Pueblo I and II periods (750 to 1150 CE), when communities were expanding.

Additionally, we have discovered evidence of the way ancestral Pueblos manipulated their environment to maximize water resources—by building reservoirs, contour terraces, and check dams (fig.

Figure 14.3. Excelsior matting, laid down on slopes, slows water runoff.

Figure 14.4. The Mesa Verde fires exposed many previously unknown archaeological sites, such as these check dams in an agricultural area.

14.4). We found that water control systems were far more common than anyone previously knew. The five new reservoirs discovered (others were already known; see chapter 15) were built near Pueblo II and III settlements and most likely filled only when snows melted and hard summer rains came down. Residents, we think, used the water for domestic instead of agricultural purposes.

By the mid-800s, Mesa Verde farmers were constructing stacked-stone terraces across broad hillsides to slow or trap runoff during rains and thereby make water more available to their crops. Soil accumulated behind the terraces as well, creating small farming plots. The post-fire surveys recorded 344 terraces associated with 89 sites, ranging from large pueblos to individual field houses.

Another technique Puebloan farmers used to control running water was to build check dams by stacking masonry blocks across intermittent streams. Before the Chapin V fire, archaeologists knew of only 191 such dams within the fire perimeter. In the post-fire surveys, they documented 1,189, many of which lay quite far downstream from village sites. From the surveys we learned that the ancient inhabitants of Mesa Verde used hillsides to direct water to cultivated fields much more intensively than previously thought. We also found that people were employing these water-control systems as early as 850 CE but increased doing so in the 900s. By 1150 their use of terraces, check dams, and reservoirs was widespread.

Although we have learned much about the ancient occupation of Mesa Verde as a result of the wildfires, our knowledge has not been gained without a trade-off. Regrettably, erosion has taken a serious toll on many irreplaceable archaeological resources. We know that burned land must be surveyed and treated within a year of a fire's occurrence or sites may be washed away before they are even discovered. By 2005, budgetary constraints had allowed us to complete surveys of only two burned areas in Mesa Verde National Park. Before we could begin surveying the Long Mesa and Balcony House Complex burns, two and three years passed, respectively. During that time, rain destroyed some sites, and new vegetation grew over others. But surveying is an ongoing process and as we continue, we can be certain that new sites will be discovered and new knowledge attained.

Julie Bell has worked as an archaeologist at Mesa Verde National Park since 1993. She was directly involved with the 1996–2003 wildfires in the park, helping with suppression, post-fire archaeological surveys, and preservation. Her interests include community studies, architectural documentation, and trade networks throughout the greater Southwest.

Figure 15.1. Cowboys watering their horses in Mummy Lake, near Far View Ruin, about 1915.

Water for the Mesa Verdeans

Kenneth R. Wright

In his essay "Living Dry," Wallace Stegner wrote, "Adaptation is the covenant that all successful organisms sign with the dry country.... And what do you do about aridity?... You must either adapt to it or try to engineer it out of existence."

In about 750 CE, the Pueblo I inhabitants of Mesa Verde began an engineering project by digging out a five-foot-deep pond that we know today as "Morefield Reservoir." Fifty years later, they started another—Box Elder Reservoir—over the mesa in Prater Canyon. These water-control systems proved so successful that the builders' Pueblo II descendants constructed two more: Mummy Lake (also known as "Far View Reservoir"; see fig. 15.1) and Sagebrush Reservoir. These four archaeological sites represent a remarkable legacy of public works engineering, continuity of technology, and the organizational skills needed to keep the reservoirs operational for hundreds of years.

Engineer aridity out of existence? Maybe not entirely, but ancestral Pueblo people between 750 and 1180 CE tried hard to do so, anticipating Stegner's call to action. Their achievements led the American Society of Civil Engineers to designate the four reservoirs as National Historic Civil Engineering Landmarks in 2004. The dedication ceremony took place while my colleagues and I were still analyzing scientific data from our study of the four sites.

On a riverless mesa where infrequent rains flash down gullies and soak through the porous ground, how did the ancient inhabitants of Mesa Verde find enough water to supply a concentrated population?

This was the question we asked in 1995 when two Mesa Verde National Park archaeologists invited my wife, Ruth, and me into the park to study several features that appeared to be reservoirs. This type of research is known as "paleohydrology."

Timber cutting, frequent forest fires, the presence of maize fields, and even the compaction of soil by ancient feet resulted in increased runoff and erosion from rains. We estimated that Mesa Verde's reservoirs filled four or five times a year—maybe more—and we concluded that they served domestic water needs. All lay within routine walking distance of settlements so that residents could easily have filled their jars and carried them home.

The four reservoirs contained plenty of potsherds in their sediments, 93 percent of them from broken jars. An antler dredging tool from Morefield Reservoir, radiocarbon-dated to about 860 CE, supplemented the sherds in dating the site to a span from 750 to 1100. Pollen analyses for all four sites showed that agricultural fields had been planted upslope.

Morefield (fig. 15.2) and Box Elder reservoirs, the two earlier ones, lie in canyon bottoms. Morefield today consists of a huge mound whose bottom and top measure 200 and 125 feet in diameter, respectively. It rises 16 feet above the present-day valley floor and 21 feet above the original bottom. It and Box Elder reservoirs ended up as mounds because, although people tried to dredge out the sediments that settled on the bottoms over the years—depositing the soil as berms around the perimeters of the ponds—the rate of sediment

Figure 15.2. This trench, dug through the Morefield Reservoir in 1997, exposed ancient sediments containing potsherds and dredging tools.

vided some protection against floods breaching the reservoir's circular berm; floodwaters would have overflowed the banks of the ditch and caused it to fail before they reached the impoundment. But because the inlet canal had to be raised to keep pace with the elevation of the reservoir, it, too, ultimately sat on a built-up berm and easily breached when overfilled. The inlet ditch for Box Elder Reservoir never developed an elevated berm because it sat on an adjacent high terrace that provided adequate elevation for gravity flow.

The two later reservoirs, Mummy Lake (fig. 15.3) and Sagebrush, were situated on mesa tops. Each measured about 90 feet across and had a perimeter formed of stone walls. From their shape, one might judge them to have been dance pavilions, but both clearly were water storage facilities with layered, water-deposited sediments. Without them, the mesa-top inhabitants would have had to rely solely on canyon-bottom springs, which were inadequate at times of large population and unreliable in times of poor rainfall.

Although the canyon-bottom sites differ from the mesa-top reservoirs, they demonstrate enough similarities that we can identify the passing along of technological knowledge from the Pueblo I to the Pueblo II period. To our surprise, when we plotted the four reservoirs on a map, we found that they sat on a line running more than six miles due east-west. This suggests to us that the builders communicated and coordinated their planning with their contemporaries and shared some assumptions about building locations with people of other times.

The early people of Mesa Verde were not engineers as we think of them today, but they set a good example to us for harvesting scarce water and making do with little. They adapted to the difficult environment, they organized to build and maintain public works projects, and they knew that water was an essential ingredient for a successful community.

inflow exceeded the rate of dredging. Every decade, the bottoms got a little higher, along with the berms.

The mound that is Morefield Reservoir contains interspersed layers of sand, charcoal, and potsherd-laden clay. The sand layers reveal 21 periods of flooding over the 350 years of the reservoir's operation, and layers of charcoal mark some 14 forest fires. The layering also indicates that the reservoir's active capacity changed over time, its maximum storage having been about 120,000 gallons.

By 1100 CE Morefield Reservoir featured an intake ditch that diverted water from the canyon bottom one-quarter mile upstream. The ditch pro-

Figure 15.3. Mummy Lake (Far View Reservoir) on Chapin Mesa, from the air, looking north. The reservoir is 90 feet in diameter. The intake ramp is visible to the left, and a staircase can be seen at the bottom.

Kenneth R. Wright is the author of *Water for the Anasazi*, published by the Public Works Historical Society, and *The Water Mysteries of Mesa Verde* (2006). He is a consulting engineer with Wright Water Engineers, Inc., and heads the Wright Paleohydrological Institute. He studied these four reservoir sites on Mesa Verde with Jack Smith, David Breternitz, and a crew of dedicated volunteers.

Figure 16.1. Cave 7, in Whisker's Draw, southeastern Utah, being excavated in 1893 by members of the Hyde Exploring Expedition.

Ancient Violence in the Mesa Verde Region

Kristin A. Kuckelman

Near a small, uninhabited cliff overhang in south-eastern Utah, now called "Cave 7," sometime during the late Basketmaker II period (200 BCE–500 CE) almost 100 men, women, and children perished in a single assault—the earliest known episode of war-fare in the northern Southwest. Someone buried their bodies, along with some of their belongings, under the overhang. In 1893 Richard Wetherill, rancher, archaeological explorer, and leader of the Hyde Exploring Expedition, discovered the remains of the victims but found no evidence of where they had lived or why so many people had congregated at this place (fig. 16.1). Basketmakers normally lived and traveled in small family groups; perhaps this large group was wintering together or had gath-ered for an important religious or social event. Why these people were killed and who the killers were will forever remain mysteries.

About 1280 CE, near the end of the Pueblo III period (1150–1300), attackers killed many residents of Castle Rock and Sand Canyon pueblos and ended the occupations of these impressive, stone masonry villages in what is now southwestern Colorado (see fig. 17.1). Within a few years of these attacks, Pueblo people no longer lived in the Mesa Verde region. Archaeologists from Crow Canyon Archaeological Center found evidence of the assaults during exca-vations in the 1990s. By carefully excavating sites of attacks and massacres such as these, other archae-ologists and I have learned much about violence among the ancestral Pueblo people of the Mesa Verde region.

Violence is a part of human society. Although the Pueblo residents of this region interacted peace-ably much of the time, violence did erupt in forms ranging from interpersonal conflict, such as battery and murder, to large-scale warfare. Many violent acts leave a trail of evidence, and important clues to the nature, scale, and timing of warfare show up in the archaeological record. Structures that have defensive architectural features or that were con-structed in defensible locations reveal that the builders feared being attacked. Intentionally burned buildings, large numbers of weapons, rock art images of warriors or battle scenes, and oral accounts of warfare related by the descendants of ancient Pueblo people suggest that conflict took place. The skeletal remains of the victims them-selves provide the most direct and telling evidence of violence: skulls and other bones that were frac-tured around the time of death ("perimortem"), bones with embedded projectile points, skeletons in awkward positions where bodies were dumped into structures, and bones that were scattered because bodies were left unburied on the prehistoric ground surface. These clues give archaeologists a valuable record of violent events.

Defensive Structures and Defensible Locations

Residents of the Mesa Verde region took a variety of precautions against attack. During some time periods, family groups built stockades or palisades around their farmsteads. We have found several such sites dating from the 600s (see fig. 3.3) and several others built in the 1000s. But because archaeologists tend to focus on refuse areas and

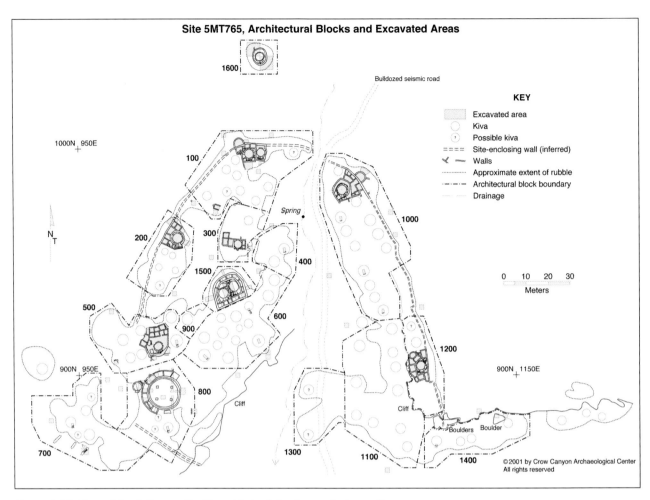

Site 5MT765, Architectural Blocks and Excavated Areas

Bulldozed seismic road

KEY
Excavated area
○ Kiva
⊙ Possible kiva
==== Site-enclosing wall (inferred)
≺ — Walls
⋯⋯ Approximate extent of rubble
—·—· Architectural block boundary
— Drainage

Spring

0 10 20 30
Meters

©2001 by Crow Canyon Archaeological Center
All rights reserved

Figure 16.2. Plan of Sand Canyon Pueblo, with its defensive enclosing walls.

main buildings—whereas people built stockades around the perimeters of their farmsteads—many stockades may remain undiscovered.

The aboveground portions of stockades deteriorated long ago, and we are unsure of the exact procedures used to construct these formidable walls. We do know from excavated post holes and post remnants that people invested a great deal of labor in building stockades. We think the posts were interlaced horizontally with willows or pliable tree branches and the entire construction coated with mud or adobe. In the 1200s, people built stone walls to enclose villages such as Sand Canyon Pueblo. These massive, durable constructions defended the villages even more effectively than timber stockades. Some stockades and stone enclosing walls have additional defensive features such as strategically placed peepholes and few access openings.

During the Pueblo III period (1150–1300; see chapter 5), people of the Mesa Verde region built stone masonry towers of various shapes and sizes that would have been useful in the event of an attack. Most towers were one or two stories high and were built with beautifully shaped and "pecked," or dimpled, blocks of sandstone. People could have escaped from some kivas (residential structures typically built underground and entered through roof hatchways) through tunnels connected to towers (see fig. 5.4), which protected them from becoming trapped during a surprise attack. Many towers were freestanding (see fig. 5.6); others adjoined adjacent buildings or the outside of a village-enclosing wall, much as military forts worldwide have been configured for centuries. From these buildings, lookouts commanded a panoramic view of the surrounding landscape and were better able to spot and defend against approaching enemies.

Figure 16.3. The placement of its doorway at the edge of a cliff made access to Hovenweep Castle, a thirteenth-century building in southeastern Utah, extremely difficult.

In the mid-thirteenth century, in the final decades before the region was completely depopulated, many people relocated from their small, scattered farmsteads to nearby canyon rims, cliff overhangs, and other defensible places. There they constructed villages around or near their water sources (see fig. 5.8). This clustering of people could have been both an offensive and a defensive, safety-in-numbers strategy. To restrict access and enhance safety, villagers constructed many single- and multiple-story buildings without doorways in the lowermost story —those ground-level rooms could be entered only through a hatchway in the roof. They erected some buildings at the very edges of canyon rims and placed the only doorway in the wall facing the canyon, so that it could be entered only from the rooftop of a lower structure inside the canyon (fig. 16.3).

It was during this time that the inhabitants of the Mesa Verde escarpment built the now internationally renowned cliff dwellings of Mesa Verde National Park. These settlements, sheltered beneath cliff overhangs, boasted excellent defensive properties: they were difficult to see from a distance, complicated to reach, and strategically dangerous to attack (fig. 16.4). In addition, most of the overhangs contained natural springs, which greatly enhanced the residents' ability to withstand prolonged attacks or sieges. The residents of cliff dwellings protected themselves even further by storing food in granaries in small cliff alcoves and on ledges that were difficult to reach (fig. 16.5). They used some small overhangs strictly as defensive refuges by constructing a masonry wall across the front of the alcove and entering the haven by

Figure 16.4. Eagle Nest, a defensively situated cliff dwelling in Ute Mountain Ute Tribal Park.

Figure 16.5. This remote granary in Grand Gulch, Utah, was well protected by its location on a ledge high off the canyon floor.

means of a ladder that could be pulled up to prevent attackers from following.

During some assaults, attackers burned buildings in an attempt either to kill the occupants or to destroy their homes. But Pueblo homes built of stone masonry did not burn readily; only the wooden timbers, which formed part of the roof, were flammable. Although some archaeologists believe that many buildings in the Mesa Verde region were burned during enemy attacks, the evidence indicates to me that most burned structures were set afire not by attackers but by the residents themselves, probably as part of a ritual "closing" of the building.

Weapons, Rock Art Images, and Oral Accounts

In warfare, the ancient Pueblo people used spears, wooden clubs, stone axes hafted on wooden handles, and bows and arrows. But they used these objects for hunting and other purposes as well; they had no weapons exclusively for warfare. They did, however, make shields of basketry or hide for combat only, so the presence of these items or depictions of them in rock art point to conflict in the region. Warriors struck fatal or debilitating blows to the heads of their enemies with shock weapons such as axes and clubs (fig. 16.6). They used bows and arrows for striking from a greater

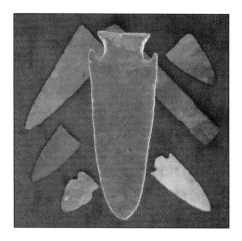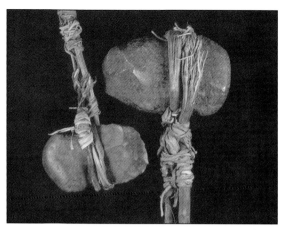

Figure 16.6. A five-inch chert blade found lodged between the ribs of a Cave 7 skeleton (left), and a pair of axes, also excavated in Cave 7.

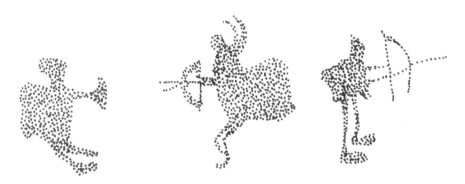

Figure 16.7. Drawings of petroglyphs on Castle Rock depicting a combative scene.

distance, although fewer of the wounds caused by arrows would have been fatal.

Shortly before the Mesa Verde region was depopulated late in the thirteenth century, Pueblo people began to depict violent scenes and warriors with shields on the faces of cliffs and boulders (fig. 16.7). An image of armed conflict at Castle Rock Pueblo was perhaps made to symbolize the violence of the times or to record the massacre that occurred there.

Oral accounts of specific prehistoric events are seldom available to archaeologists. In the mid-1800s, however, a Hopi elder related a centuries-old account of an attack on an ancestral village identified as Castle Rock Pueblo (see chapter 17). Some details in his account match the archaeological remains found during Crow Canyon's excava-

tions at the site. He said, for example, that many of the village residents were killed, causing the occupation of the village to end, and that the attack took place during mass migrations from the region. Because the elder relating the story was Hopi and because he said that the surviving villagers moved to the Hopi mesas in what is now northeastern Arizona, it is possible that some modern Hopi people descend from residents of Castle Rock Pueblo.

Wounds and Other Skeletal Damage

Many victims of interpersonal violence and large-scale attacks were struck on the head forcefully enough to fracture the skull. Some died as a result, but the presence of healed fractures on numerous skulls proves that others survived the injury. The

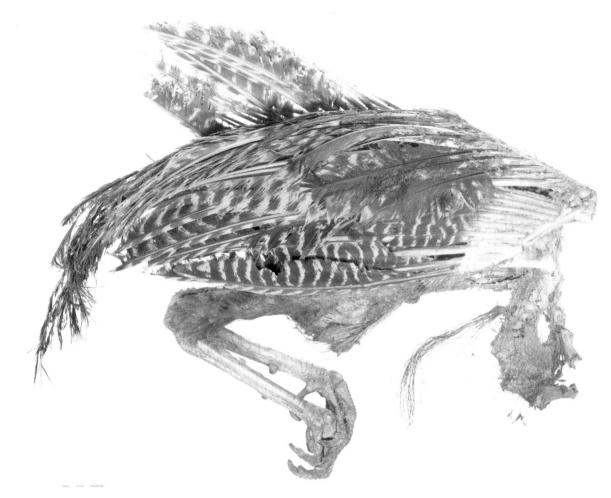

Figure 16.8. This mummified turkey was found in a rockshelter site just south of the Mesa Verde region. By the tenth century CE, Pueblo people were regularly keeping turkeys, and by the thirteenth century CE, they were an important food source.

uniform size and shape of many of these fractures indicate that they were inflicted by a single type of weapon—probably a small, sharp-bitted stone ax hafted onto a wooden handle (fig. 16.6).

Typically, ancestral Pueblo people buried their dead carefully, placing the body in an abandoned building or burying the remains either in a midden (refuse) area or beneath the floor of a room that was in still in use. The bodies of many men, women, and children who died at enemy hands, however, were not buried—they were left wherever they fell or were dropped through a nearby roof hatch or doorway, either by the attackers or by relatives or friends of the victims.

Warriors sometimes scalped or dismembered their victims. After the fatal attack on Castle Rock Pueblo, victors probably engaged in anthropophagy

(cannibalism). The practice of anthropophagy in the Mesa Verde region might have been a means to survive famines associated with severe droughts or other environmental conditions that destroyed the maize crops on which ancestral Pueblo people depended heavily for survival.

Causes of Violence

What situations and conditions caused the ancestral Pueblo people of this region to act violently? Although determining causes of human behavior is vitally important to understanding ancient cultures, we are hard-pressed to discover these causes from archaeological remains. It is probably safe to assume that personal assaults resulted from a great variety of disagreements between individuals or families and that people engaged in warfare only as a result of more serious or widespread problems. Competition over food and other resources has precipitated warfare in many cultures worldwide. In the Mesa Verde region, numerous sites with evidence of anthropophagy were inhabited during either the mid-1100s or the late 1200s, both of which were times of serious drought. The earlier of these droughts lasted from 1140 until 1180, and the latter, often called the "Great Drought," parched the landscape from 1276 until 1299.

During the early and mid-1200s, residents of the Mesa Verde region relied heavily on maize and on meat from domestic turkeys. Recent evidence from Sand Canyon Pueblo indicates that when the climate deteriorated in the late 1200s, maize crops failed and turkey flocks, which were fed maize, were decimated. People were forced to search out and eat both a wider variety and less preferred types of wild plants and animals and to compete with residents of other communities for these dwindling resources. Social, political, or religious problems might have caused conflicts during this time, but increasing violence in other parts of the Southwest and of the entire continent during the late 1200s and early 1300s suggests that the cause was a wide-ranging one such as a climate shift, instead of societal problems particular to the Pueblo people of the Mesa Verde region.

Who Were the Attackers?

The archaeological evidence of violence and warfare that we have so far unearthed in the Mesa Verde region consists mostly of the remains of the Pueblo victims and their villages. Although we have been unable to determine the identity of the aggressors of any particular attack, only a few non-Pueblo artifacts have been found at the scenes of these attacks that might indicate that the perpetrators were other than Pueblo. These artifacts consist of a few stone arrow points of a style suggesting a southern Utah origin. I believe the invaders were warriors from other Pueblo communities in the vicinity. In addition to the negative evidence just mentioned, non-Pueblo groups near the Mesa Verde region appear to have been too small to have successfully attacked pueblos as large, well fortified, and well defended as Castle Rock and Sand

Canyon, let alone to have inflicted such heavy casualties. Severe shortages of food or water might have provided ample motivation for Pueblo people in the Mesa Verde region to go to war against neighboring Pueblo communities.

Effects of Violence

Violence and warfare affected the lives of the ancestral Pueblo people of this region in many ways. Warfare sometimes determined where people chose to locate their villages and influenced their social, political, economic, and religious systems. People built defensible villages near their water sources. The clustering, or aggregating, of people must have brought new problems, such as a higher incidence of infection and contagious diseases. The increased traveling required for people to tend crops, hunt, and collect firewood heightened their exposure to ambush. When men left home on communal hunts, they left their families more vulnerable to attack. The population shrank as men, women, and children fell victim to violence. The loss of children and of women in their reproductive years reduced the population's ability to flourish; the deaths of warriors eliminated providers critical to survival. In big attacks like those on Castle Rock and Sand Canyon pueblos, the unique or specialized knowledge of particular groups was lost. Most important, intensifying violence was undoubtedly one reason people decided to emigrate from the region.

Conclusion

Among the ancestral Pueblo people of the Mesa Verde region, the incidence of interpersonal violence, the threat of warfare, and the eruption of large-scale attacks waxed and waned over more than two centuries of changing societal and environmental conditions. Because archaeologists have excavated only a tiny fraction of the archaeological remnants left by these people, we cannot determine how widespread the violence, raids, and large-scale assaults were at different times during that span. Casualties were heaviest when droughts or other environmental hazards diminished or destroyed maize crops and heightened competition for food and water. No doubt social, political, and religious issues also caused conflicts, but these types of causes leave few traces for archaeologists to find.

Conditions such as drought, resource depletion, and overpopulation have recurred throughout human history and continue to plague people today. Although drought is unpreventable, resource depletion and overpopulation might be halted through long-term, thoughtful planning. Also preventable is overdependence on one resource, such as maize, which might have been a fatal flaw in the subsistence strategy of the ancestral Pueblo people of the Mesa Verde region. Even though conflict is part of human society, we might be able to reduce its frequency by learning from past incidents of violence and warfare.

Kristin Kuckelman, senior research archaeologist for Crow Canyon Archaeological Center, has spent decades conducting field research in the Mesa Verde region. She has written many reports, journal articles, and chapters for edited volumes on the ancestral Pueblo people.

Figure 17.1. Castle Rock.

Plate 11. Long House, a cliff dwelling in Mesa Verde National Park.

Plate 12. A small cliff house in the Grand Gulch area of southeastern Utah.

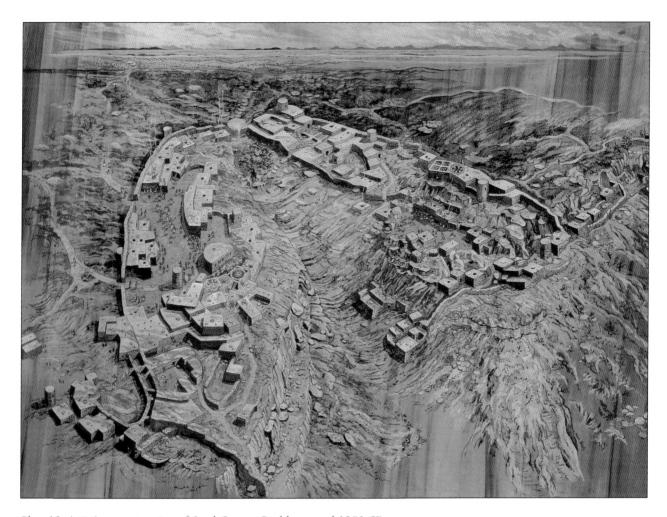

Plate 13. Artist's reconstruction of Sand Canyon Pueblo around 1250 CE.

Plate 14. A portion of an extensive panel of large Basketmaker II anthropomorphic figures along the San Juan River in southeastern Utah.

Plate 15. Indigenous corn (*Zea mays* L.) in the southwestern United States and northern Mexico today includes varieties that vary notably in ear size, kernel color, and kernel texture (flour, flint, pop, sweet, dent). The ears in this photograph represent (a) Santo Domingo blue flour, (b) Isleta white flour, (c) Hopi red flint, ((d) Hopi red flour, (e) Mojave white flour, (f) Mexican Harinosa de Ocho white flour, (g) Cochiti purple flour, (h) Acoma yellow flint, (i) Tohono O'odham yellow flower, (j-k) Chapalote brown pop/flint, (l) Mexican pink pop, (m–n) Hopi blue flint and flour, (o) Hopi red-striped flour, (p) Acoma white pop, and (q) Tesuque white sweet. Such diversity in corn has been maintained for both ceremonial and culinary needs.

Plate 16. An air tanker drops fire retardant over the headquarters area of Mesa Verde National Park during the Long Mesa fire of 2002.

Plate 17. Square Tower House, Mesa Verde National Park.

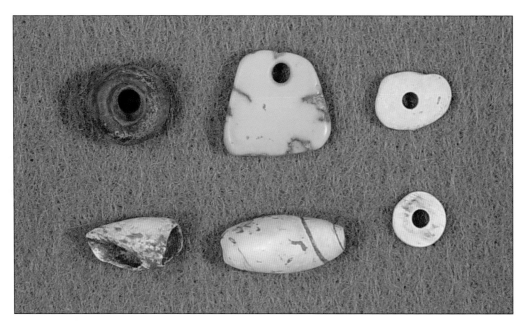

Plate 18. Stone and shell beads and ornaments from the Darkmold Site. The presence of turquoise and ocean shell at this site in southwestern Colorado implies long-distance trade during the Basketmaker II period (1000 BCE to 500 CE).

Plate 19. Pictographs in Grand Gulch, southeastern Utah.

Plate 20. Ceramic bowl with antelope design.

Plate 21. Murals in the tower of Cliff Palace. Note the triangular designs on the dado, which are discussed in chapter 11. The four vertical lines marked with 18 dots, discussed in chapter 10, are believed to be records of ancient lunar standstill events.

Plate 22. Canyon view from an ancient cave dwelling in the western Mesa Verde region.

A Hopi Story about Castle Rock

Ernest Ingersoll

On November 3, 1874, the *New York Tribune* published the following story, written by Ernest Ingersoll, a correspondent who had been accompanying the Hayden expedition in its exploration of southwestern Colorado. It appeared in print again in William Henry Jackson's chapter of the expedition's eighth annual report. John Moss, the party's guide, had recounted the legend after the explorers visited and recorded the site of Castle Rock, to which it refers. Moss had learned it from a Hopi elder while serving as Indian agent to that tribe in the mid-1860s.

Like many other Native Americans, the Hopis pass their traditional knowledge from one generation to the next within clans, each of which keeps its own stories. Some clans believe they came from the south, in what today is Arizona and Mexico, whereas others tell about their history in the north, including the area around Mesa Verde. Stories inevitably change in the retelling, and this one surely is no exception. But it speaks of a particular village and time period, of living by agriculture, of hiding in cliff dwellings, and of being mercilessly attacked by enemies. Archaeological research, including Crow Canyon's excavations at Castle Rock Pueblo, supports these aspects of the Hopi story.—DGN

Formerly, the aborigines inhabited all this country we had been over as far west as the headwaters of the San Juan, as far north as the Rio Dolores, west some distance into Utah, and south and southwest throughout Arizona and on down into Mexico. They had lived there from time immemorial—since the earth was a small island, which augmented as its inhabitants multiplied. They cultivated the valley, fashioned whatever utensils and tools they needed very neatly and handsomely out of clay and wood and stone, not knowing any of the useful metals; built their homes and kept their flocks and herds in the fertile river-bottoms, and worshiped the sun. They were an eminently peaceful and prosperous people, living by agriculture rather than by the chase. About a thousand years ago, however, they were visited by savage strangers from the north, whom they treated hospitably. Soon these visits became more frequent and annoying. Then their troublesome neighbors—ancestors of the present Utes—began to forage upon them and, at last, to massacre them and devastate their farms; so, to save their lives at least, they built houses high upon the cliffs, where they could store food and hide away till the raiders left. But one summer the invaders did not go back to their mountains as the people expected, but brought their families with them and settled down. So, driven from their homes and lands, starving in their little niches on the high cliffs, they could only steal away during the night, and wander across the cheerless uplands. To one who has traveled these steppes, such a flight seems terrible, and the mind hesitates to picture the suffering of the sad fugitives.

At the *cristone* [*crestón*, summit] they halted, and probably found friends, for the rocks and caves are full of the nests of these human wrens and swallows. Here they collected, erected stone fortifications and watch-towers, dug reservoirs in the rocks to hold a supply of water, which in all cases is precarious in this latitude, and once more stood at bay. Their foes came, and for one long month fought and were beaten back, and returned day after day to the attack as merciless and inevitable as the tide. Meanwhile, the families of the defenders were evacuating and moving south, and bravely did their protectors shield them till they were all safely a hundred miles away. The besiegers were beaten back and went away. But the narrative tells us that the hollows of the rocks were filled to the brim with the mingled blood of conquerors and conquered, and red veins of it ran down into the cañon. It was such a victory as they could not afford again, and they were glad, when the long fight was over, to follow their wives and little ones to the south. There, in the deserts of Arizona, on well-nigh unapproachable isolated bluffs, they built new towns, and their few descendants, the Moquis, live in them to this day, preserving more carefully and purely the history and veneration of their forefathers than their skill or wisdom. It was from one of their old men that this traditional sketch was obtained.

Figure 18.1. Richard Wetherill in Balcony House, photographed by Gustav Nordenskiöld in 1891.

Leaving Mesa Verde

Catherine M. Cameron

When the Wetherill brothers discovered the cliff dwellings of Mesa Verde in the winter of 1888–89, what caught the imagination of the American public was not only the seeming inaccessibility of the buildings but also the sense they conveyed of a vanished civilization (fig. 18.1). What had happened to the people who had built these impressive structures? They seemed to have departed in such a hurry that they left behind cooking pots, mugs, tools, even clothing (fig. 18.2). Where had they gone? Had they simply vanished? More than 100 years later, archaeologists have been able to answer some of these questions, but others remain in one of the Southwest's best-loved "mysteries."

The people of the Mesa Verde region did not vanish. Many of them migrated southward, and their descendants can be found today living in pueblos along the Rio Grande, atop the Hopi mesas, and at Zuni, Acoma, Jemez, and Laguna. The scale on which this migration took place was immense, and it has fascinated archaeologists and the public to this day. As many as 20,000 people may have lived in the Mesa Verde region during the 1200s CE. Although some certainly died during the turbulence that beset the century, many others emigrated, and by 1300 the region was almost completely deserted. Modern Native Americans, however, do not consider the places where their ancestors once lived to have been abandoned. What outsiders perceive as archaeological sites remain part of ongoing, active Pueblo culture.

Today, three questions about the abandonment of the Mesa Verde region still intrigue people. Why did they leave? How did they move? And where (exactly) did they go and why?

Why Did They Leave?

Although archaeologists have made remarkable advances in understanding the lifeways and development of the people who inhabited the Mesa Verde region, we have only refined our explanations of why they abandoned the region and have not settled conclusively on a single explanation. Indeed, it is likely that there was no one reason but that a combination of forces drove people out. Early scholars, such as the young Swede Gustav Nordenskiöld in 1891, argued that the residents of the Mesa Verde proper were driven off by "their enemies." Twenty years later, one of the most influential Southwestern archaeologists of the early twentieth century, Jesse Walter Fewkes, suggested that Cliff Palace was abandoned because of a "change in climate that caused the water supply to diminish and crops to fail." These two explanations for the depopulation of the Mesa Verde region are still proposed today, a century later.

The discovery of the tree-ring method of dating in 1919 proved a transforming event for the Mesa Verde region. The arid climate and the sheltered locations of many sites—in cliff alcoves or under rock overhangs—made for remarkable preservation of wooden roof beams. The Mesa Verde region quickly became one of the best-dated archaeological regions in the world. Tree rings demonstrated that Mesa Verde had suffered a significant drought from 1276 to 1299, just about the time the area was

Figure 18.2. Household tools and utensils uncovered by Alfred V. Kidder and Jesse Nusbaum in Mug House in 1908.

abandoned. Archaeologists dubbed this interval the "Great Drought," and for a considerable time it seemed the prime contender for explaining the mass migration of these farming families who depended on crops of corn, beans, and squash.

Although the Great Drought held sway for many decades as the explanation for the abandonment of the Mesa Verde region, some archaeologists began to doubt that it was the only reason. Reconstructions of past climates showed that more severe droughts had taken place before this one. The work of the archaeologist Carla Van West, of Statistical Research, Inc., demonstrated that despite the severity of the Great Drought, the land could still have supported a considerable population—it was unnecessary for everyone to have left. Climate was certainly a factor in the abandonment of the Mesa Verde region, but sophisticated environmental research showed that the decisions of these people

to emigrate might not have been stimulated simply by years of drought. For example, tree-ring expert Jeffrey Dean, of the University of Arizona, observed that the Mesa Verde region has a "bimodal" precipitation pattern, with snowfall in the winter and rainfall in the summer, that operated even in ancient times (see fig. 3.7). Farmers could have counted on winter snowfall to keep the soil moist as they planted their crops and on summer rains to nourish the growing plants. But Dean found that between about 1250 and 1450 this long-term precipitation pattern broke down in the Mesa Verde and surrounding regions. Farmers' ensuing uncertainty about their harvests might have created a strong impetus to leave.

Ruins filled with household goods suggested to early archaeologists and travelers that Mesa Verde families had run for their lives, leaving behind valuable pottery and tools. The idea that other peoples invaded the Mesa Verde region and forced the Puebloans out of their homes is an old one and still gets considerable attention from archaeologists. After Spaniards first settled in the Southwest in 1598, they learned that Navajos and Utes inhabited the Mesa Verde region. The Spanish first proposed the long held view that these tribes, hunters and gatherers who later took up farming and herding, were the invaders who drove the Pueblo families away.

More recent examinations of violence and warfare in the Southwest have offered a different picture. Archaeologists have found evidence of conflict in the Southwest throughout time, but it seems to have become especially pronounced after 1250. In his book *Prehistoric Warfare in the American Southwest*, Stephen LeBlanc argues that intense warfare took place at this time but the battles were among the Pueblo people themselves as they competed for food and other necessities made scarce by a deteriorating climate. Like Kristin Kuckelman in chapter 16, LeBlanc points to much evidence of warfare: people gathering for safety in large, defensively built communities; settlements that were burned; and the unburied remains of human victims who died violent deaths. Scholars such as LeBlanc and Kuckelman suggest that the migrations and regional depopulation that occurred across the Southwest after 1250 were the results of internal warfare. They see no involvement of nomadic peoples such as the Navajos and Utes in the vast relocation of people.

Archaeological data paint an unhappy picture of the people of the Mesa Verde region during the late 1200s. Crop failure from drought and unpredictable rainfall, resulting stresses on health, and competition for food almost certainly took many lives. Others likely made an early break for distant places where they believed they could grow their crops with greater success and security. Richard Wilshusen argues that Mesa Verdeans might have begun leaving as early as the mid-1200s; Mark Varien thinks it was later, in the late 1270s.

As population declined, it almost certainly reached a point at which some families could have achieved a comfortable living in the Mesa Verde region. So why did everyone leave? In a recent book published by Crow Canyon Archaeological Center, *Seeking the Center Place*, William D. Lipe suggests

that local leaders in the Mesa Verde area gained some measure of power from their ability to store and redistribute surplus food in years of good harvests. Even without disastrous crop failures, when crop production declined as the environment worsened, leaders might have battled one another as they tried to retain their influence. Families might also have decided to emigrate as their social system weakened and they lost faith in the ideology of their leaders. In an argument set at a larger scale, Stephen H. Lekson, of the University of Colorado, argues in his book *Chaco Meridian* that political leaders of the Mesa Verde region were instrumental in the evacuation of the area. These leaders, he suggests, moved very far south, into what is now northern Mexico, to establish the site of Casas Grandes. Clearly, the depopulation of the Mesa Verde region was the result of multiple social and environmental factors.

How Did They Move?

Archaeologists have often assumed that long-distance migrations like the one that emptied the Mesa Verde region were accomplished by single families or a few families traveling together. As anthropologists have noted for many groups around the world, people often establish relationships with other people in distant regions through trade and intermarriage. When times get tough at home, they can call on these relationships, moving to distant villages for extended stays as guests of their in-laws or trading partners. A historic document housed at the Huntington Library in San Marino, California, describes the "starving time" at Hopi in the early nineteenth century, when even nuclear families broke down as people scattered to Zuni and the Rio Grande Valley in search of food. Such migrations would be difficult to see archaeologically. A few individuals moving from the Mesa Verde area into an existing pueblo along the Rio Grande, for example, would have had little effect on the culture and practices of that town and would tend not to have left traces in the archaeological record. Some Rio Grande archaeologists argue that this is why, after the abandonment of the Mesa Verde region, they see a population increase in the Rio Grande Valley and adjacent upland areas but no clear evidence of the immigration of Mesa Verde people.

Figure 18.3. The Hopi village of Walpi during a religious ceremony, date unknown.

The oral histories of many modern pueblos, however, recount the movements of much larger groups. For example, the Hopis speak of clans that came from different directions to settle the Hopi mesas (fig. 18.3). In T. J. Ferguson and Richard Hart's *A Zuni Atlas*, the Zunis are reported to have migrated as a whole people to their present location in western New Mexico. In addition, we know that after the Pueblo Revolt of 1680 a community of Tewa Pueblo Indians from the Rio Grande Valley moved more than 200 miles west to live with the Hopis, creating their own village, Hano. These people, despite living directly adjacent to other Hopi villages, still speak the Tewa language and maintain other aspects of their Tewa culture.

Archaeologists have begun to explore the question of long-distance movement of entire communities. Lekson and his colleagues have identified several sites in southwestern New Mexico that appear to have been built by immigrants from the Mesa Verde region. At Pinnacle Ruin, for example, several lines of archaeological evidence suggest the presence of Mesa Verde people: the styles observed on painted pottery there closely resemble Mesa Verdean pottery styles; some of the walls were built using a masonry style similar to that of the Mesa Verde area; and residents created deep trash middens, a practice more typical of the Mesa Verdeans than of the local Mimbres and Tularosa people, who scattered their trash rather than piled it up. Lekson and his colleagues conclude that a large group of people—perhaps an entire town—moved out of the Mesa Verde region and traveled, as a group, 200 miles south to establish Pinnacle Ruin.

In several sites just across the Arizona–New Mexico border from Pinnacle, there are inhabitants clearly came from the Kayenta, Arizona, region. The distances they traveled were almost as great as those from Mesa Verde, again illustrating that such long-distance travel did happen. One of the best-documented cases is that of Point of Pines, an 800-room pueblo in east-central Arizona that was occupied between 1200 and 1400 (fig. 18.4). The late archaeologist Emil Haury, of the University of Arizona, documented 70 rooms in the center of the pueblo that apparently represented an immigrant enclave in

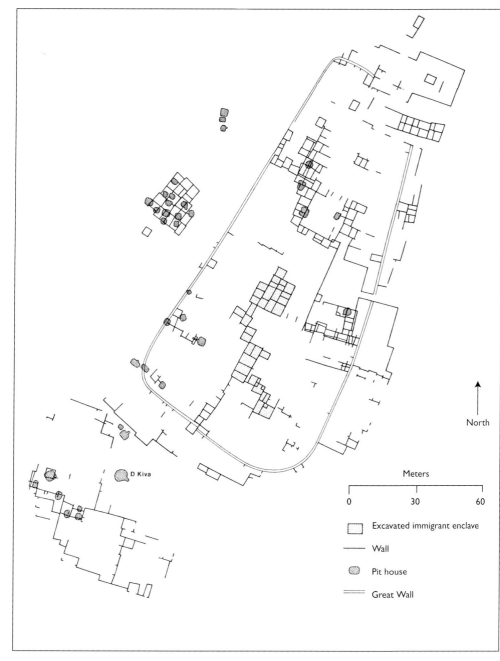

Figure 18.4. Plan of Point of Pines Pueblo in east-central Arizona showing excavated rooms inhabited by Kayenta immigrants.

region to the north. Wooden artifacts found in the unusual burned rooms had been made from trees native to the Kayenta region, and even corn and squash were of varieties from Kayenta. A Kayenta-style pot containing ritual objects—miniature baskets, wooden flower petals, a miniature bow, and cotton cloth—was found near Point of Pines; these objects strongly resembled items found in a cache in the Kayenta region. Haury concluded that in the late 1200s a group of 50 to 60 families traveled 200 miles from the Kayenta region to Point of Pines, where they lived as a separate enclave in the town. The burned rooms suggest that these outsiders were forced out after living there for about 20 years. The following hundred years in the history of Point of Pines show no remaining trace of these northerners.

this large town. The rooms were much larger than those in the rest of the pueblo and lacked the distinctive types of hearths, grinding bins, and storage cubicles found in other parts of the town. They had all been burned

As at Pinnacle Ruin, storage and cooking pots found in the enclave at Point of Pines were made in the local style, but painted serving vessels were made and decorated in the style of the Kayenta

Archaeologists are beginning to understand that migration took many forms in the Southwest and almost certainly included the movement of individuals, families, and entire communities. Equally interesting, but much less well understood, is how these people adapted to their new homes. Did they try to blend in by adopting the customs

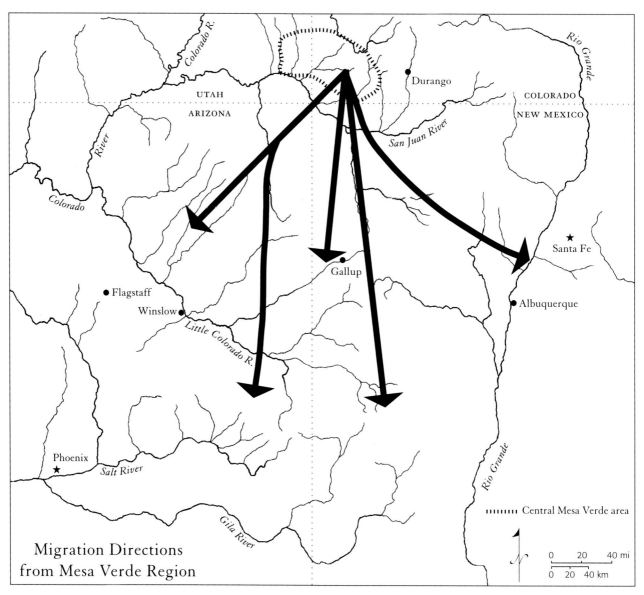

Figure 18.5. Approximate routes followed by emigrants from the Mesa Verde region.

and material culture of their hosts? Or did they maintain their own traditions, standing apart from their adopted communities? Evidence from Hano, Point of Pines, and Pinnacle Ruin suggests that immigrants maintained separate identities for considerable periods of time. Perhaps future archaeological studies of immigrant groups will show whether this was a general pattern.

Where Did They Go and Why?
Although we know that some people from the Mesa Verde region moved south, sometimes very far south, most seem to have undertaken shorter

trips with destinations in the northern Rio Grande Valley and adjacent uplands of New Mexico and in the Little Colorado River area of western New Mexico and eastern Arizona (fig. 18.5). There they likely mingled with the established residents, creating the modern pueblos of today. Many present-day Pueblo people have memories of their ancestral homes to the north.

While "push" factors, such as environmental deterioration and frightening conflicts, almost certainly motivated Mesa Verdeans to leave their northern homeland, better social, environmental, and economic conditions elsewhere might have

Figure 18.6. Petroglyph of a katsina mask, northern Rio Grande region.

attracted them to specific new places. Demographers and geographers refer to such conditions as "pull" factors. To figure out why the Mesa Verde people relocated where they did, archaeologists have begun to explore what the pull factors might have been.

Richard Ahlstrom, Carla Van West, and Jeffrey Dean have investigated what they call the "environmental gradient" between the Mesa Verde region and the northern Rio Grande region of New Mexico. Were environmental conditions so much better around the northern Rio Grande that they might have pulled migrants in from the Mesa Verde region? Ahlstrom and his colleagues believe they were. Drought, for example, was much less severe in the northern Rio Grande than in the northern San Juan region. Less environmental uncertainty and warmer temperatures, which benefited farming, might also explain why the migrants chose never to return to their former homes. In addition,

archaeologists have found some evidence for the development of irrigation techniques in the northern Rio Grande region, especially in upland areas, that might have enabled people to farm along the major river corridors for the first time.

Another possible pull factor was the dense herds of bison on the Great Plains of eastern New Mexico. These animals might have held a special attraction to the Mesa Verdeans, who had depleted the wild game in their region. Still another factor might have been that in the late 1200s other natural resources in the sparsely populated Rio Grande region—timber and fertile soil, for example—were much less depleted than they were in the Mesa Verde region, which had experienced intense human use for eight centuries.

Some archaeologists have suggested that new religious developments in the Rio Grande and Little Colorado areas exerted a strong pull on the people of the Mesa Verde. The katsina religion,

Figure 18.7. Tamaya, old Santa Ana Pueblo, along the Jemez River, 1977.

which apparently first developed around the upper Little Colorado after 1275, is still widespread among the Pueblo people today (fig. 18.6). Katsinas are supernatural beings represented by elaborately costumed dancers who perform at special ceremo-

nial events. Bill Lipe, who researched the timing of this religious movement, concluded that it appeared too late (after 1325) to have been a major pull factor for people of the Mesa Verde region. Lipe did note, however, that the old religious practices of the Mesa Verde region seem to have broken down in the late 1200s and the emigrants seem to have carried little of their symbolism with them when they left. He also suggested that the incipient religious practices of the upper Little Colorado and Rio Grande regions might have pulled on Mesa Verde farmers as they grappled with the difficult conditions in their traditional homes. Furthermore, he noted the existence of other exciting developments to the south: the beginnings of the Classic Hohokam culture in southern Arizona, the Salado cultural developments in central Arizona, and the beginnings of the great trading center at Casas Grandes in what is now northern Mexico. These distant developments might have offered opportunities and excitement that drew the people of the Mesa Verde region out of what was already becoming a hinterland.

Not Abandoned After All

Environmental deterioration made the Mesa Verde region a difficult place to be a farmer, and the resulting hard times sparked a period of intense conflict among ancestral Pueblo people. Looking south, Mesa Verdeans saw well-watered valleys (fig. 18.7) and the stirrings of exciting new social and religious developments. The movement of families and entire communities out of the Mesa Verde region may have gathered a momentum all its own, and even if a much diminished population had been able to remain, there might have been little incentive to do so.

And so the people moved, but they did not forget, nor did they lose contact with their old homes. Today, the descendants of the Mesa Verdeans live in New Mexico and Arizona. Pueblo people have histories that recount their movement through the world to reach their current locations, and many can point to archaeological sites that their people once occupied. Even those sites left behind long ago in the Mesa Verde region remain part of their world. As Rina Swentzell of Santa Clara Pueblo has written: "The place never forgets us. Even more, the structures that we build also have breath. They are alive and participate in their own cycles of life and death and of those who have lived within them. The memory of 'those gone before us' is, then, visually and psychically there to empower our present thoughts and lives."

The cliff dwellings and ancient settlements of the Mesa Verde region may appear empty and uninhabited, but they have not been abandoned by the Pueblo people. They are an ongoing part of Pueblo lives, and the rest of us owe much to Pueblo people for sharing these wonderful places with us.

Catherine M. Cameron is an associate professor of anthropology at the University of Colorado, Boulder. She was a member of the Chaco Project and has been conducting research at Bluff Great House in southeastern Utah since 1995.

Figure 19.1. Cliff houses along the Mancos River.

Mesa Verde
A Century of Research

Alden C. Hayes

The Mesa Verde archaeological district occupies a magnificent slab of geography that has probably been subjected to more intensive investigation than any other area of comparable size north of Mexico. The green-mantled tableland that gave its name to the Mesa Verde branch of ancestral Pueblo culture lies near the center of the district. The reasons for archaeologists' extra devotion to Mesa Verde are to be found in the remarkable preservation of material in the dry shelter caves and the breathtaking setting. We have been trying for some time to establish ourselves as rational scientists to be taken every bit as seriously as physicists, geneticists, and the other scholars who count and measure and discover natural laws. Still, the archaeologist who denies the romance and excitement of the first (or fiftieth) glimpse of a windowed wall of masonry, half hidden behind the piñon trees and hugging the face of a sandstone cliff, is probably not altogether honest.

I was smitten in 1958, when I was assigned to Mesa Verde National Park to make an archaeological survey as part of an extensive research project (fig. 19.2). My first cater-cornered view of Double House from the cliff above it gave me the thrill of discovery, though I knew hundreds had preceded me. During the next four years I became acquainted, in person or through their works, with many who had come before me.

Those who got there first were not necessarily writers, nor written about, so Juan Rivera might have been preceded, but according to our records he was the first European to see Mesa Verde. In 1776 he came into the country from Santa Fe by

way of the San Luis Valley and across the upper San Juan River to trade baubles to the Utes and Paiutes in exchange for unneeded children to be taken back and turned into Christian housemaids and sheepherders. He and other contemporary traders put names on the land, for when Frailes Francisco Atanasio Domínguez and Silvestre Vélez de Escalante came through from Santa Fe on the same route in 1776 to scout out a trail to San Francisco Bay, many features already had names, and they named still more. The La Plata Mountains, the Abajos, the Dolores River, the Rio de los Mancos, and Mesa Verde itself all bore those names back in the 1700s. As far as we may know, the friars did not climb the mesa, but Escalante, who was the diarist of the expedition, was interested in evidence of early inhabitants, and he described a ruined settlement on the south side of the Dolores River, which now carries his name.

Though the country must have been familiar to the wide-ranging trappers of the 1830s, the earliest recorded Anglo-Americans to see it were members of Captain J. N. McComb's party, which, in 1859, was one of several expeditions of that period dispatched by the U.S. Army to find an easy way to punch a railroad through to the Pacific coast. They did not find a feasible route in southwestern Colorado, but they camped between the foot of the Mesa Verde and the Mancos River—probably on Mud Creek—and Professor J. S. Newberry, the expedition's geologist, climbed Point Lookout on the mesa's north scarp for a sweeping view of the Four Corners country, from Shiprock to the La Sal

Figure 19.2. Al Hayes on a ledge overlooking Park Canyon in 1963.

Mountains, the San Miguels, the La Platas, and back south to Huérfano Mesa.

In 1874 four large surveying parties, each with some federal backing, were exploring, mapping, and describing the terrain of the Far West. All four of the leaders—Lieutenant George M. Wheeler,

Figure 19.3. William Henry Jackson's 1874 photograph of Two Story Cliff House in Mancos Canyon.

Major John Wesley Powell, Clarence King, and Dr. Ferdinand V. Hayden—were vying for the privilege of heading the single government agency responsible for western exploration. Hayden's expedition was the earliest, largest, and most ambitious, having claimed the Rocky Mountains as its domain for geographical studies. After exploring Yellowstone National Park and the Tetons, Hayden was working south through Colorado and the ranges surrounding South Park when he became apprehensive that Wheeler was about to trespass on his territory. To forestall that unhappy possibility and to stake his claim, he sent his photographer, William H. Jackson, to the drainage of the San Juan River. While outfitting in Denver, Jackson had heard from prospectors of mysterious empty houses built into caves in the sandstone cliffs, and he looked forward to seeing them. There was no settlement west of the La Plata Mountains at that time, but there was a small camp

of about a dozen prospectors at "Parrot City" on the headwaters of the La Plata River, just over the ridge from the present-day town of Mancos. Jackson made his way from Durango to Parrott City, where he engaged the services of Captain John Moss, an experienced mountaineer who was the leading citizen of the camp, to show him the houses in the cliffs.

After a 25- to 30-mile ride, the six-man party made camp the first night deep in Mancos Canyon. They had ridden across several mounds of rubble covered with sherds of pottery but had seen nothing of any real interest, so it was in a spirit both rueful and playful that, while digesting the evening's beans and sowbelly, they teased one of the packers about having to tote the heavy boxes of photographic equipment up the canyon wall to the apparently nonexistent cliff house. "He asked us to point out the spot," Jackson's diary reads. "The Captain pointed at random. 'Yes,' said he [the packer], 'I see it.' And behold upon my close observation there was something that appeared very like a house." Despite the failing light, they scrambled up the steep and brushy talus slope and over successive benches of perpendicular sandstone to investigate the little cliff dwelling, which Jackson named, and we know today as, "Two Story Cliff House." In better light the next morning, they returned with the unwieldy camera and 11-by-14-inch glass plates and made the first pictures of a Mesa Verde cliff dwelling (fig. 19.3). Accompanying Jackson was a young correspondent for the *New York Tribune*, Ernest Ingersoll (for Hayden knew the power of publicity), and Ingersoll's story, along with Jackson's illustrated report, quickly kindled an interest among the scholarly, as well as the merely curious, that has not diminished (see chapter 17).

The following year, 1875, Professor Hayden sent one of his principal topographers, William Henry Holmes, to make a more detailed study of the area. Holmes was a geologist, an artist, and a skilled cartographer. He climbed Mesa Verde to make a beautiful projected drawing of the country that included the southern tip of the mesa, Ute Mountain, and the Abajos. He discovered several other cliff houses and made the first known excavation when he scratched a prehistoric pot out of the dust at Sixteen-Window House. Holmes's experiences so stimulated his interest in Indian antiquities that a few years later he left the Geographical Survey to spend the rest of his working years as an archaeologist with the Bureau of American Ethnology and the U.S. National Museum.

Other results of the Hayden survey were papers by E. A. Barber on Indian pottery and stone artifacts and by Alfred Morgan on various archaeological aspects of the survey. There were other Morgans in the vicinity in the late 1870s, for Lewis Henry Morgan, the distinguished ethnologist and honorary Iroquois, made a lightning visit in 1878 and wrote a paper about Aztec Ruin on the Animas River. He certainly was the first trained anthropologist to visit the area. He was accompanied by his grand-nephew, W. F. Morgan, who wrote a detailed description of a small cliff house.

All the activity in the decade following Jackson's description of Two Story Cliff House was a matter of men following each other's footprints and seeing the same little ruins over and over. The inner recesses of the Mesa Verde were still unknown—or at least unadvertised. S. E. Osborne, a miner, left his name in Hemenway House in 1885, and Mrs. Virginia McClurg, of Denver, who was later to become the main mover behind the establishment of Mesa Verde National Park, was in Balcony House in 1886. It is hard to believe that a prospector looking for gold had not stumbled upon Cliff Palace or that a cowboy looking for a waterhole had not found the spring in Long House, but few prospectors and cattlemen are geared to talk or write about things other than mines and cattle. The Wetherills expanded the scope—and talked about it.

In 1880 Benjamin K. Wetherill, a former Indian agent and a rancher, moved to the Mancos Valley via Oklahoma and Kansas with his wife, daughter, and five sons to settle a ranch at the edge of the Ute reservation a few miles downstream from the newly established town of Mancos. Wetherill, a Quaker, had always gotten along well with Indians, and he soon made friends of the Utes, who allowed him to graze his cattle on their country.

Wetherill's sons had been running the family cattle for eight years in Mancos Canyon and its tributaries when, on a cold day in December 1888 the oldest son, Richard, and his brother-in-law, Charlie Mason, were following cow tracks up the southern end of the *potrero* we now call "Chapin Mesa." They came out onto a stretch of slickrock on the rim of a canyon, and gazing across the gulch through flurries of snow, they were amazed to see a great cave totally filled with houses—tier upon tier of them. The boys had been digging in small ruins for relics in their spare time for years and may have become a bit blasé, but this thing overwhelmed them. The cow tracks were forgotten while they explored the ruin they dubbed "The Cliff Palace" (see fig. 13.1), and the next day they discovered Spruce Tree House and Square Tower House. The third day they had to return to the line camp at the mouth of Johnson Canyon, but Richard came back to spend most of the winter digging in Cliff Palace and Spruce Tree House. For him, the cattle business was never again the same.

Richard Wetherill made a large collection that

winter of 1888–89. It did not require a great deal of earth moving, because many of the rooms had been abandoned, with household gear still sitting where it had been left—cooking pots on the hearths, food bowls on the floors, sandals in the corners, and digging sticks thrust under *vigas* (roof beams) by doorways. Feeling that the world needed to know about his discoveries, he boxed up his collection and took it by wagon to Durango, where it was exhibited in a hotel lobby. To his disappointment, his treasures elicited little interest. All the local people occasionally picked up arrowheads—this was just more old Indian stuff. So Richard took his relics to Pueblo, hoping to rouse a little more interest, but residents of that city, too, were chiefly centered on mines and livestock. One more showing, this time in Denver, was more successful, and the entire collection was sold to the Colorado Historical Society.

Back at the ranch, the Wetherills had a visitor in the summer of 1889. Frederick H. Chapin, a New England man of means and a member of the Hartford Archaeological Society, had traveled extensively in the West and was acquainted with members of Hayden's survey. From them, and from Jackson's and Holmes's publications, he knew of the cliff dwellings on the Mancos River and had determined to see them. After a trip to the mines at Ouray, he came down through Silverton into Durango, where he had difficulty even getting directions to Mancos, let alone any information about the ruins. Finally reaching the Mancos Valley by rented trap, by blind luck he found lodging at Wetherill's Alamo Ranch. He was taken by Richard and John Wetherill on an extended inspection trip down the Mancos, up onto Red Mesa south of the river, and then up onto Mesa Verde. He was so intrigued by the ruins that he returned the following summer, and in 1892 his book *The Land of the Cliff Dwellers* was published—the first detailed popular account.

The second collection of "relics" made by the Wetherill brothers, in the winter of 1889–90, was sold to an Illinois firm that exhibited it at the Field Columbian Exposition in Chicago in 1893. It was then purchased by Phoebe Hearst, who donated the artifacts to the University of Pennsylvania Museum —except for a few pieces that she took home to California, where they eventually ended up at the university's museum in Berkeley.

Another wealthy tenderfoot landed at Alamo Ranch in June 1891. Gustav Nordenskiöld, the 23-year-old son of a titled Swedish scientist and Arctic explorer, was touring frontier America to seek a cure for his tuberculosis (fig. 19.4). He happened into Denver and saw the Wetherills' exhibit at the museum. His interest whetted, he arrived at B. K. Wetherill's homestead a few days later, planning to make a quick inspection of the ruins. The few days he had intended to stay stretched into months. With Alfred or John Wetherill as a guide—or, less frequently, with Richard or Clayton—he explored the cliff dwellings, especially the less-known west side of the mesa.

Nordenskiöld introduced systematic investigation to the mesa, bringing to an end the period of "gee-whiz" discovery. He taught his guides, Richard in particular, to move slowly with a whisk broom and trowel, to record proveniences, and to label the artifacts removed. He made excavations in several ruins—rather extensive ones in Step House—and made the first orderly listing and numbering of sites. The maps, drawings, and photographs in his lavishly illustrated *The Cliff Dwellers of Mesa Verde*, published in Sweden in 1893 in both Swedish and English, still are valuable sources of information. Nordenskiöld was also the first to perceive culture change and strategically revealed chronology, when he noted in lower levels of refuse at Step House a type of crude pottery that was perhaps "the work of a people who inhabited the Step House cave before the erection of the cliff village." Three years later, the young scholar died of the disease that brought him to Colorado. The valuable collection he made that summer remains intact in the National Museum of Helsinki, Finland.

The Wetherills' direct influence on Mesa Verde diminished after 1893 as they began to look for fresher fields to the west. In Cottonwood Canyon in southeastern Utah, Richard found evidence of a preceramic occupation below the masonry houses of the cliff dwellers, confirming Nordenskiöld's hunch. He first called them the "Basket People" and later referred to them as the "Basket Makers."

Figure 19.4. Gustav Nordenskiöld.

Figure 19.5. Edgar Lee Hewett at Mesa Verde.

It was Richard, too, who introduced other terms we use today, "Cliff Dweller" and "Anasazi."

In 1895, his last year at Alamo Ranch before moving to Chaco Canyon, Richard Wetherill was once more host and guide to an eastern visitor. Dr. T. Mitchell Prudden, a physician and professor of pathology at Columbia University, for several years had spent his summers exploring the West. The writings of Jackson, Chapin, and Nordenskiöld drew him naturally to seek out the Wetherills on the Mancos River. Prudden's 1895 visit marked the beginning of nearly two decades of excursions, resulting in many articles, both popular and scientific, on the antiquities of the Southwest. Following the excavation of a series of mounds along McElmo Creek, near Cortez at the northwest foot of Mesa Verde, he made his most substantial contribution—the concept of the "unit pueblo" (the small cluster of rooms associated with a single kiva, as in fig. 4.2) and the delineation of a stage preceding the building of the more complex, classic structures.

The more adventuresome tourists continued to be packed up onto the mesa, but for the next 10 or 11 years nothing of any archaeological importance happened. Then, in 1906, Mesa Verde National Park was established. Influential in its birth was Edgar Lee Hewett (fig. 19.5), who helped draft the park legislation as well as the Antiquities Act, also passed that year.

Hewett has not been acclaimed by his peers or those who followed as an outstanding practitioner of the archaeologist's trade, but none will deny his considerable beneficial influence in two areas—the preservation of archaeological resources in parks and monuments and the training of archaeologists.

Figure 19.6. *Left to right:* J. C. "Coots" Frick, Alfred Kidder, and Jesse Nusbaum preparing to explore Mesa Verde in 1908.

A list of those who studied or apprenticed under him almost outlines a history of Southwestern archaeology. In a little book of reminiscences, Hewett explained his theory of education. Once, in Chicago, down near the lake shore, he watched a gang of wharf rats, under the guidance of an older boy, jumping off the dock to swim. He asked their leader, "How did these boys learn to swim so well?" "I taught 'em," he was told. "How did you teach them?" Hewett asked. "Pushed 'em off the pier" was the reply. Hewett felt that this was also the best technique for teaching archaeology, and he was still pushing students off the pier in his last year at the University of New Mexico in 1935.

The U.S. secretary of the interior, impressed by Hewett's work on the legislation involving Mesa Verde and the Antiquities Act, asked him to make a survey of the Four Corners country in 1907 to see what other sites might need protection. The

Archaeological Institute of America had just established a new School of American Archaeology (later the School of American Research) in Santa Fe and named Hewett as its director. To work on the Four Corners survey, Hewett brought to the Mesa Verde area two candidates for "pushing" who were to make names for themselves. He met Sylvanus G. Morley, a Harvard undergraduate from Buena Vista, Colorado, and Alfred V. Kidder, another Harvard boy, from New England, at Holly Ranch in McElmo Canyon after their long ride from Mancos (figs. 19.6, 19.7). The next morning, the three climbed the mesa above the juncture of Yellow Jacket and McElmo canyons, a vantage point from which one can see some of the biggest country in the West: from Shiprock in New Mexico to the Carrizo Mountains in Arizona, the Henrys and La Sals in Utah, and Mesa Verde and the La Platas in Colorado. With a vague wave of his arm,

Figure 19.7. Sylvanus G. Morley, about 1910.

he instructed them to make an archaeological survey and promised to return in six weeks.

In spite of this rugged initiation, Kidder and Morley were game to have another shot at it the following year. Hewett set Vay Morley to excavating Cannonball Ruin (see fig. 12.8), on the edge of McElmo Canyon, and put Kidder up on Mesa Verde with a new recruit, 20-year-old Jesse Logan Nusbaum, a gangling string bean from Greeley, Colorado. With Nusbaum taking pictures and Kidder making sketch maps, they were to record all the major cliff dwellings. The boys were agile. In 1960 I located a pretty cliff dwelling near the tip of Long Mesa so difficult of access that I had reason to hope it had not been entered since the Indians left it. After rigging a lightweight, portable rope ladder, with some trouble we entered the south end of the cave to be confronted by an inscription on the sandstone wall reading "J. Nusbaum, 1908."

Morley's report of his Cannonball excavation appeared first in the journal *American Anthropologist* with what today seems incredible speed—in the

fall of the same year the digging was done. It was reprinted as Number 2 in *Papers of the School of American Archaeology* in Santa Fe, one of the first accounts of a Southwestern excavation by an American archaeologist published in the United States. In his report, Morley went beyond a mere description of the architecture to speculate on social units and on the building of the large complex by the accretion of groups of domestic rooms around a kiva.

The School of American Archaeology had one more year in Mesa Verde country in 1910, when Hewett brought Nusbaum back to clean up and stabilize Balcony House. Not only a professional photographer, Nusbaum had also been apprenticed to his father, a bricklayer, and the results of his summer's work still stand. When the work was completed in the fall, Nusbaum dismissed his crew and, though low on supplies, stayed on with one man to await Hewett's inspection of the work. Hewett finally rode in one afternoon so late they had to build fires to illuminate the ruin. He had

Figure 19.8. Jesse Walter Fewkes in front of Mesa Verde's first museum, 1916.

come from Mancos without extra horses for his men and insisted on riding off the mesa in the dark that same evening. He left in a swirling snowstorm, leaving Nusbaum and his helper to make their way on foot the next morning. Without breakfast, they floundered through snowdrifts over the north rim and into Cortez, arriving well after midnight.

Jesse Walter Fewkes (fig. 19.8), of the Bureau of American Ethnology, is quoted in Sylvanus Morley's report of the Cannonball dig in regard to the sipapu in the kivas. The two undoubtedly met that summer of 1908, the first of many that Fewkes was to spend on Mesa Verde. After more than 20 years experience in the Southwest as an ethnologist and archaeologist, principally in Arizona, he came to the Mesa Verde area to excavate and stabilize Spruce Tree House. Although picked over by many previous visitors, the site yielded a sizable collection, the first artifacts from Mesa Verde to be

housed in the U.S. National Museum. In 1909 he returned to uncover and reinforce the crumbling walls of Cliff Palace.

After years of ethnographic and archaeological research in the Southwest, Mesa Verde was almost a retirement job for Fewkes. By this time, he was a rather benign-looking fellow with a white beard below mahogany cheekbones and white curls spilling out from under his Stetson. Most of his work was done by crews of Navajos and local ranchers while Fewkes explained things to visitors. In 1915, while excavating Sun Temple, he inaugurated evening campfire programs at which he drew parallels between the architectural features and Hopi ethnographic data. He started the excavation of Far View Ruin in 1916 and excavated Pipe Shrine House in 1922—his last year in the park.

Fewkes was a great detractor of the Wetherills, accusing them of desecrating and vandalizing the

Figure 19.9. Jesse Nusbaum

preliminary reports not followed by final ones. Unfortunately, almost no useful information was recorded in 15 seasons of fieldwork. Fewkes did make a major contribution, however. He initiated and pioneered the business of ruins stabilization.

In his next to final year at Mesa Verde, Fewkes made another contribution. He complained to Stephen Mather, director of the National Park Service, about the shoddy way the park was being run, accusing the ranger and his father-in-law, the park's superintendent, of looting the ruins and selling the plunder. After a tour of inspection accompanied by Fewkes, Mather relieved the superintendent and appointed Jesse Nusbaum (fig. 19.9), who had just completed the excavation of DuPont Cave near Kanab, Utah, for the Museum of the American Indian.

Nusbaum not only was an able administrator and a trained archaeologist but also had learned something from his old mentor, Edgar Hewett, about enlisting help from those who were in a position to be helpful. In 1924 he devoted two days to guiding John D. Rockefeller Jr. and his sons around the mesa.

ruins. Of course, in 1888 hardly anybody knew how to get the information out of a ruin. Richard Wetherill's notes were as useful as Fewkes's annual reports to the Smithsonian, which were devoted mainly to the number of rooms cleaned out, with a few comments on finds of particular interest—

Rockefeller took a lively interest in plans for the development of the park and the establishment of a museum, pledging funds to help get something started. All of Fewkes's collections had gone to the National Museum, and the park had almost nothing of the Anasazi arts to display. Partly to rectify that lack, Nusbaum elected to reexcavate Step House. This site also promised to provide information about the earlier inhabitants of the mesa, whose presence Nordenskiöld had suspected—the people whom Richard Wetherill had labeled "Basket Makers" and whom Nusbaum himself had investigated in DuPont Cave in Utah. In the fall of 1924 he trained his crew by excavating undisturbed trash in the back of Spruce Tree House, and in February 1926 he packed out to Wetherill Mesa to camp on the rim and work in Step House, where he cleaned out Basketmaker pithouses and definitely established the early use of cave sites. From this excavation and a series of others in Fewkes Canyon he gathered enough material to start the museum.

Government was easier in those days. If supervision was loose enough for it to be possible to hire relatives and make a commercial venture out of a government post, the same casualness also made it easier to do things for the public good. Nusbaum's budget was not broken for him into minute categories—so many dollars to pick up beer bottles and so many to build trails. He had a lump sum to operate the park, plus whatever he could scrounge. Without having to submit plans to a remote office of civil servant engineers and architects, he was able to build of stone and timber a headquarters, a museum, and residences for staff, using local workmen and without referring to volumes of regulations.

About the same time Nusbaum was being reintroduced to Mesa Verde, another archaeologist began a long series of excavations in the area. Paul S. Martin started digging near the head of Yellow Jacket Canyon, north of Cortez, in the summer of 1928. He was sponsored at first by the Colorado State Historical Society and later by Chicago's Field Museum of Natural History. Martin's many competent, descriptive, and promptly published reports became a body of information that, along with Earl Morris's Animas River and Red Mesa work, made it

possible to define a Mesa Verde culture area distinct from other focal hearths in the Southwest.

Earl Morris (fig. 19.10) had been a student at Hewett's field school on the Pajarito Plateau, along with Kidder, Nusbaum, and Morley. In 1913, on Hewett's recommendation, the University of Colorado entrusted Morris with a few dollars to investigate ruins in the mesa country between the La Plata and Mancos rivers. He returned to the same general vicinity and the nearby Animas Valley every summer for the next 21 years, interrupted only by brief excursions into Canyon del Muerto, the Lukachukai Mountains, or Yucatán. No better trowel hand, more astute reader of dirt, or keener observer has to date searched the earth between the San Juan and the Dolores. He wrote well, could draw, remembered what he had seen, and knew what it probably meant. Since he published his La Plata Valley report, a couple generations of archaeologists have thought that they had run into something new, only to find that Morris had made the same observation 50 years before. Most of his work was done under the auspices of the American Museum of Natural History, for which institution he excavated and stabilized Aztec Ruin, on the Animas River in New Mexico, and reconstructed the great kiva at that large pueblo.

On the basis of Morris's success at stabilizing the walls of Aztec Ruin (see fig. 4.8) and of Mummy Cave in Arizona, he was hired by the Park Service in 1935 to patch up the work done in Cliff Palace and Spruce Tree House by Fewkes some years before. To help him mix mud and lay rock, he hired James A. Lancaster, who had prior experience working for archaeologists in the area.

When Paul Martin had first come down from Denver to dig near Ackmen (now Pleasant View), he had taken on a crew of local bean farmers to help him. One of them was Al Lancaster (fig. 19.11), who showed remarkable aptitude and great enthusiasm for the work. Lancaster became dig foreman and was on tap for succeeding summers. In 1931, Martin was unable to return to the field. J. O. Brew, planning to come out from Harvard to excavate on Alkali Ridge near Blanding, Utah, wrote Martin asking for the names of men he might use. Martin had no hesitation in recommending Lancaster, who

Figure 19.10. Earl Morris.

Lancaster put in the next four field seasons at the ruins of the Hopi village of Awatovi, again for J. O. Brew, who called him "the best field man the Southwest has produced." He returned to Mesa Verde in 1939 to take charge of a continuing program of stabilization and maintenance of the park's excavated sites (see fig. 20.4). Lancaster had a part to play in almost all research on Mesa Verde from that time onward—even after his so-called retirement in 1964.

What was known about cultural sequence and change on Mesa Verde by 1940 was derived largely by inference from the work of Martin, Morris, and Brew in adjacent valleys and on their separating ridges. Except for Nusbaum's Basketmaker pithouses in Step House cave and a pithouse excavated on Chapin Mesa by Ralph Linton in 1919 while he was assisting Fewkes, excavation on the mesa had been confined mostly to the cliff dwellings and large surface ruins of the "Classic" or "Great Pueblo" period. In 1939 and 1940 Lancaster and Terah Smiley, of the University of Arizona, added to Basketmaker material by digging more pithouses on Chapin Mesa.

Nusbaum, who had been appointed consulting archaeologist to the secretary of the interior, with his office in Santa Fe, was touring the park in 1939 when he spied bulldozers at work in Soda Canyon, far below the mesa's rim, on Ute reservation land. Knowing the floor of the canyon to be paved with ruins, he protested to the superintendent of the

made a valuable hand for Brew and stayed with him through three seasons of work in a series of open sites on Alkali Ridge. When Martin was gearing up for a return to his work around Yellow Jacket, he learned that his skilled foreman had transferred his allegiance to Brew and Harvard. The news lodged a thorn of resentment in Martin that he never forgot.

After learning the rudiments of ruins stabilization from Earl Morris at Cliff Palace in 1935,

Figure 19.11. James A. Lancaster, 1963.

Ute agency, and by threatening to phone Secretary Harold Ickes about the matter, he was able to get the road work halted until some salvage archaeology could be performed. This was a landmark episode. It set a precedent for the archaeological salvage work still being done today, establishing government responsibility for conserving antiquities on government land (see chapter 20). The road work was held up for two years until funds could be found to support investigation of the archaeological sites in the right-of-way. The nation's first highway salvage project was born.

Erik K. Reed was sent up from the Santa Fe office of the National Park Service in the spring of 1942 to do the job. Reed's excavations at five sites and his survey of Mancos Canyon, just below Mesa Verde's southern toe, provided the basis for an attempt to describe a sequential development that could apply also to archaeology on the mesa itself.

Harold Gladwin was a wealthy, retired industri-alist who, having found it difficult to get definitive answers to his questions about the prehistoric Southwest, set up a foundation he called "Gila Pueblo," headquartered in Globe, Arizona. He hired archaeologists and proceeded to look for answers, starting his search in central Arizona and working outward in ever-widening circles. Although his team collected tree-ring samples from many sites on and around the mesa in the mid-1930s, it was not until 1947 that he was prepared to put a shovel into the ground. To do the digging, he dispatched Deric O'Bryan, a man who knew the park well. O'Bryan, Jesse Nusbaum's stepson, had lived on the mesa as a boy, accompanying Nusbaum on the Step House dig and other expeditions.

Martin had dug around Yellow Jacket hoping to establish a cultural sequence and on Alkali Ridge Brew had looked for evidence of stages between the so-called Modified Basketmaker culture and the Classic Pueblo, but previous work on Mesa Verde itself had been mostly reportorial and descriptive: "This is what we found." On his return to Mesa Verde, O'Bryan came with a list of nine questions he hoped to answer. Problem-oriented archaeology had arrived at Mesa Verde. Among the things he wanted to know were, What was the evidence on the mesa of Paleoindian hunters, of the postulated Basketmaker I period, and of the preceramic agriculturalists of Basketmaker II? How did the Modified Basketmakers of Mesa Verde compare with those of adjacent areas? Was there a locally definable Pueblo II or early "Developmental" Pueblo? And what had caused the entire region to be abandoned at about 1300 CE?

Over the next two summers, O'Bryan carried out extensive excavations at four sites, showing a continuous occupation from the Modified Basketmaker culture of the seventh century into the Great Pueblo period of the twelfth. His findings answered some of his questions and enabled him to propose a sequence of five progressive phases—a system that has stood up fairly well in the light of evidence uncovered by subsequent work.

O'Bryan's excavations made apparent the gradual changes in architecture and minor artifacts, but the park had no examples from the earlier stages to show to its visitors. Don Watson, the

Figure 19.12. Douglas Osborne (center) and Mesa Verde staff with pottery from Wetherill Mesa, 1962.

park archaeologist in 1950, with Al Lancaster by his side, completed an intensive survey of the sites on Chapin Mesa and located several good prospects for filling the gap. He and Lancaster, with the help of others on staff—Philip Van Cleave and Jean Pinkley—excavated four sites on the Ruins Loop Road between headquarters and the view point across the canyon from Cliff Palace. The purpose of the excavations was primarily to create "exhibits in place" as adjuncts to the park's interpretive program, but they did more than that. They were also good digs that provided valuable information.

For four years, starting in 1953, Robert and Florence Lister ran a field school in archaeology at Mesa Verde for the University of Colorado, during which they excavated a series of Pueblo III houses in the vicinity of Far View. The digs and the team's stabilization of walls fulfilled three objectives: they provided on-the-job training in field techniques for students, they enriched the body of data, and they produced new exhibits to show to park visitors. Bob Lister, like several of his predecessors, had a link to Mesa Verde in that he had been a student of

Edgar L. Hewett's at the University of New Mexico.

In 1958 the National Park Service undertook what was perhaps the first large-scale, multidisciplinary research project in the United States when it fielded the Wetherill Mesa Archaeological Project, conceived by chief park archaeologist John Corbett and supervised by Douglas Osborne (fig. 19.12). The ostensible reason for the project, and the excuse for the expenditure of government funds, was the preparation of ruins for public exhibition on the west side of the park, to help accommodate the crowding caused by increased traffic. Of course, the archaeologists also hoped to learn more about what had happened a thousand years earlier, and why. Generous support from the National Geographic Society helped with the theoretical, or less immediately pragmatic, aspects of the project.

Between 1958 and 1963 the Park Service accomplished an intensive survey of Wetherill Mesa and excavated and stabilized Mug House as well as Long House, the second largest cliff dwelling in the park (see pl. 11). Step House was reexcavated, with the discovery of more pithouses, and prepared for exhibit. Five mesa-top sites exemplifying occupations from the mid-600s to the mid-1200s were excavated, and testing was done in a half-dozen more. Needed stabilization was also conducted in several other large cliff dwellings on Wetherill Mesa. The year-round crew of about 15 (including laboratory help) was expanded to about 50 in the summer. Included on the permanent staff were George S. Cattanach, Arthur H. Rohn, and Richard P. Wheeler. Al Lancaster was still digging, as well as supervising all the stabilization work. And Edgar Hewett's long arm was still reaching to Mesa Verde through Doug Osborne and me. Like Lister, we had been Hewett's students during his last year on the campus at the University of New Mexico.

Following the completion of the Wetherill Mesa Project in 1965, we knew in much finer detail what had happened at Mesa Verde, but certainly many questions remained about why. To probe some of those questions, Lister returned with his research team from the University of Colorado. Much of their work involved survey and salvage excavation for the Bureau of Land Management and the Ute Mountain Ute Reservation. They also dug several sites at the east side of the park where the Park Service planned to expand camping facilities. The team continued to look for answers to questions that archaeologists had been asking for years, such as, What factors contributed to the wholesale depopulation of the Four Corners area? And because every new addition to our knowledge through excavation gives rise to new questions, another emerged: In what ways was Mesa Verde culture affected by the rise of the "Chaco Phenomenon?"

A signal accomplishment of the University of Colorado was the completion of a rod-by-rod survey of the park. A project started by Don Watson in the 1930s and continued on the west side of the mesa by the Wetherill Mesa Project had left three-quarters of the park unsurveyed. Nearly a century after Jackson's discovery of Two Story Cliff House, we still did not know how many archaeological sites we had, to say nothing of their location or type. Back in 1959 park superintendent Chester A. Thomas had put on a show-and-tell program for local officials, newspaper reporters, and chambers of commerce to describe the Wetherill Mesa research. After saying a few words about the survey I was conducting, I was asked by a young woman with notepad and pencil at the ready, "Mr. Hayes, how many undiscovered ruins are there in Mesa Verde?" Now, thanks to the exhaustive work of park research archaeologist Jack E. Smith, one might be able to answer that question: "Ma'am, there are none."

The late Alden Hayes wrote this essay in 1985 for a previous School of American Research publication. Had he been here to revise it, he would certainly have amended the end of the essay in light of the discovery of hundreds of sites after wildfires on Mesa Verde between 1996 and 2003 (see chapter 14). Hayes was an archaeologist with the National Park Service who conducted research on the Mesa Verde and throughout the Southwest. After retiring, he wrote books, worked as an archaeological river guide, and taught at Crow Canyon Archaeological Center.

Figure 20.1. Excavators at Goodman Point Pueblo, summer 2005.

Mesa Verdean Archaeology since the Mid-1960s

David A. Breternitz

I have worked and lived in southwestern Colorado for some 40 years and have had the good fortune to take part in the exciting archaeological advancements of the Mesa Verde region. In contrast to the early years discussed by Alden Hayes in the preceding chapter, when archaeological investigations were concentrated on Mesa Verde National Park, research in recent decades has expanded to include the larger Mesa Verde culture area. What is more, the number of researchers, academic institutions, and governmental agencies involved has proliferated.

Most of the research carried out since the 1960s can be attributed to a series of laws, rules, and policies emanating from federal and state legislation and designed to promote the preservation of the country's historical and cultural heritage. Most notable are the National Historic Preservation Act of 1966 and the 1969 Executive Order 11593. The latter mandates that all federal land management agencies inventory the cultural resources under their jurisdiction.

Archaeological Surveys

Surveys, which locate, document, and evaluate cultural resources in a given project area, account for most of the archaeology conducted in southwestern Colorado in recent decades. Although surveys do not involve excavation, they have contributed a great deal to our knowledge of the extent and variety of archaeological sites in the region. Some surveys have preceded timber sales or tree-thinning operations (necessitated by fire danger caused by drought and bark beetle infestations) on land managed by

the Bureau of Land Management (BLM) and the US Forest Service.

Typically, during a survey, a crew of archaeologists walks across the landscape, keeping 10 to 15 meters apart. When someone observes evidence of past cultural activity—potsherds, stone artifacts, or remains of structures, for example—the crew stops, closely examines the evidence, creates a map and a site form, takes photographs, and tabulates visible artifacts.

Between 1965 and the mid-1970s, the University of Colorado (UC) inventoried BLM land in southwestern Colorado and documented 1,617 sites, most of which now lie within the boundaries of the new Canyon of the Ancients National Monument. This project helped inform federal managers of the extent and importance of cultural resources on land under their jurisdiction and, incidentally, was a factor in the creation of Executive Order 11593 in 1969. Amazingly, this project cost taxpayers only $18.55 per recorded site.

A few years later, UC archaeologist Jack Smith directed a complete inventory of sites in Mesa Verde National Park, recording 3,892 sites. Between 1996 and 2003, a series of forest fires denuded large tracts of the park, exposing a multitude of previously invisible sites. As Julie Bell describes in chapter 14, the fires stimulated renewed surveying, which resulted in even more accurate and detailed archaeological documentation and added more than 600 sites to those already known.

Energy development, which often involves laying oil and gas pipelines, constructing electrical

Figure 20.2. University of Colorado field school students working at Coyote Village (MV820). *Left to right:* Cory Breternitz, Steve Hallisy, and Don Schelly.

transmission lines, and building roads, lies behind much of the survey work that has been done in the Mesa Verde area and the Southwest as a whole. Two examples are the MAPCO (fig. 20.3) and Northwest Pipelines projects, which were directed by Jerry Fetterman, of Woods Canyon Archaeological Consultants, and Alan Reed and Susan Chandler, of Alpine Archaeo-logical Consultants, between 1990 and 2002. These companies conducted research at a variety of sites, including Archaic residential sites, Basketmaker III stockaded settlements, Pueblo II habitations and hunting camps, and eighteenth-century Navajo brush shelters and forked-stick hogans. Because several rights-of-way for these linear projects paralleled previous rights-of-way, they investigated some of the sites two and even three times.

Shell Oil Company developed carbon dioxide resources in southwestern Colorado in the 1980s. For this project, archaeologists created a predictive model of the significant cultural resources around

the proposed well pads, pumping plants, and pipeline distribution facilities. The modeling allowed them to advise the company of the chances of encountering cultural sites within any specific 400-by-400-foot square within the well field. It proved to be 80 percent accurate and enabled engineers to bypass archaeological sites, avoid construction delays, and cut costs. In addition, archaeological resources were saved.

In 1966, "chaining" (clear-cutting by pulling an anchor chain attached to two bulldozers across a wooded landscape to create grazing land) on the Ute Mountain Ute Reservation south of Cortez, Colorado, required extensive archaeological survey. Student crews from the Mesa Verde Research Center and Santa Fe's Laboratory of Anthropology walked the areas to be chained and flagged visible sites, which were then spared destruction. Beginning about the same time, the tribe began planning its Ute Mountain Ute Tribal Park, just south of Mesa

Figure 20.3. Archaeologists Jerry Fetterman and Vern Hensler wrap a wood sample for tree-ring dating at a Pueblo II site during the MAPCO pipeline project.

Figure 20.4. James A. Lancaster (top of ladder) during the 1934 stabilization of Balcony House.

Verde National Park. Toward that end, archaeological crews surveyed a new road in Mancos Canyon and conducted test excavations in numerous cliff dwellings. By collecting tree-ring samples, they were able to further our knowledge of when these sites were occupied. Besides doing archaeological research, they built trails and stabilized ruins to prepare them for public visitation. Today, Ute guides lead daily tours to some of these sites in spring, summer, and fall.

One of the smaller Pueblo II sites excavated in connection with the Mancos Canyon road construction yielded the first scientific proof of prehistoric cannibalism in the Mesa Verde region. In 1992 Tim D. White published these findings in his book *Prehistoric Cannibalism at Mancos 5MTUMR-2346*. Seven years later, Christy G. Turner and Jacqueline A. Turner treated the subject comprehensively in their book *Man Corn*.

Ruins Stabilization

As public interest in archaeology and antiquity grew throughout the twentieth century, so did the need to preserve sites from the effects of visitors and natural erosion. Personnel at public parks also had to consider public safety. Stabilization was not a new concept: Jesse Walter Fewkes had stabilized some of the Mesa Verde cliff dwellings in the early 1900s. But in 1974 the University of Colorado actually developed a credit course in stabilization for both undergraduate and graduate-level students. At the time, everyone recognized James A. Lancaster as the leading ruins stabilization expert (fig. 20.4). Al was a local man and bean farmer. The problem was that he had only an eighth-grade education and the university could not accredit him to teach a college course. To solve the difficulty, I was listed as the instructor in the course catalogue, even though my experience was at about the same level as that of the students.

Figure 20.5. Joe Ben Wheat (right) with a student at the University of Colorado's Yellow Jacket Field School.

Figure 20.6. W. James Judge (center) teaching students at Fort Lewis College's field school at the Pigg Site in southwestern Colorado.

We first worked at Lowry Ruin, an outlying Chacoan great house near Pleasant View, and from there we went on to Escalante Ruin, another great-house site perched on the hill behind the Anasazi Heritage Center, near Dolores. Since then, CU has contracted with the Bureau of Land Management to stabilize Cannonball Ruin, the McLean Basin Towers, Sand Canyon Cliff Dwelling, and other sites. Today, several private firms continue stabilization projects.

Research and Training Programs

Field schools have been training archaeology students and contributing to our knowledge of ancient North America since Edgar Lee Hewett started one at Santa Fe's School of American Archaeology in 1907. From 1965 to 1977 the Mesa Verde Research Center provided instruction to more than 350 students (some were repeaters) in the park. In addition to the previously noted survey work in Ute Mountain Ute Tribal Park, the students excavated sites in Morefield Canyon, on Wetherill Mesa, and around Far View Ruin. The data resulting from this work helped to enhance the park's interpretive program for the visiting public.

Joe Ben Wheat (1916–97), a leading Southwestern anthropologist, directed a University of Colorado field school for some 15 years at a series of Basketmaker II through Pueblo II sites near Yellow Jacket, 15 miles north of Cortez (fig. 20.5). This long-term field project added to our understanding of the way ancestral Pueblo culture evolved over many centuries.

In the 1990s, Fort Lewis College, in Durango, conducted summer field schools at the Pigg Site and Puzzle House, which were part of the prehis-

Figure 20.7. William D. Lipe at a rock art site on Cedar Mesa.

toric Lowry community near present-day Pleasant View, Colorado. W. James Judge, an experienced Chaco archaeologist, directed the field school (fig. 20.6). His students and he found that Puzzle House, which saw three occupations (650, 1100, and 1180 CE), held valuable information about the cultural dynamics of the Lowry community and life there following the abandonment of Chaco Canyon in the mid-1100s.

Students from Fort Lewis College have also been excavating the Darkmold Site near Durango since its discovery in 1998 (see chapter 2). An open-air, single-family dwelling dating between about 2,150 and 1,500 years ago (Basketmaker II to early Basketmaker III), the site has afforded a glimpse into early sedentary life in the Southwest and produced good evidence for the emergence of corn agriculture. An interesting find by Mona Charles, who led the research, and her students was the existence of bell-shaped pits in the floor, thought to have been used for storing corn.

Two field school projects in the mid-1970s produced significant findings. Students from San

Jose University, under the tutelage of Joe Winter, worked in Hovenweep National Monument, concentrating their research on the role and function of the famous and enigmatic stone towers found at the heads of canyons. William D. Lipe and R. G. Matson, of Washington State University, led students in research into the Basketmaker II period and early agriculture on Cedar Mesa in southeastern Utah (fig. 20.7).

Crow Canyon Archaeological Center, a private organization with a campus northwest of Cortez, offers archaeological laboratory and field experience to members of the public. The center has conducted research at several important ancestral Pueblo sites in the Montezuma Valley and conducted educational programs for individuals and groups of all ages. Its surveys and excavations have greatly enhanced our understanding of the prehistoric occupation of the area north and west of Cortez. From 1983 to 1993, Crow Canyon conducted systematic investigations at Sand Canyon Pueblo, a large, horseshoe-shaped village at the head of a canyon in the McElmo drainage (see pl.

13). Excavations revealed that the town, whose houses and public buildings are surrounded by a wall, was planned in its design and built between the 1250s and 1270s. Of particular interest to researchers was the reason the inhabitants of the valley left their many small, dispersed pueblos to aggregate in large sites like Sand Canyon Pueblo.

Large, Federally Sponsored, Construction-Related Projects

The largest archaeological data-recovery contract in American history went into effect in 1978 after the federal government decided to dam the Dolores River in order to create an agricultural irrigation system in the Montezuma Valley. Over a seven-and-a-half-year period, members of the Dolores Archaeological Program (DAP) recorded 1,626 sites, of which 102 were tested or fully excavated. To accomplish the task, the University of Colorado, which was the contractor, along with its subcontractor, Washington State University, employed 550 people and spent just under $10 million on the archaeological research alone. An equal amount was later spent on related archaeological work, historical studies, and building and fitting the Anasazi Heritage Center. The center attests to the foresight of the federal agencies involved in retaining all the recovered artifacts in the area. As anyone who has visited the center knows, it includes an excellent museum.

I had the honor of being the senior principal investigator for the project's duration—it was a highlight of my professional career—and I took special pride in the fact that all contract obligations were completed on time and under budget (fig. 20.8). In addition to its archaeological findings, the DAP served as a training ground for many students and initiates, among whom a remarkable number chose to continue their professional careers in archaeology in the Four Corners area.

The DAP filled a void in our knowledge of Mesa Verdean prehistory in the Dolores area, especially in terms of population dynamics. Notably, DAP research showed that the aggregation of families into village-size communities began in the 800s CE. In most of the region, the subsequent 200 years saw the demise of village life as people

Figure 20.8. David A. Breternitz during the Dolores Archaeological Program years.

dispersed back into smaller, scattered sites. Then, in the 1100s and 1200s, we recognize the reoccurrence of aggregation as large communities developed again, just before the well-known abandonment of the area by 1300.

Recently, the DAP's entire database was brought up to date and made available online, so researchers can conduct comparative analyses that were impossible in the mid-1980s. Electronic data storage and communication now make it possible for work like this, completed decades ago, to influence new research programs.

The major excavation program associated with the Animas–La Plata Project, which is contracted to SWCA Environmental Consultants, began in 2002 (fig. 20.9). This is another large-scale, federal public works project requiring extensive archaeological clearance. Water will be taken out of the Animas River near Durango, pumped over the hill

Figure 20.9. Excavation of a pithouse during the Animas–La Plata project.

into the La Plata drainage, stored in a reservoir, and then distributed to farmers and municipal water systems. The Southern Ute, Ute Mountain Ute, and Navajo tribes will benefit from the project. As of this writing, archaeologists are excavating numerous hamlet sites and a large village, the Sacred Ridge Site, all dating between about 650 and 800 CE.

Miscellaneous Archaeological Activities

In 2004 the announcement that the American Society of Civil Engineers had named four prehistoric reservoirs in Mesa Verde National Park as National Historic Civil Engineering Landmarks caught the attention of the national press. During the previous 10 years, the Wright Paleohydrological Institute, headed by Kenneth R. Wright, had been conducting multidisciplinary investigations at four prehistoric water collecting and reservoir systems in the park. It also studied soils and drainage systems and, through pollen studies, retrieved data on ancient plant regimes. In chapter 15, Wright tells more about the reservoirs and how they ameliorated problems of drought on Mesa Verde.

The excavation of Stix-and-Leaves Pueblo, a site on private land excavated by Bruce Bradley in the early 2000s, provided insights into tenth-century life in the area north of Mesa Verde. We had understood from previous research that between 925 and 950 CE, the people of this area left their villages and either moved into small hamlets or emigrated, probably to the south. Stix-and Leaves Pueblo, however, remained inhabited until after 959. Each site investigated helps to fill out our picture of the past.

The Archaeological Conservancy

Since the early 1980s, the Archaeological Conservancy, a national nonprofit organization based in Albuquerque, New Mexico, has made the Mesa Verde area a major focus of its preservation efforts, acquiring 11 ruins that were threatened by development. These include Mud Springs, the Hedley Ruins, Yellow Jacket Pueblo (the largest Puebloan site in the Mesa Verde region), Albert Porter Pueblo, the Brewer Archaeological Preserve, and the Hampton Ruins. The Archaeological

Conservancy also promoted the creation of Canyons of the Ancients National Monument, which was accomplished by presidential proclamation at the end of the Clinton administration.

Environmental Studies

A series of studies relating the past environment to archaeological investigations and interpretations has greatly enhanced our understanding of Mesa Verdean prehistory. Kenneth L. Petersen, for example, used tree-ring records and pollen studies to reconstruct the general climatic picture, primarily for the years from 575 to 1300 CE. Carla Van West, then a doctoral candidate at Washington State University, also contributed importantly to this field. Using the Palmer Drought Severity Index as her basic tool, she analyzed 4,500 grid squares (each 200 by 200 meters) for a block of land 701 square miles in area. Initially, she dealt with the 900–1300 time period, but she has subsequently extended her study back to around 600 CE. Her work enables researchers to calculate the agricultural potential of each grid square for every year included in the study and to relate this information to the ever-changing distribution of archaeological sites over the landscape.

The Current Status of Research and Knowledge in the Mesa Verde Region

At one time, what we knew about the Mesa Verde region consisted principally of the archaeological record for Mesa Verde National Park. Today, scholars recognize that the core area of this ancestral Pueblo culture was in the farmlands and valleys west and north of the park and in southeastern Utah. Although what happened on Mesa Verde was important, it was atypical of cultural developments in the wider region. The larger picture is one of smaller-scale, localized developments. Just as the modern small towns of Mancos, Dolores, and Dove Creek have their individual histories, so did each of the many ancient hamlets. Recent research shows that each local area had its own identity based on location, population density, access to natural resources, and trade contacts both within and beyond the region.

I find the potential for understanding the prehistory of these small population enclaves exciting. The more we succeed in putting together the small pieces of the puzzle, the more we will understand the full picture of what happened in the region. In the 1920s an archaeologist described research in the American Southwest as a "sucked orange." His assessment has proved false: the dynamic, multidisciplinary studies that are taking place bode well for new and deeper insights into the prehistory of Mesa Verde, the Southwest, and beyond.

David A. Breternitz, a professor emeritus at the University of Colorado, Boulder, has conducted archaeological research in the Mesa Verde region for 40 years and was senior principal investigator for the Dolores Archaeological Project. He lives in Dove Creek, Colorado.

Suggested Reading

Adams, Karen R.
2000   "Anthropogenic Ecology of the North American Southwest." In *People and Plants in Ancient Western North America*, edited by Paul E. Minnis, pp. 167–204. Smithsonian Books, Washington, DC.

Adler, Michael
1994   "Population Aggregation and the Anasazi Social Landscape: A View from the Four Corners." In *The Ancient Southwestern Community: Models and Methods for the Study of Prehistoric Social Organization*, edited by W. H. Wills and Robert D. Leonard, pp. 85–101. University of New Mexico Press, Albuquerque.

Blackburn, Fred M., and Ray A. Williamson
1997   *Cowboys and Cave Dwellers: Basketmaker Archaeology in Utah's Grand Gulch*. School of American Research, SAR Press, Santa Fe, NM.

Breternitz, David A., Christine K. Robinson, and G. Timothy Gross, compilers
1986   *Dolores Archaeological Program: Final Synthetic Report*. United States Department of the Interior, Bureau of Reclamation, Engineering and Research Center, Denver.

Breternitz, David A., A. H. Rohn Jr., and E. A. Morris
1974   *Prehistoric Ceramics of the Mesa Verde Region*. Ceramic Series no. 5. Museum of Northern Arizona, Flagstaff.

Cameron, Catherine M., ed.
1995   Migration and the Movement of Southwestern Peoples. Special Issue of *Journal of Anthropological Archaeology* 14, no. 2.

Cole, Sally J.
1990   *Legacy on Stone: Rock Art of the Colorado Plateau and Four Corners Region*. Johnson Publishing, Boulder, CO.

Hayes, Alden C., and James A. Lancaster
1975   *Badger House Community, Mesa Verde National Park*. Publications in Archeology no. 7E, Wetherill Mesa Studies. National Park Service, Washington, DC.

Kohler, Timothy A., George J. Gumerman, and Robert G. Reynolds
2005   "Simulating Ancient Societies." *Scientific American* (July):77–83.

Kuckelman, Kristin A., Ricky R. Lightfoot, and Debra L. Martin
2002   "The Bioarchaeology and Taphonomy of Violence at Castle Rock and Sand Canyon Pueblos, Southwestern Colorado." *American Antiquity* 67, no. 3:486–513.

LeBlanc, Steven A.
1999   *Prehistoric Warfare in the American Southwest*. University of Utah Press, Salt Lake City.

Lightfoot, Ricky R., and Mary C. Etzkorn
1993   *The Duckfoot Site*, vol. 1, *Descriptive Archaeology*. Occasional Paper no. 3. Crow Canyon Archaeological Center, Cortez, CO.

Lipe, William D., Mark D. Varien, and Richard H. Wilshusen, eds.
1999   *Colorado Prehistory: A Context for the Southern Colorado River Basin*. Colorado Council of Professional Archaeologists, Denver.

Lister, Florence C.
2004   *Troweling through Time: The First Century of Mesa Verdean Archaeology*. University of New Mexico Press, Albuquerque.

Lister, Robert H., and Florence C. Lister
1987   *Aztec Ruins on the Animas*. University of New Mexico Press, Albuquerque.

Noble, David Grant
2000   *Ancient Ruins of the Southwest: An Archaeological Guide*. Northland Publishing Company, Flagstaff, AZ.

Nordenskiöld, Gustav
[1893] *The Cliff-Dwellers of the Mesa Verde*. Rio
1979   Grande Press, Glorieta, NM.

Ortiz, Alfonso
1969   *The Tewa World: Space, Time, Being, and Becoming in a Pueblo Society*. University of Chicago Press, Chicago.

Plog, Stephen
1997   *Ancient Peoples of the American Southwest*. Thames and Hudson, London.

Rohn, Arthur H.
1969   *Mug House, Mesa Verde National Park, Colorado*. Archeological Research Series no. 7-D, Wetherill Mesa Excavations. National Park Service, Washington, DC.

Thompson, Ian
2004   *The Towers of Hovenweep*. Canyonlands Natural History Association, Moab, Utah.

Van West, Carla R.
1994   *Modeling Prehistoric Agricultural Productivity in Southwestern Colorado: A GIS Approach*. Reports of Investigations no. 67. Washington State University Department of Anthropology, Pullman, WA, and Crow Canyon Archaeological Center, Cortez, CO.

Varien, Mark D.
1999   *Sedentism and Mobility in a Social Landscape: Mesa Verde and Beyond*. University of Arizona Press, Tucson.

Varien, Mark D., ed.
2000   Special issue of *Kiva: The Journal of Southwestern Anthropology and History* 66, no. 1. Arizona Archaeological and Historical Society, Tucson.

Varien, Mark D., and Richard H. Wilshusen
2000   *Seeking the Center Place: Archaeology and Ancient Communities in the Mesa Verde Region*. University of Utah Press, Salt Lake City.

Wilshusen, Richard H., Melissa J. Churchill, and James M. Potter
1997   "Prehistoric Reservoirs and Water Basins in the Mesa Verde Region: Intensification of Water Collection Strategies during the Great Pueblo Period." *American Antiquity* 62, no. 4:664–81.

Wilshusen, Richard H., and Scott G. Ortman
1999   "Rethinking the Pueblo I Period in the San Juan Drainage: Aggregation, Migration, and Cultural Diversity." *Kiva* 64, no. 3: 369–99.

To read research reports on the Mesa Verde region published online, see the Crow Canyon Archaeological Center's website, http://www.crowcanyon.org/research.html.

Picture Credits

Abbreviations:

CCAC	Crow Canyon Archaeological Center
DCA	Department of Cultural Affairs
MNM	Museum of New Mexico
MVNP	Mesa Verde National Park
SAR	School of American Research

Color sections, after pages 48 and 136: Plates 1, 2: courtesy Adriel Heisey, photographer; plates 3, 11, 14, 17, 19, 22: courtesy David Grant Noble, photographer; plates 4-7: courtesy William Stone, photographer; plates 8-10: courtesy George H. H. Huey, photographer; plate 12, courtesy Bruce Hucko, photographer; plate 13: painting by Glenn Felch, courtesy CCAC, photograph by David Grant Noble; plate 15: courtesy Karen Adams, photographer; plate 16: courtesy MVNP, photograph by Charlie Peterson; plate 18: courtesy Fort Lewis College, photograph by Ian Crosser; plate 20: courtesy MVNP; plate 21, courtesy Laurel Casjens, photographer.

Front matter: Frontispiece: courtesy George H. H. Huey, photographer; maps 1, 2: SAR, drawn by Molly O'Halloran; pp. vii, xiv: courtesy David Grant Noble, photographer.

Chapter One: Figs. 1.1–1.4, 1.6, 1.7: courtesy MVNP; fig. 1.5: courtesy Bruce Hucko, photographer.

Chapter Two: Figs. 2.1, 2.2, 2.5: courtesy David Grant Noble, photographer; fig. 2.3: from H. M. Wormington, *Prehistoric Indians of the Southwest*, 3rd ed. (Denver: Denver Museum of Natural History, 1956), fig. 9, courtesy Denver Museum of Nature and Science; figs. 2.4, 2.7: photographs by Ian Crosser, courtesy Fort Lewis College; fig. 2.6: courtesy MVNP; fig. 2.8: drawing by Jack Pfertsh.

Chapter Three: Fig. 3.1: photograph by Larry Harwood, courtesy University of Colorado Museum of Natural History; fig. 3.2: after Joel M. Brisbin and Mark D. Varien, "Excavations at Tres Bobos Hamlet (Site 5MT4545), a Basketmaker III Habitation," in *Dolores Archaeological Program: Anasazi Communities at Dolores. Early Anasazi Sites in the Sagehen Flats Area*, compiled by A. E. Kane and G. T. Gross (Denver: US Department of the Interior, Bureau of Reclamation, Engineering and Research Center, 1986), 117–210; fig. 3.3: after fig. 3.7 in James N. Morris, *Archaeological Excavations on the Hovenweep Laterals*, Four Corners Archaeological Project, Report no. 16, vol. 1 (Cortez, CO: Complete Archaeological Service Associates, 1991); fig. 3.4, drawing by Michael Robbins; fig. 3.5, painting by Paul Folwell; fig. 3.6: adapted from fig. 2.9 in Joel M. Brisbin, Allen E. Kane, and James N. Morris, "Excavations at McPhee Pueblo (Site 5MT4475), a Pueblo I and Early Pueblo II Multi-component Village," in *Dolores Archaeological Program: Anasazi Communities at Dolores: McPhee Village*, compiled by A. E. Kane and C. K. Robinson (Denver: US Department of the Interior, Bureau of Reclamation, Engineering and Research Center, 1988); fig. 3.7: SAR, drawn by Molly O'Halloran.

Chapter Four: Figs. 4.1, 4.6: courtesy David Grant Noble, photographer; fig. 4.2: adapted from fig. 13 in Robert H. Lister, *Contributions to Mesa Verde Archaeology, II: Site 875, Mesa Verde National Park, Colorado* (Boulder: University of Colorado Press, 1965); fig. 4.3: from H. M. Wormington, *Prehistoric Indians of the Southwest*, fig. 21, courtesy Denver Museum of Nature and Science; fig. 4.4: adapted from Mary Errickson, *Archaeological Investigations on Prehistoric Sites: Reach III of the Towaoc Canal, Ute Mountain Ute Reservation, Montezuma County, Colorado*, vol. 1 (Salt Lake City: Cultural Resources Program, Bureau of Reclamation, Upper Colorado Region, 1993); fig. 4.5: adapted from Jervis D. Swannack Jr., *Wetherill Mesa Excavations: Big Juniper House, Mesa Verde National Park, Colorado* (Washington, DC: National Park Service, Department of the

Interior, 1969), 25; fig. 4.7: courtesy Field Museum of Natural History; fig. 4.8: adapted from a drawing by Jerry Livingston, courtesy National Park Service.

Chapter Five: Fig. 5.1: photograph by Don Watson, courtesy MVNP; fig. 5.2: courtesy Adriel Heisey, photographer; fig. 5.3: courtesy CCAC; figs. 5.4, 5.6: courtesy David Grant Noble, photographer; fig. 5.5: photograph by Gustav Nordenskiöld, courtesy MVNP; fig. 5.7: from pl. 39 and figs. 1 and 2 in W. H. Holmes, "Report of the Ancient Ruins of Southwestern Colorado, Examined during the Summers of 1875 and 1876," in F. V. Hayden, *Tenth Annual Report of the United States Geological and Geographical Survey of the Territories Embracing Colorado and Parts of Adjacent Territories* (Washington, DC: Government Printing Office, 1878); fig. 5.8: drafted by Neal Morris, courtesy CCAC; fig. 5.9: courtesy Palace of the Governors (MNM/DCA), neg. no. 37070.

Chapter Six: Fig. 6.1: courtesy Tessie Naranjo; figs. 6.2, 6.5: courtesy David Grant Noble, photographer; fig. 6.3: photograph by Paul Logsdon; fig. 6.4: SAR, drawn by Molly O'Halloran; fig. 6.6: courtesy Palace of the Governors (MNM/DCA), neg. no. 4128; fig. 6.7: courtesy Palace of the Governors (MNM/DCA), neg. no. 42740.

Chapter Seven: Fig. 7.1: courtesy MVNP collections, photograph by David Grant Noble, figs. 7.2, 7.8: photographs by Lynn Lown, SAR collections; fig. 7.3: photograph by Alden Hayes, Clifford Chappel collection at the Anasazi Heritage Center, courtesy MVNP; fig. 7.4: courtesy MVNP; figs. 7.5, 7.6, 7.7: photographs by Fred Mang, courtesy MVNP; fig. 7.9: photograph by David Grant Noble, courtesy Edgar Gilliland; fig. 7.10: photograph by J. W. Fewkes, courtesy MVNP.

Chapter Eight: Fig. 8.1: photograph by Kevin Black, courtesy Colorado Historical Society; figs. 8.2, 8.4, 8.6: courtesy Village Ecodynamics Project; fig. 8.3: courtesy Palace of the Governors (MNM/DCA), neg. no. 3984; fig. 8.5: courtesy Museum of Northern Arizona; fig. 8.7: courtesy Ruth Van Dyke, photographer.

Chapter Nine: Fig. 9.1: courtesy Adriel Heisey, photographer; fig. 9.2: courtesy James Duffield, photographer; fig. 9.3: courtesy J. R. Lancaster, photographer; fig. 9.4: courtesy Alvin Reiner, photographer; fig. 9.5: courtesy David Grant Noble, photographer; fig. 9.6: courtesy Jonathan Till, photographer; fig. 9.7: courtesy Bruce Hucko, photographer; fig. 9.8: drafted by Jonathan Till and Phil Geib, courtesy Catherine M. Cameron.

Chapter Ten: Fig. 10.1: drawing by J. E. Kindig, alignment lines by J. McKim Malville; fig. 10.2: courtesy Donna Glowacki, photographer; figs. 10.3, 10.5: adapted from figs. 11 and 8 in J. McKim Malville and Kenneth R. Brownsberger, "Ceremonial Features of Yellow Jacket, 5MT5," in *Archaeoastronomy: The Journal of the Center for Archaeoastronomy*, vol. XI; figs. 10.4, 10.6: courtesy of J. McKim Malville, photographer; fig. 10.7: courtesy Preston Fisher, photographer; 10.8: courtesy Adriel Heisey, photographer.

Chapter Eleven: Fig. 11.1: courtesy Field Museum of Natural History; fig. 11.2, top, middle: drawing by Sally J. Cole, adapted from figs. 5.24 and 3.42 in Morris, *Hovenweep Laterals*; fig. 11.2, bottom: drawing by Sally J. Cole, adapted from fig. 32 in Lamar Lindsay, *Westwater Ruin (Five Kiva Ruin)* (Salt Lake City: Utah Navajo Development Council, 1979); fig. 11.3, top: drawing by Sally J. Cole, adapted from a field drawing by Carole Graham; fig. 11.3, bottom: drawing by Sally J. Cole, adapted from a field drawing by Victoria Jeffries; fig. 11.4: courtesy Myers Walker, photographer; fig. 11.5: drawing by Sally J. Cole, adapted from fig. 205 in Constance S. Silver, chapter 15 in *Prehistoric Adaptive Strategies in the Chaco Canyon Region, Northwestern New Mexico*, vol. 2, *Site Reports*, assembled by Alan H. Simmons (Window Rock, AZ: Navajo Nation,

1982); fig. 11.6: drawings by Sally J. Cole, adapted from (top) fig. 89, (center) fig. 62, (bottom) fig. 79 in Watson Smith, *Kiva Mural Decorations at Awatovi and Kawaika-a* (Cambridge, MA: Peabody Museum of American Archaeology and Ethnology, Harvard University, 1952).

Chapter Twelve: Fig. 12.1: photograph by Fred Mang, courtesy MVNP; figs. 12.2, 12.3, 12.8: courtesy MVNP; fig. 12.4: photograph by Christopher Pierce, courtesy CCAC; fig. 12.5: courtesy Robin Lyle, photographer; fig. 12.6: photograph by David M. Grimes, courtesy CCAC; fig. 12.7: courtesy Scott Ortman, photographer; fig. 12.9: courtesy Palace of the Governors (MNM/DCA), neg. no. 21661.

Chapter Thirteen: Fig. 13.1: courtesy George H. H. Huey, photographer; figs. 13.2–13.6: courtesy MVNP.

Chapter Fourteen: Fig. 14.1: photograph by Julie Bell, courtesy MVNP; fig. 14.2: left, photograph by Laurel J. Casjens, courtesy MVNP, right, courtesy MVNP; fig. 14.3: photograph by Tori Cooper, courtesy MVNP; fig. 14.4: courtesy MVNP.

Chapter Fifteen: Fig. 15.1: photograph by Jesse Nusbaum, courtesy MVNP; fig. 15.2: courtesy Ruth Wright, photographer; fig. 15.3: courtesy MVNP.

Chapter Sixteen: Fig. 16.1: courtesy University of Pennsylvania Museum, neg. no. S4-139872; fig. 16.2: drafted by Neal Morris, courtesy CCAC; figs. 16.3, 16.4, 16.5: courtesy David Grant Noble, photographer; fig. 16.6: photographs by Bruce Hucko, courtesy American Museum of Natural History, acc. nos. H-12981 (left) and H-13035 (right); fig. 16.7: drawings by Kristin A. Kuckelman, courtesy CCAC; fig. 16.8: courtesy MVNP.

Chapter Seventeen: Fig. 17.1: courtesy Palace of the Governors (MNM/DCA), neg. no. 60720.

Chapter Eighteen: Fig. 18.1: photograph by Gustav Nordenskiöld, courtesy MVNP; fig. 18.2: photograph by Jesse Nusbaum, courtesy Palace of the Governors (MNM/DCA), neg. no. 60657; fig. 18.3: courtesy Palace of the Governors (MNM/DCA), neg. no. 90981; fig. 18.4: adapted from fig. 4.27 in Emil W. Haury, *Point of Pines, Arizona: A History of the University of Arizona Archaeological Field School* (Tucson: University of Arizona Press, 1989); fig. 18.5: SAR, drawn by Molly O'Halloran; fig. 18.6: courtesy David Grant Noble, photographer; fig. 18.7: courtesy Peter Dechert, photographer.

Chapter Nineteen: Fig. 19.1: from pl. 35 in Holmes, "Report on the Ancient Ruins of Southwestern Colorado"; figs. 19.2, 19.11, 19.12: photographs by Fred Mang, courtesy MVNP; fig. 19.3: photograph by William Henry Jackson, courtesy MVNP; figs. 19.4, 18.8: courtesy MVNP; figs. 19.5, 19.6, 19.7, and 19.9: courtesy Palace of the Governors (MNM/DCA), neg. nos. 44296, 139158, 10313, 60487; fig. 19.10: courtesy University of Colorado Museum of Natural History, no. MO-10.

Chapter Twenty: Fig. 20.1: courtesy CCAC; fig. 20.2: courtesy David A. Breternitz, photographer; fig. 20.3: courtesy Woods Canyon Archaeological Consultants; fig. 20.4: courtesy MVNP; fig. 20.5: photograph by Ken Abbott, courtesy University of Colorado, Boulder; fig. 20.6: courtesy W. James Judge; fig. 20.7: courtesy Scott Ortman, photographer; fig. 20.8: courtesy Cory Breternitz; fig. 20.9: courtesy SWCA Environmental Consultants.

Index

Note: Page numbers printed in *italics* refer to illustrations; entries beginning with an upper-case P refer to plate numbers. Numbers in **bold** indicate maps or plans.

Great Sage Plain, 40, 41–45
Guernsey, Samuel, 13

Hallisy, Steve, *166*
Harrington, John P., 51–52
Hart, Richard, 142
Haury, Emil, 142–143
Hayden, Ferdinand V., 150–152
Hayes, Alden, xvii, *150*
Health, Basketmaker II, 14, 15
Hearst, Phoebe, 153
Hedley Pueblo, 43
Hensler, Kathy, 105–106
Hensler, Vern, *167*
Herraduras, 80
Hewett, Edgar Lee, 51, *154*, 154–157, 159, 163, 168
Hibben, Frank C., 98
Holcomb, Manuel, *48*
Holly House, 89, *90*
Holmes, William Henry, xvi, 39, 106, 152
Hopi: Castle Rock conflict oral history, 132, 137–138; corn
    planting, *46*; kivas, 88, 97; migrations, 141, 142;
    mural designs, 94; Walpi, *142*
Horizon scene murals, 97–99
Horseshoe Ruin, P4
Hovenweep National Monument: P3; Hovenweep Castle,
    85, *129*; Square Tower, 42, *42*; summer solstice at
    Holly House, *90*; towers, *78*, 78–79, 89, *90*, P4
Hunter-gatherers, 9–10, 11; archaeological record, xv;
    plant usage, 4–6, *5*; protein sources, 6, *6*; technology,
    10, 11, *12*, 17
Hurst, William, xvii
Hyde Exploring Expedition, *126*

Ingersoll, Ernest, 137, 152

Jackson, William Henry, xvi, 39, 151–152
Judge, W. James, 36, *168*, 168–169
Juniper berries, 4, *5*

Katsina religion, *145*, 145–146
Kayenta immigrants, 142–143
Khun, Gia, *48*, 49
Kidder, Alfred V., 13, *155*, 155–156
King, Clarence, 150–151
Kivas: Basketmaker III, 23; Chaco Canyon murals, 97; cir-
    cular, *31*; container metaphor, 107, *108*, 109; develop-
    ment, 30–31; Escalante great house, *28*; great, 78;
    Lowry great house, *92*, 94; Mule Canyon Indian
    Ruins, *41*; multiwall structures, 43; murals, *94*, 94–97,
    95, *97*, *98*; Perfect Kiva, 85; pottery use in, 106; reli-
    gious symbolism in, 31; and social organization, 112,
    113–114, 116, *116*; uses, 31–32, 114; Yellow Jacket
    Pueblo, 86, 88–89
Knobby Knee Stockade, **21**, 21–23

Kodak House, P8
Kohler, Timothy A., 3, 6, 40
Kokopelli, 16, *63*, 97
Kuckelman, Kristin, 44, 45–46, 85, 141

Lacy, Lee, *105*
Laguna Pueblo, 97
Lancaster, James A. (Al), 159–160, *161*, 162, 163, *167*,
    167–168
Land management, 33, 34
Landscape murals, 97–99
Langton, Chris, 67
LeBlanc, Stephen, 141
Lekson, Stephen H., 35, 36, 44, 79, 89, 141, 142
Lineages. *See* clans
Lines across time, 89, 90, 139, 147
Linguistic information, 51, 52–53
Lino Gray pottery, 102
Linton, Ralph, 160
Lipe, William D., 43, 141, 146–147, 169, *169*
Lister, Florence, 162
Lister, Robert, 162
Lizard man, 88, 89
Location of high devotional expression (LsHDE), 86. *See
    also* sacred landscapes
Long House, P11
Lowry Pueblo, 34, *92*, 94; great house, *92*, P6

Maize. *See* corn
Marriages, 36
Martin, Paul S., 93, 94, 159–160, *161*
Martinez, Maria, *109*
Mason, Charles, xv, 152
Material culture: Basketmaker II, *15*, 16; Late Archaic, 12
Mather, Stephen, 158
Mathews, Meredith, 6
Matrilineal organization, 111–112
Matson, R. G., 16, 169
McAnany, Patricia, 98
McClurg, Virginia, 152
McComb, J. N., 149–150
McPhee Pueblo, 26
McPhee Village, **24**, 24–26
Mesa Verde National Park, **viii, ix**, 52, P1, P2, P7, P8, P11,
    P16, P17; established, 39, 152, 154; north rim, *xv*;
    number of sites in, 165. *See also specific sites*
Mesa Verde Research Center, 168
Mexican influence, 61, 62
Middens, 83
Migrations: and climate, 73; ethnographic data, 50–54,
    56–57, 141, 142, 144, 147; from Kayenta, 142–143;
    Mogollon, 16; and pottery, 103; Pueblo I, 26–27; on
    rock art, 22; routes, **144**; in simulation project, 70;
    and social stratification, 87; Tewa stories, 56–57. *See
    also* abandonment

Residences: Basketmaker II, 13–14; Basketmaker III, 20–21; cliff dwellings, 111, 112–114, 129, *130, 148*; kivas as, 114; Late Archaic, 11, 12; pithouses, 20–21, 23–24; Pueblo II, *30*, 32–33, 42; Pueblo III, 40–41, 42; Pueblo I-III pattern, 30; ritual destruction, 22. *See also specific sites*

Rice grass, 5

Rio Grande Pueblos, 88

Ritual architecture, 90–91; Holly House, *90*; Sun Temple, *91*; Yellow Jacket Pueblo (5MT5), **84,** 85–90, *87,* **87, 88**

Rituals: of abandonment, 22, 26, 131, 143; feasting, 25, 89, 106, *107*; locations, 77–78, 79–80, 89; and political organization, 25; pottery exchanges, 44

Rivera, Juan, 149

Roads, 35, 79–80, 89

Roads through time, 79

Rock art, *76, 145, 169,* P19; Basketmaker II, *8,* 15–16, P14; Basketmaker III, *22, 81*; content, 81–82, 131–132, *132*; fire damage, 119, *120*; as sacred landscapes, *76,* 80–82, *81,* 88, 89. *See also* murals

Rockefeller, John D., Jr., 158–159

Rock enclosures, 80, *80*

Rockshelters, 11

Rohn, Arthur H., 116, 163

Sacred landscapes, **75,** *76,* 76–79, *77, 83*; astronomical sites, 82–83, 90–91; cairns and rock enclosures, 80, *80*; evolution, 78; mundane as, 83; murals, 97–99; natural features, *76, 77*; and origins, 52–54, 56; roads and trails, 35, 79–80, 89; rock art, *76,* 80–82, *81,* 88, 89. *See also* great houses; kivas

Sagebrush Reservoir, 123, *124*

Salmon Ruin, 35, 36

Salvage archaeology, xvi, 161, 165, 166–167, 170–171

Salzer, Matthew, 3

Sand Canyon Pueblo, P13; conflict, 44, 127, 134; defenses, 128, **128**; kivas, 43; pottery, *107*

Sand (Sandy) Lake, 51–54, 56

San Juan River rock art, 81

San Luis Valley, *50*

Santa Ana Pueblo (old), *146*

Santa Clara Pueblo, 49, *49, 53,* 54, *55*

Santana, *109*

Schelly, Don, *166*

Sedentism, 19, 21, 61

Settlements: and agriculture, 13–14, 29; Basketmaker II, 15; Basketmaker III, *20,* 20–23, *21*; and conflicts, 73, 134, 170; ebb and flow, 170; location, 20, 78; Pueblo I, 19, 23–26, *24,* 87; Pueblo II, *30,* **32,** 32–33, 35–36, 42; Pueblo III, 39, *39,* 40–44, 88–89. *See also specific sites*

Simulation project, *66,* **68,** 68–72, *69, 71*; corn production, *69*

Sipapu, 31, 88–89, 106

Skeletons, 13, 127, 132–133

Smiley, Terah, 160

Smith, Jack E., 34, 163, 165

Smith, Watson, 96, 98

Snowmelt, 2

Social organization: Chacoan influence, 35–37; clans, 111–115; decision-making in, 72; ethnographic data, 111; expressed in pottery, 63–65; kivas in, 112–114; matrilineal, 111–112; moieties, 43, 56, 115–116; regional, 36; rituals for cultural integration, 25; Spruce Tree House, **117**; stresses prior to abandonment, 141; in villages, 114–116, *116,* **117**; in Yellow Jacket area, 87

Solstices, 85, 86, *87,* 89–90, *90, 91*

Speaker Chief Complex, 116

Spear points, 9

Split-twig figurines, 11, *13*

Spruce Tree House, *xiv, 38,* 116, *116,* **117,** 152, P2

Square Tower House (Mesa Verde), 152, P17

Square Tower (Hovenweep), 42, *42*

Stegner, Wallace, 123

Stein, John, 79

Stockades, 22, 127–128

Storage. *See* food storage

Storage, water, 102

Storytelling, 49

Structures: container metaphor, 107, *108,* 109; defensive, 127–129, *128, 129, 130,* 131, *131*; and moieties, 115–116; multiwall, 42–43, *43,* 89; use through time, 43–44, 139; for village identity, 114–116. *See also specific classes*

Sun Temple, 85, 89–90, *91*

Swentzell, Rina, 147

Swink, Clint, *105*

Tamaya, *146*

Tchamahia, P9

Temperatures, 3, 45–46

Tewa people, *48*; land of, *50,* **51,** *52*; migration, 142; origins, *49,* 49–54, 56–57; Santa Clara Pueblo, *53, 55*

Textiles, *61,* 94, 106–107, *107*

Thomas, Chester A., 163

Till, Jonathan, xvii

Toll, Wolcott, 36

Tools, 60, P9; Basketmaker II, 15, *15*; Basketmaker III, 21, 24; Pueblo I, *18,* 24; Pueblo III, *140,* 140–141, 143

Towers, *42*; defensive, 128; early, 42; Hovenweep, *78,* 78–79, 89, *90,* P4; Mesa Verde, 89, P17; symbolic significance, *78,* 78–79; Yellow Jacket Pueblo, 89

Trade: Late Archaic, 11–12; local, 44; long-distance, 36; pottery, 104, 105–106

Trails, 79, *79*

Tres Bobos Hamlet, *20*

Triwall structures, 42–43, *43*

Turkeys, 6, 72, *133,* 134

Turner, Christy G., 37, 167
Turner, Jacqueline A., 167
Twin Rocks, 77

Ute ancestors, xv

Van Cleave, Philip, 162
Van Dyke, Ruth, 26
Van West, Carla, 140, 145, 172
Varien, Mark, 30, 36, 37, 141
Village Ecodynamics Project, 40
Villages: advantages, 25; identity in, 114–116, *116*, **117**; movement to, 19, 41; Pueblo III, 39, *39*, 43

Warfare. *See* conflict
Water resources, 2–3, *34*; drought, 3–4, 36, 45–46, 134, 139–140; dry farming, 1, 3, 33–34, *46*; management, *2*, 78, 120–121, *121*; precipitation, 2, 3, 26, 140; reservoirs, 34, 122, *122*, 123–124, *124*, *125*; rock art near, 81; as sacred, 76, 78; settlement location, 15, 20; storage containers, 102
Watson, Don, 162, 163
Weapons: Archaic, *11, 12*; Basketmaker II, *11, 12*; development of, 17; fire, 129, 131; Paleoindian, 9, 10; in rock art, 131, *132*; stone points, *60*

Weaving. *See* textiles
Wetherill, Benjamin K., 152
Wetherill, John, 153
Wetherill, Richard, xv, 13, 127, *138*, 152–154, 157–158

Wetherill Mesa Archaeological Project, 111, 162–163
Wheat, Joe Ben, 86, 87, 88, 168, *168*
Wheeler, George M., 150–151
Wheeler, Richard P., 163
White, Tim D., 167
Wilcox, David, 36
Wildfires, 10, *118*, 119–121, *120*
Willow-twig figurines, 11, *13*
Wilshusen, Richard, 29, 141
Wilson, C. Dean, 101
Windes, Tom, 26
Winter, Joe, 169
Women, archaic, 11
Wright, Kenneth R., 34, 171

Yellow Jacket Pueblo (5MT5), 41, **84**, 85–90, **87**, *87*, **88**
Yucca, 5
Yucca House, 74, 85

Zunis, 142